Equality Unfulfilled

The year 1972 is often hailed as an inflection point in the evolution of women's rights. Congress passed Title IX of the Education Amendments of 1972, a law that outlawed sex-based discrimination in education. Many Americans celebrate Title IX for having ushered in an era of expanded opportunity for women's athletics; yet fifty years after its passage, sex-based inequalities in college athletics remain the reality. *Equality Unfulfilled* explains why. The book identifies institutional roadblocks – including sex-based segregation, androcentric organizational cultures, and overbearing market incentives – that undermine efforts to achieve systemic change. Drawing on original surveys with student-athletes, athletic administrators, college coaches, members of the public, and fans of college sports, it highlights how institutions shape attitudes toward gender equity policy. It offers novel lessons not only for those interested in college sports but for everyone seeking to understand the barriers that any marginalized group faces in its quest for equality.

James N. Druckman is the Payson S. Wild Professor of Political Science at Northwestern University, Illinois. He is the author of several books, his most recent being *Experimental Thinking: A Primer on Social Science Experiments* (2022).

Elizabeth A. Sharrow is an associate professor in the School of Public Policy and the Department of History at the University of Massachusetts Amherst. She has won multiple awards for her scholarship on Title IX.

Cambridge Studies in Gender and Politics

Cambridge Studies in Gender and Politics addresses theoretical, empirical, and normative issues at the intersection of politics and gender. Books in this series adopt incisive and comprehensive approaches to key research themes concerning the construction and impact of sex and gender, as well as their political and social consequences.

General Editors

Karen Beckwith, *Case Western Reserve University* (Lead)
Lisa Baldez, *Dartmouth College*
Christina Wolbrecht, *University of Notre Dame*

Editorial Advisory Board

Nancy Burns, *University of Michigan*
Matthew Evangelista, *Cornell University*
Nancy Hirschmann, *University of Pennsylvania*
Sarah Song, *University of California, Berkeley*
Ann Towns, *University of Gothenburg*
Aili Mari Tripp, *University of Wisconsin – Madison*
Georgina Waylen, *University of Manchester*

Books in the Series

J. Kevin Corder and Christina Wolbrecht, *Counting Women's Ballots*
Mala Htun, *Inclusion without Representation in Latin America*
Mala Htun and S. Laurel Weldon, *The Logics of Gender Justice*
Aili Mari Tripp, *Women and Power in Postconflict Africa*
Kristin N. Wylie, *Party Institutionalization and Women's Representation in Democratic Brazil*
Rachel E. Brulé, *Women, Power, and Property: The Paradox of Gender Equality Laws in India*
Ana Catalano Weeks, *Making Gender Salient: From Gender Quota Laws to Policy*

Equality Unfulfilled

*How Title IX's Policy Design Undermines
Change to College Sports*

JAMES N. DRUCKMAN
Northwestern University, Illinois

ELIZABETH A. SHARROW
University of Massachusetts Amherst

CAMBRIDGE
UNIVERSITY PRESS

CAMBRIDGE
UNIVERSITY PRESS

Shaftesbury Road, Cambridge CB2 8EA, United Kingdom

One Liberty Plaza, 20th Floor, New York, NY 10006, USA

477 Williamstown Road, Port Melbourne, VIC 3207, Australia

314–321, 3rd Floor, Plot 3, Splendor Forum, Jasola District Centre,
New Delhi – 110025, India

103 Penang Road, #05–06/07, Visioncrest Commercial, Singapore 238467

Cambridge University Press is part of Cambridge University Press & Assessment,
a department of the University of Cambridge.

We share the University's mission to contribute to society through the pursuit of
education, learning and research at the highest international levels of excellence.

www.cambridge.org
Information on this title: www.cambridge.org/9781009338325

DOI: 10.1017/9781009338356

First published 2023

A catalogue record for this publication is available from the British Library.

Library of Congress Cataloging-in-Publication Data
NAMES: Druckman, James N., 1971– author. | Sharrow, Elizabeth A., author.
TITLE: Equality unfulfilled : how Title IX's policy design undermines
change to college sports / James N. Druckman, Elizabeth A. Sharrow.
DESCRIPTION: Cambridge, United Kingdom ; New York, NY : Cambridge
University Press, 2023. | Series: Cambridge studies in gender and politics |
Includes bibliographical references and index.
IDENTIFIERS: LCCN 2023002761 | ISBN 9781009338325 (hardback) |
ISBN 9781009338356 (ebook)
SUBJECTS: LCSH: Sex discrimination in sports – United States. |
College sports – Social aspects – United States. | College sports for
women – United States. | United States. Education Amendments of 1972. Title IX.
CLASSIFICATION: LCC GV709.18.U6 D78 2023 |
DDC 796.04/30973–dc23/eng/20230310
LC record available at https://lccn.loc.gov/2023002761

ISBN 978-1-009-33832-5 Hardback
ISBN 978-1-009-33836-3 Paperback

To Nicole Druckman and James and Susan Sharrow

Contents

Figures

Tables

Preface

The year 1972 is often hailed as an inflection point in the evolution of women's rights. Congress passed Title IX of the Education Amendments of 1972 that outlawed sex-based discrimination in education. Many celebrate Title IX as a transformative policy that ushered in an era of expanded opportunity and support for women's athletics. This may be true relative to a baseline of women's near exclusion. Yet the reality is that sex-based inequalities in college athletics remain enormous, fifty years after the passage of Title IX. This book explains why. It identifies institutional perversions – including sex-based segregation, androcentric organizational cultures, and overbearing market incentives – that undermine efforts toward equality. Drawing on large-scale, original data collections with more than 7,000 student-athletes, athletic administrators, college coaches, members of the public, and college sports fans, the book highlights how institutions shape attitudes about gender equity initiatives. It offers novel lessons not only for those interested in college sports but for anyone seeking to understand barriers that any marginalized group faces in its quest for equality.

Acknowledgments

This book is the culmination of more than twenty years of conversations, collaboration, and consternation. Over the years and as our dialogue deepened, our ideas and approaches productively coevolved on every level of this project. Our names are listed in alphabetical order, but the book is the product of equal, deeply enmeshed, and impossible to disentangle contributions.

We first discussed gender inequality in sports – and the institutions designed to address it – at the turn of the century when we both were at the University of Minnesota. At the time, we did not necessarily envision a research collaboration, hopeful as we were that serious progress toward equality would be made in the ensuing decades. Yet our discussions continued and our dismay grew while progress, such as it is, left us underwhelmed. By early 2016, we both were working on college sports-related scholarly topics, and we decided to pursue a joint project. We found, perhaps surprisingly, that student-athletes – both women and men – express strong normative support for equality in college sports. This left us with an important question: If support for equality among key stakeholders remains quite high, what explains the persistence of sex-based inequalities? This book is our answer. It melds various research traditions, multiple literatures, normative and positive considerations, and attention to theoretical and applied concerns. While the book directly addresses sex-based inequalities in college sports, the findings – we believe – have direct relevance to understanding intergroup relations in virtually any context, particularly when one of the groups has a marginalized status. It speaks to general issues of segregation, organizational culture, socialization, and politics and markets. Our hope is that the arguments and evidence help scholars, practitioners, and interested members of the public understand how political structures that appear to promote equality can have perverse impacts that, in some sense, work to undermine it.

Of course, our more than twenty years of conversations and more than six years of collaboration mean that we have had the privilege of receiving advice, feedback, and help from more people than we can name here. Let us first thank the most crucial people – our partners. Despite having little to no interest in sports, Nicole Druckman listened intently, for years, to ideas about why college sports work the way they do. More important, though, is the inspiration that comes from her perspectives, work, and persistence, all aimed at repairing the world. Mara Toone, herself a former athlete and current women's sports fan, has been an unflagging supporter of this project from the start. She too (alongside Sam Seaborn, resident canine scholar) has listened to and enthusiastically participated in discussion about our questions, research design, and conclusions. Her commitment to social critique and demanding more from an unjust world is a daily inspiration. We also thank Susan and James Sharrow for their decades of support of all kinds, and for unwittingly ensuring that we would meet at the University of Minnesota.

We also give special thanks to scholars who went beyond reasonable expectations to offer guidance. Linda Tropp offered masterful insights about interpersonal contact, helping us, as well, to understand the nuance and profoundness of her own work. Ethan Busby also provided excellent advice regarding intergroup contact, specifically imagined contact. Jaime Schultz provided much-needed perspective about how to think about sports, at crucial points. Alice Eagly tutored us on gender stereotypes. Matt DeBell spent considerable time explaining how best to implement sample weights; John Bullock, Jean Clipperton, and Jay Seawright provided additional guidance on data analyses. Tasha Philpot's and Monica Schneider's support and enthusiasm for the project provided affirmation when needed. Bridgette Davis, whose friendship arrived during the late stages of writing, buoyed the final revisions immeasurably. Dara Strolovitch, as colleague, mentor, and friend, has provided steadfast support for our work on Title IX and the (perhaps unlikely) study of sport as a site of political marginality.

Several others provided superb feedback and advice; an incomplete list includes Leann Banaszak, Matt Brundage, Camille Burge, Sue Carroll, Miceal Canavan, Delton Daigle, David Day, Elizabeth Demers, Kelly Dittmar, Kathy Dolan, Andrew Flores, Jane Fountain, Jeremy Freese, Dan Galvin, Elizabeth Goodyear-Grant, Gretchen Hendricks, Greg Huber,

Jenn Jackson, Diana Jain, Josh Kalla, Suji Kang, Yanna Krupnikov, Aleks Ksiazkiewicz, Regina Kunzel, Chris Kuzawa, Matt Levendusky, Lauren McCarthy, Cecilia Mo, Matt Nelsen, Monique Newton, Matt Notowidigdo, Julie Novkov, Cleo O'Brien-Udry, Laura Paler, Jennifer Piscopo, Onnie Rogers, Kira Sanbonmatsu, Alex Scacco, Andres Schelp, Jonathan Schulman, Morty Shapiro, Evelyn Simien, Patricia Strach, Dawn Teele, Rob Van Houweling, Chagai Weiss, Cara Wong, Kim Yuracko, and Christina Xydias. Additionally, Jake Druckman and Sam Druckman provided extremely distinct views on sports that proved valuable in thinking about fans and nonfans (respectively).

We also have been exceptionally fortunate to work with editors of this remarkable series: Lisa Baldez, Karen Beckwith, and Christina Wolbrecht, as well as Rachel Blaifeder from Cambridge University Press. Additionally, we thank many who offered feedback on presentations of the work at Cornell University, Duke University, Northwestern University, Tulane University, the University of Illinois at Urbana-Champaign, and the University of California, Berkeley. We also received superb comments from members of the Inter-Group Relations Workshop, the Gender and Political Psychology Network and members of panels at the annual meetings of the American Political Science Association and the Midwest Political Science Association. We are also grateful to the Education Politics and Policy Section of the American Political Science Association for their recognition of our 2021 paper version of Chapter 3, which provided a welcome boost during revisions of the manuscript.

Our work would not have been possible without the diligence of a large number of people who assisted with data collection. Adam Howat, Jake Rothschild, Maya Novak-Herzog, and Andrew Thompson invested considerable time on multiple aspects of the research. We also thank, for their foundational help, Madison Alvis, Robin Bayes, Marika Cerbone, James Crisafulli, Amanda Sahar d'Urso, Elizabeth Donoghue, Dylan Doppelt, Julia Driscoll, S. R. Gubitz, Katie Harvey, Ben Hempker, Joe Horner, Kirsten Huh, Casey Kelleher, Maryarita Kobotis, Sangjun Lee, Jeremy Levy, Ali McCoy, Stephen Monteiro, Justin Murphy, Malika Antoine Nicholson, Elizabeth Osborn, Kumar Ramanathan, Jacob Rothschild, Natalie Sands, Richard Shafranek, Summer Tuman, Anna Wang, Samuel Webber, Matt White, Abigail Williams, and Hannah Winslow. Of course, we also thank the thousands of student-athletes, coaches, athletic administrators, and members of the public who responded to our surveys.

Finally, we owe particular gratitude to women and gender-diverse student-athletes and the organizations that support them. We hope that they find some worth in this book, and a possible roadmap toward a better future.

I

Gender Equality in College Athletics

Assessing Fifty Years of Title IX

Nineteen seventy-two was a monumental year for women's sports. The
United States Congress passed Title IX of the Education Amendments
of 1972, a law that prohibited discrimination based on sex in educational programming including school-sponsored sports.[1] In the eyes of
many Americans, this signified the start of progress toward equality in
college athletics. Yet, more than a half century later, the quest for parity
remains unfulfilled. The glaring inequalities exposed during the National
Collegiate Athletic Association's (NCAA's) 2021 men's and women's
basketball championships made this freshly clear. Men's teams participating in what has become known as the "March Madness" tournament
enjoyed an elaborate training facility, piles of participant swag and gifts,
and unlimited steak and shrimp buffet-style meals. Meanwhile, participants in the women's tournament disclosed via social media that their
teams had access to paltry training support, minimal commemorative
gear, and prepackaged, calorie-controlled meals. In fact, there was no sign
that the women's tournament was part of "March Madness." Instead of
the iconic "March Madness" insignia used to promote the men's events
on jerseys, television broadcasts, tournament facilities, and fan apparel,
the courts on which the women played were emblazoned with the mere
text "NCAA Women's Basketball." University of Connecticut acting
head coach Chris Dailey commented, "I think it looks a little embar-
rassing on the court when you see 'Women's Basketball' and nothing

---

[1] Throughout, we employ the language of sex, gender, male, female, women, and men carefully and provisionally. We offer a detailed discussion about our use of language later in
this chapter.

connected to March Madness. There are women playing, so clearly it's women's basketball. I think everyone can get that. So, I think that certainly it's something that needs to be discussed" (Associated Press 2021).

Significant public discussion ensued. The NCAA leadership initially claimed that insufficient space at the host hotel was the reason for the women's negligible training facilities (Hensley-Clancy 2021b). But Sedona Prince, a University of Oregon player, gave the lie to their claims in a viral TikTok video. Prince's post revealed a near empty ballroom, featuring only one tower of hand weights and a pile of yoga mats, reserved for the women to train. She also posted the video on Twitter where it was retweeted over 210,000 times.[2] Athletic training staff posted contrasting images of the men's facilities that included dozens of weightlifting stands, barbells, and heavy weight plates to simultaneously accommodate multiple teams. Journalists in every major American news outlet began to cover the story.

Women athletes, coaches, and fans alike expressed indignation on social media at the revelations. Former longtime head coach of the University of Notre Dame's women's basketball program, Muffet McGraw (2021), tweeted:

While I appreciate the outrage, the fact that there's a huge disparity between men's and women's sports is hardly breaking news. We have been fighting this battle for years and frankly, I'm tired of it ... The fact that there are inequities in facilities, food, fan attendance, and swag bags is not what bothers me. What bothers me is that no one on the NCAA's leadership team even noticed ... Well time's up gentlemen. This generation of women expects more and we won't stop until we get it.

The NCAA president, Mark Emmert, eventually responded that "it is pretty self-evident that we dropped the ball in supporting our women's athletes, and we can't do that ... What do we need to do better? How do we make up for those shortcomings from this day going on and create the kind of gender equity that we all talk about ... to make sure it's a reality, not just language?" (Dinich 2021). Under intense public pressure, athletic leadership thus acknowledged the issues.

Nevertheless, only a few months after the basketball tournaments, evidence of inequalities emerged again, this time in college baseball and softball. The 2021 NCAA-sponsored men's baseball "College World Series" ensured the players had rest days between games and offered recreational golf outings and recuperative massages. In sharp contrast,

---

[2] See https://twitter.com/sedonaprince_/status/1372736231562342402?lang=en.

teams in the NCAA-sponsored "Women's College World Series" soft-ball tournament endured a lack of showers at the stadiums and few, if any, off days between games. Many teams even played two games a day, with some games starting near midnight since the inflexible women's tournament schedule did not account for weather delays (Leonhardt 2021). And this, despite fan interest in women's softball ranking near the top of all college sports, regularly exceeding viewership of the men's College World Series (Elchlepp 2021). Patty Gasso, coach of the 2021 national champion softball team from the University of Oklahoma, retorted, "we're still not being treated [the same n]or [do we] have the same opportunities, amenities that others do. And it's sad for me... It's kind of shameful, it really is, and I am committed to help this change" (Hoover 2021).[3]

These events invite deeper investigation into gender inequalities in college athletics. They also highlight the important advocacy roles of student-athletes (i.e., varsity collegiate athletes who compete for school-sponsored teams), coaches, and leaders within the system. Indeed, the day after Prince's video of the women's lackluster basket-ball tournament training facilities went viral, the chair of the NCAA Committee on Women's Athletics (CWA), Suzette McQueen, took action. She wrote to NCAA president Emmert that the basketball tour-nament conditions "undermined the NCAA's authority as a propo-nent and guarantor of Title IX protections" (West 2021). The NCAA agreed to an external equity review of its championships.[4] The review, the first phase of which was released in August 2021, offered a damn-ing evaluation of sex bias in NCAA championship practices, referring to the inequities as "significant and systemic" (Kaplan Hecker & Fink LLP (KHF) 2021a, 108). It also noted that while Title IX does not directly apply to the NCAA itself, it "does apply to the vast majority of NCAA's member" colleges and universities and thus federal policy

---

[3] Similar critiques of subpar venues and media coverage also emerged during the 2021 NCAA women's volleyball tournament (Olson 2021).

[4] The review came in response to the CWA and a letter from thirty-six Democratic Mem-bers of Congress (Hensley-Clancy 2021c) and was conducted by the law firm Kaplan Hecker & Fink (aka KHF). Five months later, the review concluded that "it is beyond dispute that there were significant disparities" between the treatment of the men's and women's championships and that the "experience" for participants in the women's tour-nament "was markedly different from and inferior to that of the men's" (KHF 2021a, 7). On September 29, 2021, the NCAA announced it would allow the women's tournament to use the March Madness trademark and change the budgeting model of the tourna-ments. The long-term material effects of these efforts remain to be seen.

"provided [the taskforce] with a helpful lens for assessing the gender equity of the NCAA championships" (4).[5]

The NCAA subsequently ensured that the 2022 basketball tournaments did not repeat the same massive public displays of inequalities – men and women were provided similar facilities and food, and both tournaments employed the "March Madness" label in marketing, television broadcasts, merchandise, and arena insignia. The recommendations emerging from the external report and the changes made by the NCAA to the 2022 tournaments may suggest the subtle hope of movement toward real equality in collegiate sports. However, in the aftermath of the external review the NCAA made no commitments to directly address the deeper gendered inequalities that pervade college sports (see KHF 2021b). Even the 2022 changes to the basketball tournament, while certainly important, remained relatively superficial. For instance, no changes were made regarding revenue distribution (e.g., how money is allocated in the men's and women's tournaments) – an issue that the external report noted as a central factor in the subordination of the women's events (KHF 2021a, 93–95). Reacting to the 2022 revised practices and the initial shifts toward more equitable management by the NCAA, one columnist aptly noted: "That's all fine and good. It's also low-hanging fruit. Fifty years after the passage of Title IX ... the NCAA was goaded into these simple changes after an internally ordered reviewer blistered the organization for an old-school, male-centered approach ... The true test has yet to come. Simple changes go only so far" (Streeter 2022a). The future for high-profile championships *and* quotidian opportunity and spending practices that we detail later in this chapter (and which pervade colleges and universities across the country) remain unclear.

In this book, we provide an assessment of gender equality in collegiate athletics fifty years after the passage of Title IX. Although much has evolved for women in sport since 1972, we illustrate the consequences of quiescence in recent years. There has been an absence of vigorous leadership among the most empowered stakeholders (i.e., the NCAA, members of Congress and federal bureaucrats, high-level university administrators). We seek to understand why and explore the possibility of agitation toward change in policy. We investigate whether protests

---

[5] Title IX specifically targets "education programs" but not, according to the US Supreme Court, the NCAA itself (see *NCAA v. Smith*, 525 U.S. 459, 469 (1999)). However, the NCAA does provide guidance on gender equity considerations to its member institutions who must comply with federal law.

and demands from key actors, like those instigated in 2021, are likely to generate improved future practices. We also interrogate how the structures of college sports – that is, the institutions that govern it – protect the status quo and undermine initiatives for change. Our framework and analyses are relevant for those who study the politics of college sports and beyond. We illustrate how institutions – particularly those that promote segregation as a vehicle for equal treatment, that prioritize cultural norms of the historically dominant group, and that enable profit-seeking as a goal within colleges and universities – can undermine the political quest for full equality.

We begin by establishing, in this chapter, the context of policy and practice in which recent events at NCAA tournaments emerged. As we detail, all conversations about equality in American collegiate sports are indebted to the passage of civil rights laws in the 1970s. We first summarize the history of Title IX, and we characterize the cultural mythos that often frames it as a unique policy success. Next, we raise questions about the accuracy of this frame and present evidence that interrogates it. Our skepticism stems from a pervasive reality: Despite federal law that outlaws sex discrimination in educational institutions, significantly inequitable practices persist. We illustrate this, provide an outline for the book, and gesture toward the needed policy change – and troubling institutional roadblocks – that will define the future of efforts to obtain equality. To be clear, lackluster leadership that neither enforces Title IX nor attends to the need for nuanced evaluations of how well it currently functions have rendered the insufficiencies of the status quo. Our aim is to lay bare the consequences of inaction and to diagnose and explore alternative possibilities (and structural limitations) to pursue meaningful progress.

1.1 THE PROMISE AND THE REALITY OF TITLE IX

In order to look to the future, we should first explain the past. The policy framework for this book emerged forty-nine years before the events of 2021, in a year that is often hailed as an inflection point in the evolution of women's rights. Therein, the US Congress passed the Education Amendments of 1972, including Title IX that states: "No person in the United States shall, on the basis of sex, be excluded from participation in, be denied the benefits of, or be subjected to discrimination under any education program or activity receiving Federal financial assistance."[6]

[6] 20 U.S.C. §1681.

Sports are not enumerated in the law, nor were they the main focus of lawmakers before its passage (Edwards 2010; Rose 2018). However, the initial spotlight on sex bias in classrooms, graduate admissions, and faculty appointments swiftly expanded to encompass extracurricular, school-sponsored athletics programs during debate over policy design in the 1970s (Sharrow 2017). In recent years, most journalistic coverage and the majority of Americans celebrate Title IX as a pivotal policy that ended the exclusion of girls and women in athletics and offered them full educational opportunities in the classroom.[7] Much like the 100th anniversary of women's suffrage in 2019, the 50th anniversary of Title IX in 2022 invited inevitable assessments of sex nondiscrimination policies and their consequences.

This dominant story of Title IX's success is a powerful one. On its fortieth anniversary, President Barack Obama (2012a) declared that Title IX has "helped to make our society more equal in general." Undeniably, a great deal of evidence substantiates this claim. In higher education, women outnumber men in college enrollment and now receive graduate degrees at parity with men in many fields (Rose 2018). Improved higher educational attainment opened the workplace for women (Hanson, Guilfoy, and Pillai 2009). In collegiate sports, competitive opportunities for women have ballooned roughly twelvefold since the early 1970s (NCAA 2017a; Wilson 2022). In turn, women and girls who participate in sports are more likely to live healthier lives (Callison and Lowen 2022; Kaestner and Xu 2010; Staurowsky et al. 2015). These impacts sharply contrast with the uneven effectiveness of gendered policies aimed at pay inequity, parental leave, access to childcare, and workplace sexual harassment. On balance, sex-based oppression and inequalities remain thorny problems. Yet Title IX is often discussed (both implicitly and explicitly in media, policy reports, and scholarship) as an exceptional, liberal feminist policy *success*. Although activists and elected officials continue to seek improved policy enforcement, including in its application to sports, Title IX is commonly framed as "the most important step for gender equality since the 19th Amendment gave us the right to vote" (Bernice Sandler quoted in Wulf 2012).

But what *is* the status of women in college athletics a half century after Title IX became law? How close do current practices come to achieving

---

[7] Several studies show that much journalistic attention employs progressive narratives of Title IX's success, promoting the idea that discrimination is a vestige of the past (Roessner and Whiteside 2016; Whiteside and Roessner 2018). Public opinion has long supported Title IX (Sigelman and Wilcox 2001; YouGov 2017).

sex equality? Although there is some merit to Title IX's success story, it also hinges on a powerful dose of underexamined folklore. While equitable opportunities for women have expanded over the past half century, the promise of *full equality* remains unfulfilled, particularly in athletics. As we document later in this chapter, men are persistently provided greater numbers of athletic roster spots, significantly more financial support for their teams, and the preponderance of coaching and athletic leadership opportunities. Likewise, the benefits of expanded athletic opportunity have disproportionately favored cisgender, able-bodied, White women from middle-to-upper-income families, revealing the intersectional shortcomings of the policy (see NWLC and PRRAC 2015; Pickett, Dawkins, and Braddock 2012).[8]

Political disputes over the efficacy of Title IX often pivot to whether better enforcement could end inequality. On Title IX's fortieth anniversary, President Obama (2012b) also noted, "We have come so far. But there's so much farther we can go. There are always more barriers we can break and more progress we can make. As president, I'll do my part to keep Title IX strong and vibrant." Scholars (e.g., Yanus and O'Connor 2016), public figures (e.g., Romero and Yarrison 2012), advocacy groups (e.g., Barnett and Hardin 2011; NCWGE 2022; Staurowsky et al. 2020), and journalists (e.g., Barra 2012; Hardin and Whiteside 2009; Wulf 2012) typically embrace status quo policy design even while recognizing persistent inequalities. This perspective suggests that extant inequalities can be addressed through better policy administration and oversight, ultimately pursuing equality *within* existing policy parameters.

If the conventional wisdom about Title IX is correct, then movements for better enforcement should be sufficient to secure equality. However, there is plentiful evidence of insufficiencies in the status quo, such as that revealed during the 2021 basketball tournaments. This evidence persists despite fifty years of policy implementation. Even the ostensibly more equitable 2022 NCAA basketball tournaments remain the exception rather than the norm. As we noted, initial changes to the tournament structures do not address systemic issues (such as tournament revenue sharing), and they have not produced a widespread shift to routine, non-tournament practices across institutions where leadership also remains lacking. Ultimately, the events of 2021 and 2022 merely reveal the practices of the NCAA. Although the NCAA is a key player in college sports whose choices reveal much about the gendered order of college sports,

---

[8] Throughout, we have opted to capitalize "White" (see Ewing 2020).

narrowly focusing on their tournaments does not fully capture the status of equality, nor the quality of efforts to implement federal policy.[9] As we will show, when we take an overall look at nationwide practices, the average and overall gendered athletic participation, resource allocation, and leadership inequalities at colleges and universities across the country are stark. This evidence raises questions about whether extant policy, if better enforced, will suffice in its current form.

Rather than reifying the assumption that mere pressure toward policy enforcement will be sufficient to produce full equality, we adopt a critical perspective. We set out to study whether existing structures provide adequate vehicles for the push toward parity, and if not, why? As the circumstances in 2021 illustrate, public attention to inequality implies that student-athletes, coaches, leadership, and fans are well poised to propel needed adjustments to the status quo. Indeed, such exogenous pressures on the NCAA were key to securing the external gender equity review, and research shows that policy stakeholders are often crucial actors in advocating for enforcement or transformation (e.g., Campbell 2003).

But how likely is it that such groups *will* push for widespread policy change? In this book, we tackle this question head-on. We do this by scrutinizing whether and how initiatives for gender equity could emerge from student-athletes, college sports coaches and athletic administrators, the mass public, or college sports fans. The success of such initiatives, we argue, will be key to defining the future possibilities for equality.

Ours is more than a speculative argument. We test our predictions with multiple original, direct solicitation surveys with student-athletes, coaches, athletic administrators, and the American public, including fans (total N = 7,500 respondents). Our surveys query support for gender equity initiatives (i.e., policies that aim to improve equality of outcomes); our findings reveal substantial institutional hurdles in the pursuit of equality.

Drawing on theories of interpersonal contact (among student-athletes), organizational culture (among athletic administrators and coaches), socialization effects of sports participation (among the public), and political economy (among fans), we reveal how potential pathways to reform are blocked by four institutional conditions. First, sex-segregated athletic training and competition – incentivized under the status quo policy

---

[9] Indeed, the aforementioned external equity review explicitly focused on the narrow issue of college basketball tournaments and not on the larger systemic inequalities that we document later in this chapter.

design – block coalition formation among student-athletes. Those competing in the "men's" versus "women's" categories are less likely to push for full equality. Second, organizational culture (i.e., assumptions taught to and brought to bear on those who work within an organization) inhibits progressive leadership among women working as coaches and administrators in college athletics by conservatizing their preferences. Third, sex-segregated youth athletic experiences – specifically in high school – indelibly socialize young men to accept the marginalization of women. Such consequences endure into adulthood regardless of men's interest in sports later in life. Fourth, the economic pressures from college sports fans who prefer the status quo impede reform. These rarely acknowledged conditions present core roadblocks to change.

Our findings offer underappreciated perspectives on public policy. First, efforts to obtain sex equality have not been achieved merely through bureaucratic implementation of Title IX in its current form. Nuanced evaluations of Title IX's legacy must grapple with this fact. Second, our results demonstrate how institutions and policy design can shape policy preferences in ways that undermine potential efforts to obtain equality now and in the future. The status quo is (and will likely stay) unequal, at least in part, because coalitions to demand equality remain suppressed. When steady efforts to promote equality are constrained by existing structures, it reveals the need for fundamental institutional and cultural change. Finally, we provide lessons from this case study of Title IX for those who seek to design policy and institutions that address the marginalization of any excluded group. We situate our book within the landscape of efforts to promote egalitarianism via policy interventions in the United States and demonstrate that our findings have broad implications for the future of gender equality.

1.2 CONTEXT AND CASE LOGIC: CIVIL RIGHTS AND THE UNFINISHED JOURNEY TO EQUALITY

Of all possible windows into the status of gender equity, why study non-discrimination policy in sports? Although intercollegiate and interscholastic athletic programs have drawn much of the attention and debate about Title IX, the law itself is one of many federal civil rights policies. Civil rights policies such as Title IX are designed to protect against discrimination and improve the status of marginalized groups in America. Title IX's focus on school-sponsored athletics is one component of its general ban on sex discrimination in educational programming of all types. Thus, it is imperative to study policy impacts on equality in sports because athletic teams are components of American education.

We follow a long tradition of normative Western political thought by focusing on questions of equality (e.g., Fraser 2009; Klinkner and Smith 1999; Smith 1997; Young 2000). Although equality constitutes a core tenet of full citizenship in democratic societies (Smith 2022), history and feminist critique demonstrate that ascriptively liberal political orders, even those in the contemporary United States, can still fall short on the full incorporation of women into society and public life (see Brown 1988; Mettler 1998; Ritter 2006). In recent years, and particularly (though not exclusively) after the election of Donald Trump to the American presidency, both political scientists and theorists alike have grown increasingly concerned about women's status in American democracy (e.g., Brown 1995; Honig 2021; Strolovitch, Wong, and Proctor 2017; Threadcraft 2016). Evidence suggests an uneven efficacy for sex-equity policies at work (Edelman 2016; Edelman and Cabrera 2020), policies securing reproductive rights and autonomy (Solinger 2019; Ziegler 2015), and policies designed to prevent violence against women (Sidorsky and Schiller 2023; Sweet 2021). Such gendered policies are regularly under scrutiny, often underenforced, and increasingly under threat. Notably, the day after the fiftieth legislative anniversary of Title IX in June 2022, the US Supreme Court ruled in *Dobbs v. Jackson Women's Health Organization*, effectively ending federal abortion rights granted by the 1973 *Roe v. Wade* decision. Gendered backlash – to borrow a term coined by Susan Faludi (1991) to describe conservative political pushback to the feminist movement's policy success – is imminent. Such events underscore the need for rigorous analyses of public policies intended to promote gender equality. To the extent that Title IX *has* been a successful tool for addressing inequality in the male-dominated realm of athletics, there may be lessons for solving women's oppression elsewhere in society.

By the same token, identifying points of policy failure is crucial if Title IX is to be appropriately used as a model for other policies. In other domains, much is known about the difficult task of societal change via public policy. Civil rights policies in particular have proven uneven in their effectiveness at addressing workplace inequalities (Dobbin 2009; Edelman 2016), lack of equitable educational access (Bell 2004; Bowen and Bok 1998), and the needs of people with disabilities (O'Brien 2001; Pettinicchio 2019). More generally, multiple studies document the unfinished and often retrogressive business of addressing race-based discrimination (Barnes 2021; Fording, Soss, and Schram 2011; Pollock 2008), legacies of homophobia (Canaday 2009), and other forms of bias at the intersections of race, gender, class, and sexuality via public policies (Crenshaw 1991; Michener and Brower 2020). Similar appraisals of policy inadequacies under Title IX should also inform the next era of policy design and implementation, particularly if or when feminist movements must respond to backlash.

Political scientists have said relatively little about the influence of Title IX on intercollegiate sports (although see McDonagh and Pappano 2007). Anecdotally, scholars theorize that Title IX's implementation educated women on their gendered political rights (Mettler and Soss 2004, 61) but with limited rigorous assessment of how or with what effect. This silence persists despite increasing interest in the political consequences of public policy with respect to mobilizing beneficiaries (Campbell 2003; Michener 2018), stimulating their long-term civic participation (Mettler 2005), and rendering shifts in public opinion (Lerman and McCabe 2017; Mettler and Soss 2004). Elsewhere in the field, scholars recognize the important impacts of women as elected representatives, social movement leaders, and voters, despite their chronic underrepresentation in political institutions (e.g., Dittmar, Sanbonmatsu, and Carroll 2018; Lawless 2015). Yet scholars give limited attention to the ways that women have been influenced by and in turn have come to shape subsequent policy debates about Title IX. Given Title IX's ostensibly transformative effects, the void of political science research is noteworthy.

Other disciplines have had more to say, albeit with different foci. For instance, economists demonstrate that Title IX's implementation in sports positively altered women's workforce participation (Stevenson 2010) and physical health (Kaestner and Xu 2010). Sociologists analyze how policy facilitates expansive shifts in understandings of gender (Cooky and Messner 2018; Messner 2002; Schultz 2014) and how girls' sports participation increases the likelihood of completing a college degree (Troutman and Durfur 2007). Policy historians and legal scholars provide context for the ongoing battles over interpretation and compliance (e.g., Belanger 2016; Brake 2010; Buzuvis and Newhall 2012; Rose 2018; Sharrow 2021b). Beyond sports, recent scholarship traces the centrality of women's activism in reshaping Title IX's application to addressing sexual misconduct on college campuses (Brodsky 2021; Reynolds 2019).

This scholarship reveals the importance of insider-advocates in Title IX's history. Our previous research on student-athletes' opinions about equality in college athletics made us curious about the potential for policy reform movements, emerging from either beneficiaries or other interested parties (Druckman et al. 2014a; Druckman, Rothschild, and Sharrow 2018; Sharrow 2017). We aimed to study such possibilities for shaping the future of policy across the *constituencies* of American collegiate sport. We also suspected that Title IX's implementation and repercussions would be attenuated by the historic *structures* of college sports – particularly as they relate to sex-differentiated competition, one topic that has been more thoroughly problematized in political science research (McDonagh and Pappano 2007; Sharrow 2021a). Thus, we set out to research this book based on an instinct that analyzing college sports provides a rare opportunity to study policy constituents, possibilities for policy change, and the impacts of contemporary institutional segregation on policy opinions and policy coalitions.

1.2.1 Governance and Organization of College Sports

More generally, understanding policy in college sports provides insights about the politics of women's inclusion into historically exclusionary spaces. Intercollegiate athletics before Title IX were notoriously male-centric in both competitive venues and governance structures (Cahn 1995). The first men's intercollegiate competition was in 1852 and the NCAA, the now-dominant college sports governing entity, began organizing competitive athletics for men in 1910.[10] College leaders made no efforts to nationally organize women's sports competition until 1941. Even then, it was the Division for Girls and Women's Sport of the American Association for Health, Physical Education and Recreation, not the NCAA, that convened the first national collegiate women's championship in golf.

Athletic programming was similarly sidelined in congressional debate on discrimination against women in education and was scarcely considered

---

[10] The NCAA does not govern all American college athletics, although it organizes and oversees the preponderance of institutions (nearly 1,300) and student-athletes (over 460,000 annually). Elsewhere, the National Association of Intercollegiate Athletics governs athletics at small colleges in North America, the National Junior College Athletic Association governs athletics for community/junior colleges in the United States, and the National Christian College Association (NCCA) governs competition among some Christian colleges in the United States and Canada. Neither club sports nor intramurals are governed by the NCAA. Many club sports have distinct governing bodies (e.g., the National Intramural-Recreational Sports Association, National Federation of Collegiate Club Sports Leagues). Only varsity athletics sponsored by NCAA member institutions fall within our study design.

until *after* the 1972 passage of Title IX (Edwards 2010; Sharrow 2017). In 1971–72, only 15 percent of collegiate varsity athletic opportunities were available to women (Staurowsky et al. 2022), an imbalance that swiftly drew the attention of activists interested in defining the breadth of sex nondiscrimination. Federal policy deliberation throughout the 1970s concerned the means for addressing this imbalance. Aggressive lobbying efforts from men's coaches, organized through the NCAA, argued that men's sports should be allowed to retain their independence. Although final federal regulations disconfirmed the notion that men's teams were entitled to act with disregard for women's equality, vestiges of the idea that men's sports are the "real" college sports whereas women's competition is merely a sideshow persist in contemporary athletics.

In practice, the regulations incentivized creation of "separate but equal" women's teams. Today, Title IX remains a nondiscrimination policy that requires similar, but not identical, treatment of women and men in school-sponsored sports (see Brake 2010, chaps. 6 and 7). Policy design to define and combat sex discrimination under Title IX addresses issues of access, opportunity, treatment, and resource allocation. Schools need to provide proportional athletic opportunities (including scholarship dollars) and equivalent treatment and benefits to women and men (US Department of Education Office for Civil Rights [OCR] 1979). As feminist legal scholars note, Title IX blends "measures of equality that are substantive and results oriented" (Brake 2010, 8), requiring institutions to ensure nondiscrimination in sports through a variety of means that we detail in what follows. Ultimately, contemporary college sports are built on guidelines crafted in the 1970s and in which policymakers merely required existing, male-dominated, athletic departments to add new women's teams without otherwise requiring them to change their administrative practices or personnel. Moreover, equal spending is *not* required under law.[11] ⬆ important

In practice, policy thus protected rather than challenged central structures of androcentric athletic institutions. It required the creation of new sex-segregated teams, largely governed by preexisting men's leadership, as the "nondiscriminatory" solution to long-standing exclusions. Policy guidelines did not require coed teams, joint practice facilities, or shared coaches across sex-separated structures, nor did such practices widely emerge organically. Policymakers imported binary organizational logics to entrench separate "men's" and "women's" teams, presuming and

[11] For the history of congressional debate over equal funding, see Suggs (2005, chap. 4).

privileging access for cisgender athletes (Sharrow 2017). Thus policy design, not merely preexisting norms or customs, cemented growth in "separate but equal" sports teams (Sharrow 2013, 2021a).[12] Legalized sex segregation paired with limited policy interference into athletic leadership sustained, rather than disrupted, the preexisting dominance of men's sports and leadership.

Decades hence, sex-based segregation in athletics is profoundly normalized. Whereas sex segregation is outlawed or outmoded in almost every other social realm (see Sharrow 2021a; Strum 2004), alternative organizational bases for school-sponsored sports are rarely discussed (with the obvious exception of organizing competition by age or skill – i.e., junior varsity teams – in interscholastic sports). The institutionalization of segregation through policy design is key to this normalization. Early in life, children invariably engage in sex-integrated play at school and in their neighborhoods. Hextrum (2021, 97) aptly explains, "Institutions formalize, and in turn gender, children's play. Schools route children's play into formalized and regulated channels ... eliminating opportunities for youth to design their own physical contests. In these formal settings ... institutions' representatives ... taught them the right way to play. This 'right way' retained a masculine athletic structure." Various other organizational principles could be (and occasionally are) deployed to structure athletic competition, such as height, weight, age, or ability (Cooky and McDonald 2005; Hextrum 2021, 98; Sharrow 2021a). However, Title IX's policy guidelines consider only sex for organization of teams (and even then, tend to narrowly conflate "sex" with sex assigned at birth except where participation guidelines for gender-diverse participants broaden eligibility).

The institutions that govern and oversee sex-separate competition – that is, sports governance organizations – also developed in segregated contexts. The NCAA now publicly supports current policy guidelines, though its record on Title IX reveals periods of aggressive resistance to sports equity. During initial debates over how to construct equity policy in sports, the NCAA sued the US Department of Health, Education, and Welfare (HEW) in an attempt to invalidate the federal regulations in 1978.[13] It contended that HEW, the agency of the federal bureaucracy

---

[12] During the twentieth century, access to physical education and recreation increased significantly for girls and women, also often in segregated spaces. Women physical educators were key players in debates over integrated physical education (Verbrugge 2012).

[13] *National Collegiate Athletic Association v. Califano*, 444 F. Supp. 425 (D. Kans., 1978), affirmed, 622 F. 2d 1382 (10th Circ. 1980).

then charged with administering Title IX, exceeded its authority in promulgating requirements for its member institutions.[14] The court ruled against the NCAA, finding that it did not have the legal standing to contest the regulations (Schubert, Schubert, and Schubert-Madsen 1991). During that period, women's athletics was governed by the Association for Intercollegiate Athletics for Women (AIAW), founded in 1971. By 1981, only two years after the federal government finalized Title IX's enforcement guidelines, the NCAA abruptly changed its stance on women's sports and began hosting its own women's championships. The AIAW suffered significant loss in membership and financial income as a result of the NCAA's decision to monetize women's championships (Festle 1996). It filed an unsuccessful antitrust lawsuit against the NCAA to retain governance of women's collegiate athletics (Wushanley 2004). Thus, the AIAW, unable to compete with the financial incentives offered to participating schools by the NCAA, ceased operations in 1982. In the years that followed, the NCAA incorporated women's sports into its governance structure and replicated Title IX's policy design by instituting sex-separate national championships.

1.2.2 Equity Guidelines and the "Three-Part Test"

Throughout the 1980s and 1990s, political institutions were the venue for significant policy debate about enacting Title IX. As the NCAA asserted its leadership over intercollegiate competition, scores of women pushed for policy enforcement at their individual institutions in efforts to obtain equal opportunities. This meant that many women employed direct pressure on leadership by filing federal-level complaints to the OCR in the US Department of Education or pursuing lawsuits (Brake 2010; Reynolds 2019). These actions facilitated growth in women's athletic teams by demanding action on federal policy guidelines at colleges around the country.

One particular lawsuit, *Cohen et al. v. Brown University*, inspired clarification of enforcement mechanisms that paradoxically made policy more detailed and less enforceable (OCR 1979; see also Brake 2010; Sharrow 2013).[15] Since the *Cohen* decision, OCR specified that schools must pass the "three-part test" of compliance with Title IX (OCR 1996).

---

[14] The US Department of Education, founded in 1979, now oversees implementation and enforcement of Title IX.

[15] The case was brought by women student-athletes at Brown University where athletic administrators demoted their varsity gymnastics and volleyball teams to club status; the

College athletic departments must either: (1) provide participation opportunities and scholarships for women and men that are substantially proportionate to their undergraduate enrollments, (2) demonstrate a history of continuing expansion for the "underrepresented sex" (i.e., women), or (3) show evidence of having accommodated the "interests and abilities" of the underrepresented sex. Although political debates about compliance rules resurfaced in the early 2000s (see Sharrow 2020; Suggs 2005, chap. 10), the "three-part test" remains the dominant policy guideline.

However, current federal standards provide such leeway for unequal practices that no institution has ever confronted a loss of federal funding – Title IX's ultimate enforcement provision – from a policy investigation. This is the case even though many schools remain at least partially noncompliant with the "three-part test" (e.g., Sigelman and Wahlbeck 1999; Yanus and O'Connor 2016). As the size and scope of intercollegiate athletic competition ballooned over the past decades (Clotfelter 2019), sports governance and federal civil rights policies hived men's sports away from women's and entrenched sex-segregated practices that often obscure, rather than reveal, the extent of inequality.

Today, the NCAA's main purpose involves overseeing ninety national championships across twenty-four sports. The federal government retains full authority to enforce the law, but the NCAA wields sufficient power and clout over the decisions of its nearly 1,300 member institutions to aggressively incentivize compliance. They have the latitude to craft membership rules that could, in theory, require participating schools to comply with federal guidelines. Although the NCAA no longer expresses open hostility to policy requiring equal treatment and opportunity for women in sport, they have yet to forcefully pursue it in their sports championships, as evidenced by the events in 2021. Gaps between commitments to equity in principle and practice remain.

1.3 INEQUALITY IN CONTEMPORARY COLLEGE SPORTS

In our introductory example we described the stark inequalities at the men's and women's 2021 NCAA championships. Here we take up our central framing more systematically, asking: Are women college athletes

---

student-athletes charged that by ceasing support for women's teams while continuing to fund disproportionate opportunities for men Brown violated Title IX (*Cohen et al. v. Brown University*, 101 F.3d 155 [1996]).

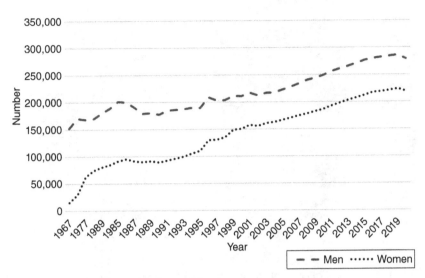

FIGURE 1.1 US college athletic participation, 1967–2021
Source: NCAA Sports Sponsorship and Participation Rates Report 2021. (Data are noncontiguous from 1967 to 1982; specific numbers are available for 1967, 1972, 1977, and 1982–2021.)

↳Answering a question

a marginalized group – that is, one targeted by policy but persistently facing systematic discrimination and frequent exclusion in the status quo (Young 2000)? We address this question with a new analysis of data on gendered dynamics in sports participation opportunities (i.e., roster spots on varsity sports teams), resource allocation, and athletic leadership.

Figure 1.1 presents NCAA-sponsored athletic participation opportunities for men and women from 1967 to 2021 (based on data from the NCAA). The monotonic increases in athletic opportunity for both groups are striking. Whereas limited varsity athletic programming was available for women fifty years ago, there is now substantial evidence that federal policy opens inroads for inclusion. However, the figure also exposes enduring inequalities – as women's participation increased, so did opportunities for men. Despite policy implementation, *full equality* of opportunity, wherein the two trend lines would eventually converge, remains elusive.

Participation opportunities illustrate only part of practice in college sport. We further explore the status of differential treatment by collecting data from the US Department of Education's Equity in Athletics Data Analysis Tool, for the 2018–2019 academic year (the year during which we collected most of the data in this book) (US Department of Education

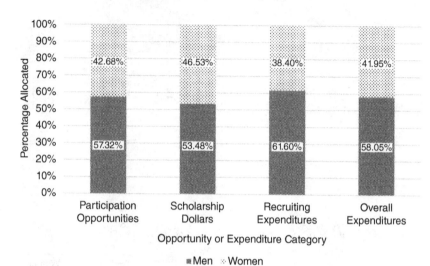

FIGURE 1.2 College athletic opportunities and expenditures, 2018–19

(DOE) 2021a).[16] In Figure 1.2, we present the results, displaying national average percent allocations to men and women (derived across percentages calculated within each institution) for participation opportunities, scholarship spending, recruiting expenditures, and overall expenditures. These data cover all NCAA schools across NCAA divisions.[17] We provide narrower breakdowns of averages by NCAA division and among schools with and without football programs and additional details on the primary data sources in the appendix. (Throughout the book, we regularly refer to both general and chapter-specific information available in our online appendix at www.cambridge.org/Druckman-Sharrow_EqualityUnfulfilled.) We also return to a longer discussion of the roles of football and men's basketball in debates over gender equity at the end of this chapter.

[16] Per allowable federal guidelines, the participation data include male "practice players" on women's team rosters, if individual institutions elect to report them. This practice, common in Division I women's basketball, allows institutions to report men who practice (but never compete) on women's teams (e.g., mocking likely opposition plays to prepare for games) *as* "women" (also see Fink, LaVoi, and Newhall 2016).

[17] The NCAA divisional structure was created in 1973 to align institutions for competition; national championships and elements of governance are organized within divisions. Division I institutions are generally the largest athletics programs with the most sizable budgets; they are further subdivided based on whether or not they offer football programs and at what level (i.e., Football Bowl Subdivision [FBS – formerly NCAA Division IA] or Football Championship Subdivision [FCS – formerly NCAA Division IAA]). They grant partial or full athletic scholarships to many (but not all) athletes and compete at the highest level. Division II institutions are also allowed to grant athletic scholarships. Division III institutions cannot grant athletic scholarships (see Shannon 2018).

The first bar in Figure 1.2 shows, consistent with Figure 1.1, that men receive substantially greater average participation opportunities: 57.32 percent versus 42.68 percent for women, on average, leading to a 14.64 percentage point gap that favors men.[18] As a point of reference, women comprise about 57 percent of the nationwide undergraduate population – an enrollment gap that favors women by about 14 percentage points (NCES 2021). Thus, based on the pure proportionality expectation in the "three-part test" of Title IX compliance, the disparity among student-athletes is even more striking. Athletic opportunities *should* mirror the gender proportion of enrolled undergraduate students if Title IX is fully enforced. That is, proportionality in athletic opportunities should technically favor women, based on their higher undergraduate enrollment levels. Enforcing proportionality could lead to *greater* athletic opportunities for women, at least on average.[19]

In the second bar, we present the average percentage of scholarship dollars allocated to men and women. This reveals a gender gap of 53.48 percent to 46.53 percent on average (a 6.95 percentage point disparity that favors scholarship spending for men). These participation and scholarship inequalities persist *despite* policy guidelines that explicitly pressure colleges and universities to pursue parity in these practices.

The third bar in Figure 1.2 reports the enormous 23.20 percentage point (61.60 percent to 38.40 percent) average athlete recruiting expenditure differential between men's and women's sports. The final bar displays the average overall expenditure allocation with 58.05 percent going to men and 41.95 percent going to women (a 16.10 percentage point difference). In the appendix, we show that among the largest NCAA Division I Football Bowl Subdivision (FBS) programs, that overall average expenditure disparity is significantly larger. In those programs, men enjoy 41.5 percentage points more of the average overall spending per institution – an average of $21.5 million per year at each Division I FBS school. Cumulatively, among NCAA Division I programs alone, these disparities favor excess spending on men's athletics at over

---

[18] We also calculated the differences in the number of teams overall and here, there are consistently more women's teams, but they tend to have fewer athletes, particularly compared to the size of men's football rosters, many of which host over 100 student-athletes. On average, NCAA colleges and universities host 1.11 more teams for women.

[19] Each institution is technically required to provide athletic opportunities on the basis of sex proportionate to their undergraduate enrollment. So, while the nationwide comparison is based on aggregated trends, strict proportionality would require schools to invert their current practices, providing 57 percent of athletic opportunities to women (or whatever percent women are enrolled in their undergraduate population). As we note, the federal government has been loath to enforce this.

$3.1 billion annually. While Title IX does not strictly require equal spending, the size of spending disparities nonetheless reveals the hyper-prioritization of men's teams.

Of course, the status of women in collegiate athletics has improved over time. The resource and spending inequalities pre-Title IX were inarguably dramatically larger when very few opportunities and limited expenditures were devoted to women's sports. However, focusing only on change over time suggests that the salient points of comparison in assessing equality would merely compare women's treatment now to their treatment in 1972, a half century ago.[20] Instead, we argue that the vital counterfactual for assessing the status quo requires comparison of men's and women's treatment in contemporary practice – a higher bar but a better metric by which to assess the status of equality.

With this metric in mind, we also observe gross inequalities in professional athletic leadership opportunities. For instance, before Title IX, over 90 percent of women's teams were coached by women (Acosta and Carpenter 2014; National Coalition for Women and Girls in Education [NCWGE] 2017). Despite the increase in women's teams, there has been a dramatic decrease in the proportion of women collegiate coaches over the past five decades. Men now hold 59 percent of the coaching positions for women's teams, in addition to nearly every appointment coaching men's programs. Further, during the period of our studies, nearly 24 percent of NCAA Division I women's teams had all-male coaching staffs (LaVoi, Boucher, and Silbert 2019).

In Figure 1.3, we present data on employment of men and women in collegiate coaching and athletic administration from 2018 to 19. (We again provide more acute breakdowns in the appendix.) The first bar of Figure 1.3 displays the overall distribution of men and women across coaching positions, including head and assistant coaches, for all (men's and women's) sports, revealing dramatic inequalities.[21] Across NCAA schools, only slightly more than one quarter of all coaching positions are occupied

---

[20] Some commentators often jump to this perspective, particularly to suggest that men's sports ought to remain at the center of collegiate athletics (e.g., Gavora 2002; Will 2002).

[21] The data on coaches include volunteer coaches. Volunteer coaches are prevalent in college sports, and they work directly with student-athletes and within teams. The title "volunteer" is often deceptive; the number of paid coaches is regulated by the NCAA and those labeled "volunteers" are, in many cases, compensated by external revenue generated by youth summer sports camps, clinics, etc. Also, to be clear, our population of coaches does not include trainers; trainers are treated as athletic administrators (typically, as part of the athletic performance staff). More detail is available in Chapter 2.

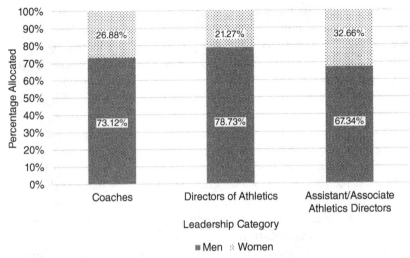

FIGURE 1.3 College athletic leadership opportunities, 2018–19

by women (a 46.24 percentage point disparity that favors men's employment) and, as mentioned, nearly all the women coach women's teams.

We find similar disparities among athletic administrators: Men inhabit 78.73 percent of athletic director positions and 67.34 percent of assistant and associate athletic director jobs. Women hold only 21.27 percent and 32.66 percent of those directorship positions, respectively (gaps of 57.46 percentage points and 34.68 percentage points that favor men's leadership) (see also Whisenant 2003).[22] This underrepresentation of women is strikingly most similar to industries such as manufacturing (29.4 percent women) and agriculture (26.2 percent women), according to the US Bureau of Labor Statistics (2021). Moreover, as we will discuss in subsequent chapters, women are also underrepresented on NCAA governing committees that determine the rules and regulations for intercollegiate athletic competition, where men hold 60 percent of the positions. Definitively, athletic administrative leadership and coaching remain overwhelmingly male-dominated: The 2020 Racial and Gender Report Card on College Sport (Lapchick 2020) gave the industry a grade of C+ for gender hiring.

These employment statistics accentuate the limitations of potential Title IX "spillover effects." That is, the expansion of women's teams

[22] Among the sixty-five schools in the Power Five Conferences (that largely include the football teams with the highest revenue), women hold only five or 7.69 percent of the athletic director position (as of May 2021) (Phillips 2021).

could have stimulated a larger talent pool of prospective female coaches and/or athletic administrators poised to enter the field, as well as increased college athletic employment possibilities. But increasing a possible pipeline for women in leadership through expanding women's athletic opportunity has failed to render a durable shift in women's athletic industry leadership. Such contradictory gender dynamics of bounded expansion at the points of entry into athletics (e.g., increased opportunity for participation, increased numbers of women's teams with new coaching opportunities) and spiraling retraction in representation up the leadership hierarchy (e.g., diminished proportion of women in leadership) are cause for concern. As we know from research in other domains and as we explore more fully in Chapter 4, women's underrepresentation in governance and management positions substantially restricts representation of their interests (Karpowitz and Mendelberg 2014).

Overall, our analyses make clear that across participation, resources, and leadership college athletics overwhelmingly benefit men. Relative to a standard of full gender equality with men (rather than in comparison to the benchmark of historic exclusions), disparities are stark. The data reveal that rather than reflecting a one-off error in tournament planning, the inequities that defined the 2021 basketball tournaments exemplify broader trends: inequalities remain an enduring tradition.

The data also underscore the importance of studying college athletics. An uncritical assessment of Title IX's effects, or an unnuanced assumption that moderate shifts toward inclusion are sufficient, could lead policymakers to replicate its tactics and policy design in other gendered policy realms. Although women student-athletes have greater athletic opportunities now than fifty years ago, women remain underincorporated, vastly underfunded, and dramatically constrained in their professional opportunities compared to men. Questioning how facets of a celebrated civil rights policy regime retain hurdles to equality can prevent duplication of the same incomplete outcomes in other policy domains, thereby preventing the perpetuation of disparities elsewhere in society.

1.4 THEORIZING ROUTES TO POLICY CHANGE

With these intractable imbalances in mind, we sought to understand *why* they persist. What prevents more progressive policy efforts to address inequalities? We begin by identifying initiatives that aim to address gender inequality in college sports. In so doing, we again emphasize that our focus on equality reflects a normative stance, not a legal one. The goal

of Title IX was not necessarily equality, per se: The point was to eliminate sex discrimination that by itself does not ensure equal outcomes.[23]
Moreover, in its implementation, as we note, Title IX does not strictly
prohibit lop-sided spending patterns nor any type of gendered dispropor-
tionality in leadership. The proposals we next delineate and on which
we subsequently focus are demonstrably forward-looking initiatives that
would propel a movement toward gender equality. Given the absence
of momentum toward full equality from those who could aggressively
pursue it (e.g., lawmakers), our attention turns to the latent forces that
could, in theory, force new forms of change.

1.4.1 Policy Proposals for Gender Equality

The policy agenda around sex discrimination and inequality in college
athletics includes several proposals. Consideration among political elites
and the general public is dominated by episodic discussion of better
enforcement of Title IX and equal athletic opportunities. The history of
Title IX reveals such conversations in congressional proceedings, formal periods of public comment, and federal-level public hearings (Kihl
and Soroka 2012; Sharrow 2013, 2020).[24] Media coverage, particularly
around Title IX's "anniversary," frequently highlights policy implementation struggles (Hardin et al. 2007; Whiteside and Hardin 2008).[25] As
we noted, despite the clarification of the proportionality standard in the
status quo, college athletics continue to underserve women (including
when it comes to participation) leaving enforcement concerns squarely
on the policy agenda, but typically among a host of low-salience issues.

Recent events propelled increased attention to policy protections
against sexual harassment. At the confluence of #MeToo and the activism regarding Title IX's application to addressing sexual violence on college campuses, egregious and well-publicized incidents of sexual abuse
rocked the sporting world. Most notably, Larry Nassar, a former elite
and collegiate athletic trainer, was convicted for multiple sexual assaults.

---

[23] That said, policy interpretations make liberal use of the language of "equal opportunity"
in formal guidance to schools (see, e.g., OCR 2020).

[24] For example, Members of Congress sponsored legislation to this end in spring 2021
("The Patsy T. Mink and Louise M. Slaughter Gender Equity in Education Act of 2021,"
H.R. 4097, 117th Cong. [2021]). Discussion of these topics often cohere around annual
celebrations of National Girls and Women in Sports Day, observed each February.

[25] At the same time, this focus is often on mere enforcement instead of more radical changes
as scholars find that recent reporting often frames sex discrimination as a relic of the past
(Whiteside and Roessner 2018).

His more than 250 accusers who included many former college athletes (and members of the US gymnastics team) testified at Nassar's sentencing hearing in January 2018, heightening public attention to the trauma endured by survivors. Later that year, Michigan State University – where Nassar had been employed as an athletic trainer – announced a $500 million settlement with Nassar's victims in a civil lawsuit regarding its lack of action to protect athletes from abuse. Unlike other sexual abuse scandals (e.g., at Pennsylvania State University), the NCAA did not sanction Michigan State University. Nassar's court proceedings came on the heels of sexual assault cases incriminating football players at Baylor University, which also ultimately went unsanctioned by the NCAA (see Luther 2016). Instead, the NCAA Board of Governors passed policy to heighten engagement with campus-level sexual violence prevention among member institutions, starting in 2017 (NCAA 2017b). This action was limited, but it intensified attention to the issue among key stakeholders. Moreover, as we designed our empirical studies (in 2017–2018), the Trump administration was rewriting Title IX policy guidelines with respect to procedures for addressing campus sexual misconduct, including within collegiate athletics. These conversations continued under the Biden administration whose US Department of Education hosted public hearings on the topics in June 2021 (Gravely 2021), ultimately releasing new proposed regulations on campus sexual misconduct in June 2022 and transgender inclusion and gender identity nondiscrimination in April 2023.[26]

In addition to enforcement policies, advocates often argue for more aggressive equity initiatives, particularly in terms of athletic spending. A sixty-page status report published by the NCAA on the occasion of Title IX's forty-fifth anniversary (NCAA 2017a) drew significant media attention to spending imbalances and reinvigorated public debate about equal spending among men's and women's sports (Meredith 2017). Opponents of Title IX often contend that full equality for women could trigger dire financial consequences under the current model of college athletics (Gavora 2002).[27] Consequently, the absence of spending equality policies

---

[26] The issue of sexual harassment in sports remained in the public conscience into the fall of 2022, with a blistering report about abusive behavior and sexual misconduct by coaches in the National Women's Soccer League (Yates 2022).

[27] Opponents of Title IX who make this argument claim that "revenue sports" – namely football and men's basketball – are "needed" to fund women's sports. If equality were required, they argue that rosters in some sports would have to be trimmed (e.g., fewer football players) and would consequently bring in less revenue. We return to a discussion of this argument later in this chapter.

has galvanized focus on whether equal treatment imperatives should include spending rules, particularly when issue salience is high.

A final set of proposals would boost pathways for women as coaches and administrators, in light of their abysmal underrepresentation in athletic leadership (see Sabo, Veliz, and Staurowsky 2016). Such policies could emulate those used in other domains. For example, since 2003, the National Football League (NFL) requires that all teams with a vacancy in the head coaching or senior football operations position must interview at least one candidate of color in their finalist pool (i.e., the "Rooney Rule").[28] Similarly, college athletics could require that final interviews for the athletic director position and head coach positions for women's teams include women candidates on the shortlist.

Possible Solution

With these various issues and trends in mind, we identified six specific proposals that would promote gender equality in athletics through public policy and which have recently circulated in policy discussions: (1) the increased enforcement of Title IX by officials, (2) the creation of equal athletic opportunities for women and men, (3) the increased enforcement of sexual harassment laws as they pertain to stakeholders in college athletics, (4) the creation of rules requiring equal spending for women's and men's sports, (5) the creation of requirements to interview at least one woman in the finalist pool for a women's team's head coach position, and (6) the creation of requirements to interview at least one woman in the finalist pool for an athletic director job. Each of these "gender equity initiatives," as we call them, are proposals aimed at changing current practices to make them more equitable with the long-term objective of achieving full equality. As we describe in Chapter 2, we use these proposals to formulate our main policy measures.

A policy agenda with proposals requires active constituents to advocate for policy change. Literatures across political science suggest that policy change, particularly in the absence of aggressive leadership from lawmakers, typically requires an activated lobbying force. We next provide an overview of our theory of three possible routes through which actors could pursue these initiatives, elaborating both the circumstances required for and possible hurdles that may limit transformation from the status quo.

---

[28] In 2022, the Rooney Rule added a requirement that all teams must have at least one minority individual on their offensive coaching staff (recent rule changes now designate that women, regardless of racial or ethnic identity, can be designated as a "minority").

1.4.2 Change from the "Bottom Up": Student-Athletes as Activists

Policy change could come from the *bottom up*, driven by athletes-as-policy-stakeholders. Student-athletes are the primary target population of Title IX's athletic regulations. Women's collegiate sports history includes many changes resulting from athlete activism (see Belanger 2016; Brake 2010; Cahn 1995). Indeed, in the midst of the national news and uproar about the aforementioned 2021 NCAA basketball tournament inequalities, coach Cori Close of the University of California, Los Angeles, said of the student-athletes: "They're the ones that have the most powerful voice. If this was not being bolstered by student-athletes and led by the student-athletes, I don't think it would have near as much power" (Baccellieri 2021). For example, as soon as the 2021 women's tournament concluded, players mobilized through social media and shared highlight videos, creating a tournament montage to advance their concerns about gendered disparities using the hashtags #OurShiningMoment and #OurFairShot. The latter hashtag promoted a new, durable initiative to advance discussion of gender inequalities in college basketball (WBCA 2021).

However, such change from "below" is not easy. Student-athletes' lives remain highly regulated, and they possess scant direct power to influence regulations that determine their training and competitive autonomy. On the other hand, there exists a long history, going back to at least the 1930s, of student-athletes pushing for change on racial inclusion gender equality, and compensation opportunities (Druckman, Howat, and Rothschild 2019; Epstein and Kisska-Schulze 2016). The level of success among particular subgroups of student-athletes (i.e., women) can be contingent on the size of their support coalitions – a heterogeneous majority of student-athletes advocating for change carries more potential than a smaller homogenous group.

When it comes to gender equity initiatives, we might expect female student-athletes to express support given their status as targeted policy beneficiaries from the historically marginalized group. Yet, as detailed in Figure 1.2, women, despite being a decisive majority of the population enrolled in undergraduate programs nationwide, comprise a clear minority of student-athletes (43 percent). To embolden their efforts, it may be essential to form a majority coalition with male student-athletes – that is, an alliance between those who are disempowered by the status quo (women) and those who are not (men). Such a coalition would not only generate strength in numbers but also carry symbolic weight. Many detractors of sex equality presume a zero-sum relationship between women's and men's opportunities and resources. That is, women's quest for additional opportunity is often framed by opponents as an attempt to "take" a fixed number of existing opportunities "from men." Such framing persists against the evidence of continued, parallel growth among men's sports in the wake of Title IX revealed in Figure 1.1.[29] Majoritarian coalitions of both women and men could propel successful movements for full equality.

In Chapter 3, we fully develop this theory. We extend work on social movements and interest group coalitions among marginalized groups to argue that coalitions can have a powerful impact in pressing for change (e.g., Han, McKenna, and Oyakawa 2021; Strolovitch 2007; Tormos 2017; VanDyke and Amos 2017). We also draw on political science research that suggests how policy advocates can drive change from within institutions (Campbell 2003; Katzenstein 1998; Mettler 2005). We argue that coalition formation requires meaningful engagement across groups and, given the unique structures that define the collegiate student-athlete experience, present a new theory of interpersonal contact as it relates to policy change.

Theorizing in this realm requires moving beyond the enormous existing literature on intergroup contact that mostly focuses on prejudice reduction (e.g., Paluck et al. 2021). We identify conditions under which an out-group (i.e., male student-athletes) may become more supportive of policies that benefit a marginalized group (i.e., female student-athletes). These include: (1) when the out-group understands the plight of the marginalized group (i.e., female student-athletes) and (2) when the out-group trusts the policymaking institutions (e.g., colleges, NCAA) to not substantially undermine their own interests. We argue that interpersonal contact is a mechanism through which the first condition can be met. Intergroup conversations about the contours of their experiences as student-athletes have the potential to educate the advantaged group (i.e., men) about the inequitable circumstances facing the marginalized group (i.e., women) (see Harnois 2017; Wiley et al. 2021). We theorize that such contact provides a potential pathway for the emergence of coalition and change from the *bottom up*. However, this occurs only when the advantaged group trusts the policymaking institutions (e.g., Lupia and McCubbins 1998); this addition of trust and a focus on policy beliefs, rather than group attitudes, constitute a novel theoretical contribution to work on contact.

---

[29] Men's participation opportunities have grown in sum, but we acknowledge the nuance obscured by these nationwide numbers. It is the case that some men's sports have been unduly eliminated at some schools during the past fifty years. However, overall growth in men's football rosters during that time – at many of the same schools that cut smaller men's teams – reveals that if administrators are engaging in any "zero-sum" choices they more aptly pit men's football against lower-profile men's sports. We discuss this further in Chapter 3.

We further hypothesize constraints on the potential for coalitions. The context of life as a student-athlete is key. College athletes spend an inordinate amount of time with and among their teammates while they train, travel, compete, study, and often when they eat and socialize (Ottaway 2018). Doing so also means spending unusually little time (compared to other college students) with those of the other sex. This is because Title IX creates incentives for institutions to support separate teams for women and men, hyperstructuring the social and competitive structures in athletes' lives and thereby diminishing cross-sex interactions. Consequently, exogenous institutional segregation of student-athletes significantly impedes the prospect that men will experience or identify with the inequitable plight of their marginalized female counterparts. We theorize that this limits the likelihood of policy coalition formation (see also Han, McKenna, and Oyakawa 2021; Htun and Weldon 2012; Tormos 2017; Weldon 2011), undermining change from the bottom up.

In Chapter 3, we present survey and experimental data to assess our argument. The data show that, indeed, male student-athletes exhibit more support for gender equity initiatives when they trust their schools and the NCAA and when they have high levels of interpersonal contact with female student-athletes. Thus, support for equity benefits increases among men who train and compete in sex-integrated environments (e.g., on track and field or swimming and diving teams where training in shared facilities is more common, often under shared coaching staff). Yet most male student-athletes do not live in such settings, as integrated or coed teams are the exception rather than the norm. Consequently, there is relatively limited cross-sex contact for male student-athletes and therefore many express lower levels of support for equity initiatives.

The chapter accentuates a possible route to policy change while also identifying how sex segregation inhibits it. The argument reveals, more generally, that an underappreciated barrier to policy change for marginalized groups emerges from segregated settings. It casts light on the problematic impacts of sex-segregated athletics – impacts theorized but rarely investigated by social scientists. Furthermore, our findings underscore the urgency for assessment of male-exclusive and male-dominated environments where, in college sports, the data show that men more easily secure and hoard opportunities and resources.

1.4.3 Change from the "Top Down": Leaders as Representatives

Given the relatively disempowered status of student-athletes, we also consider the possibility that athletic leadership might push to alter the status quo. Change could come from the *top down*, driven by those in a position to directly enact policies. Policymakers in the context of college sports include athletic department administrators (e.g., those in the athletic director's office, medical personnel, and academic support services) and coaches. Athletic administrators oversee Title IX compliance, hiring of coaches, and allocating resources. They can directly affect legislation via the NCAA rulemaking committees and must implement policy (both from the NCAA and the federal government) at individual schools. For instance, in the wake of the 2021 basketball tournament inequities, the external equity review panel recommended that the NCAA host the men's and women's semifinals and finals (i.e., Final Fours) at the same site and offer financial incentives to schools to improve their women's basketball programs (KHF 2021a). Athletic administrators have the power to pursue such policies in the long run and across their sports programs.

While coaches have relatively less direct policy control (although they too can sit on NCAA committees), they make hiring decisions within their team staffs and often serve as important intermediaries between student-athletes and higher-level athletic administrators. Additionally, coaches can raise awareness about equity concerns, as female basketball coaches did following the 2021 tournament. The Women's Basketball Coaches Association institutionalized the aforementioned initiatives to demand gender equity that initially emerged organically among the student-athletes in women's college basketball named "Our Fair Shot."[30] Athletic administrators and coaches further serve, in essence, as representatives of student-athletes in policy conversations. While they act as highly imperfect representatives given the lack of direct accountability mechanisms, they nonetheless are best positioned to advance student-athletes' interests to higher administration. We consider athletic administrators and coaches as leaders who can enact change from the top down in Chapter 4.

Of course, equity policies could be prompted by women and/or men in leadership positions. We focus on isolating the specific role of women for three reasons. First, theories of representation suggest that those who are descriptively representative of the beneficiary population are more likely to pursue substantive changes on behalf of the group, particularly when they have shared experiences (Dittmar, Sanbonmatsu, and Carroll 2018; Mansbridge 1999). Along these lines, many women in sports leadership are former participants in college sports. Fifty percent of women athletic

---

[30] The demands articulated in the "Our Fair Shot" campaign addressed many of the resource proposals we identify in our main measures, including demands for equal institutional support, training facilities, and recruiting dollars. See https://ourfairshot.com.

administrators and nearly 90 percent of women coaches are former college athletes.[31] Second, women administrators and coaches, like female
student-athletes, directly benefit from sex nondiscrimination policies that
secure the rights and opportunities for women in the workplace (e.g.,
increasing the number of women in leadership). Support for women's
sports can also increase job quality and security for coaches of women's
teams. Third, recent history includes examples of initiatives driven by
women to increase women's leadership and representation, including
the creation of positions such as the "Senior Woman Administrator"
(intended to vest authority in the senior-most female athletic director
within a school) and the publication of reports on the status of gender
parity in college sports (e.g., NCAA 2017a). Across many colleges and
universities, aggressive implementation of Title IX has stemmed from
advocacy by female leaders (Cahn 1995; LeBlanc and Swanson 2016).
In short, given the relative stagnation in the move to equality and the
related inaction to better pursue it through assertive leadership in recent
years, we hoped to identify potential subcurrents for change within athletic administration. On gendered policy issues, this drew our attention
to the possible roles of and constraints on women as changemakers.

We bring together work on policy feedback, organizational culture,
and gender in sports to theorize how status quo institutions can undermine possibilities for leader-driven policy change by women. Political
science research suggests that representative processes can successfully
evoke minority interests in governing bodies (Dittmar, Sanbonmatsu,
and Carroll 2018; Reingold 2000; Tate 2003). Women in positions of
power could work to enact change on behalf of women's interests using
their institutionalized power and/or in coalition with empowered men
from the "top down."

Yet research also suggests that when women enter collegiate athletic leadership positions, they find themselves embedded in an organizational culture – that is, patterns of behaviors and beliefs that are
imparted to new members of the organization (Schein 2004) – defined
by male domination, normalized gendered inequality, and scant support
for progressive gender initiatives (see Darvin, Hancock, and Williams
2021; Hindman and Walker 2020; Kane 2016). Women in sports leadership thus confront a double-bind between the need to support the aims
of their employer and the pressure to pursue equity commitments on
behalf of women as a group (see also Katz, Walker, and Hindman 2018).

---

[31] These percentages come from data we present in Chapter 4.

reasons why isolating female positions

Circumstances are exacerbated (and constituted) by the reality that, as among student-athletes, women comprise a minority of athletic administrators and coaches.[32] As such, we theorize that they engage in coping strategies that often involve altering their personal perspectives to better assimilate in their work environment (Miscenko and Day 2016; Wille and De Fruyt 2014). Likewise, those who advance up the hierarchy of a male-dominated industry likely reflect some selection effects that reward those who best conform to the extant culture.

We suggest that socialization (and/or selection) stemming from organizational culture leads women in athletic leadership roles (whether as administrators or coaches) to express lower levels of support for policy change compared to those below them in the institutional hierarchy (i.e., female student-athletes). We expect that women who have ascended the hierarchy – such as those who head athletic departments or head coaches – will exhibit significantly less support due to cultural entrenchment. These factors, we argue, make change from the *top down* less likely.

Male-dominated leadership structures suppress otherwise-possible change both directly and indirectly. They directly quell change by cultivating conservative leaders and incentivizing minimal responsibility to the requirements of status quo equity policy. Women in leadership within male-dominated organizations are less likely to unilaterally press for change or to build coalitions with male administrators when allies are few. Indirectly, androcentric hierarchies in sport suppress leadership opportunities for women and create a culture that socializes or selects women less supportive of full equality. We expect that quiescence, not change, is valued among those who advance in the hierarchy and therefore lead at the top level. Athletic administrators *could* lead towards change, yet we know relatively little about what constrains those with professional and group-based gendered interests (i.e., women) from successfully doing so.

In Chapter 4, we use data from surveys of coaches and athletic administrators to evaluate our expectations. The results reveal that female leaders indeed exhibit lower levels of equity initiative support than those held by female student-athletes – particularly among those leaders higher up the hierarchy. Organizational culture of college sports, where female administrators and coaches remain in the clear minority, is a hurdle to

---

[32] This mirrors women's underrepresentation in other governing institutions in the United States (CAWP 2021) and undermines the possibility of a majoritarian coalition of women policymakers who could unilaterally and aggressively enact "women's interests" in college athletics.

equality. This underscores the general lesson that marginalized groups pursuing change from the top down must contend with organizational cultures that resist such transformation.

This case also highlights how policies themselves can shape organizational culture: here, by normalizing basic, numeric gender inequalities and views. Policy design remains grounded in the era of its formulation, when women were largely excluded from college sports. This outdated baseline remains the salient point of comparison, rather than full equality. In short, the limits of policy design normalize an intransigent organizational culture that breeds, that is, feedbacks to, inequalities.

1.4.4 Change from the "Outside In": The Public as Policy Demanders

A final possible route for change is from outside the system – that is, from the public writ large and/or consumers of college sports advocating from the *outside in*. Although policy targets particular beneficiaries (e.g., student-athletes), Title IX is a civil rights law and therefore the ultimate constituents are the American public. The public supports Title IX (Igielnik 2022; Sigelman and Wilcox 2001; YouGov 2017).[33] But, whether there is widespread acknowledgment of extant inequalities or support for more progressive initiatives remains unclear. The stability of Title IX's policy milieu and its high popularity after fifty years of implementation makes significant shifts to the policy (via state or federal legislation) relatively unlikely compared to other issues (Mettler 2016).[34] However, we suggest that understanding mass opinion remains essential since legislators might enact policy change in anticipation of public reactions.

Research suggests that the public can influence sporting debates (Sharrow 2020; Thorson and Serazio 2018; Wallsten et al. 2017). Such possibilities remain clear as evidenced when the 2021 NCAA basketball tournament inequities were met with public outcry – including substantial social media engagement – that prompted the NCAA to address immediate inequalities and pursue an equity review. One

---

[33] An April 2022 Pew poll shows that 63 percent who know about Title IX and sports view the impact on gender equality as being positive and only 17 percent view it negatively (with the rest saying it has no impact) (Igielnik 2022).

[34] Notably, even recently proposed state-level legislation that challenges the rights of transgender girls and women to compete in sports typically reifies the import of Title IX and argues that transgender athletes should be excluded from the law's protections, *not* that the law itself should change to better serve all constituents (Sharrow 2021b).

media source noted that "the situation was seized on by everyone ... As a result, the NCAA installed a full weight room for the women sooner than had been originally planned, and it expanded the food options" (Baccellieri 2021).

We also recognize that change can come directly via the marketplace. College sports operate as an industry largely dependent on economic support from fans (Nixon 2014). In a capitalistic system, what fans want out of the "product" and how they react to industry conditions and values matter. Collegiate sports fans hold particular sway given the outsized role of consumer demands in the college sports economy (Clotfelter 2019). Examples of change to sports from the outside in include fan pressure on schools to change their Native American mascots (Billings and Black 2018; Guiliano 2015) or fans organizing to insist that the NCAA move championship competitions away from states with discriminatory public policies (Kliegman 2021). In Chapter 5, we consider the role of the public in pressing for policy change, whether via demands as citizen constituents of nondiscrimination policy or as fans with market-driven preferences.

We extend work on socialization effects to theorize some additional important factors. We expect that familial socialization will play a role. Specifically, we theorize that having a daughter who plays (or played) sports will increase parents' (both mothers and fathers) support for gender equity initiatives, as suggested by previous work (Sharrow et al. 2018). However, we also theorize that another socialization force might dwarf the impacts of familial effects. Specifically, we suggest that participation in a sex-segregated athletic system at an early age, namely in high school, normalizes the separation and gendered priorities/hierarchy within athletics, particularly among men. We focus on high school as that, historically, demarcates a clear transition from youth sports (where sex-integrated teams are not rare) to more competitive athletics governed by sex segregation. As such, we explore whether men who played high school sports remain more opposed to gender equity initiatives than men who did not play sports in high school. In contrast, we expect that women who played in high school directly experienced inequalities and, thus, if anything, will remain supportive of change for collegiate athletics. This chapter explores, in part, whether the impacts of sex segregation on constituent opinions toward equity policies have enduring consequences in the fight for gender equality. It shows how institutional settings can have long-term consequences on policy opinions and views of equality. Moreover, since a greater share of men participated in high school sports (55 percent) than there are men who have daughters who play sports (16 percent), we discuss how this competing trend can dominate the impact of increased support from parenting a daughter who plays (or played) sports.[35]

Finally, we theorize how the economic structure of college sports shapes support for gender equity initiatives, through a smaller subset of the public – fans. We draw on the political economy literature on "private politics" (e.g., Abito, Besanko, and Diermeier 2019; Druckman and Valdes 2019) and scholarship on fandom to theorize that those who financially invest in college sports (e.g., attend or watch games) develop a status quo bias against any change, including novel gender equity initiatives. This reflects their investment in the product and the overwhelming media bias that places higher value on and coverage of men's sports (see Cooky et al. 2021; Musto, Cooky, and Messner 2017).

We test our predictions with a representative survey of the public, including college sports fans. The data reveal the barriers expected by our theory. We find a long-term impact of experiencing sex segregation in sports on men's enduring attitudes toward equity policies later in life. We also detect that economic barriers stemming from the privileged status given to men in college athletics suppress support among fans. Structural barriers hinder change, this time from the outside in.

1.5 REFORMING COLLEGE SPORTS

In Chapter 6, we situate our findings in a larger context. We point out the peculiarity of college sports institutions, relative to those that govern other social spaces – they invoke conflicting missions of revenue generation and education, incentivize sex segregation rather than integration, and normalize massive gender disproportionalities in leadership roles. We summarize how these structures have halted the quest, by student-athletes, athletic leaders, and the public, for gender equality. We also generalize lessons from our findings to other domains. For instance, our exploration into the impact of segregation on policy opinions reveals that any type of separation can diminish the possibility of policy coalitions that benefit marginalized groups. Even if segregation stems from geographic sorting or histories of discrimination (rather than standing institutional rules), it can lead to inequitable practices. We provide examples from work on racial segregation regarding housing and education policy and the role of partisan sorting

---

[35] These percentages come from data we present in Chapter 5.

in the emergence of antidemocratic attitudes. Further, sex segregation specifically facilitates and/or rationalizes discriminatory policies toward transgender people, a topic of contemporary relevance given the number of states that have recently passed anti-trans laws (Sharrow 2021b).

When it comes to organizational culture, our findings offer insight into theories of representation. We investigate whether descriptively representative individuals better represent the preferences of those from their shared identity groups. We find this is, all else constant, the case for female leaders in colleges sports (i.e., relative to male leaders, their preferences are closer to those of female student-athletes); however, the preferences of women in higher athletic leadership positions are less representative of women student-athletes as well as women lower in the athletic hierarchy. This accentuates how formal positionality matters, with leaders having to navigate an organizational culture that may not cohere with the interests of their constituent groups. In less-democratic contexts that lack accountability mechanisms – such as college sports – this can result in the disenfranchisement of relevant stakeholders.

Finally, we discuss the implications of our findings for work on policy feedback and socialization. On questions of policy feedback, we illustrate the uncertainties of determining key policy constituents when policies have a commercial element. We ultimately question how the quasi-private market of college athletics renders ambiguity around whether student-athletes, the tax-paying public that funds Title IX enforcement, or fans should determine the future of the law. On topics of policy socialization, we draw a connection between early socialization experiences, such as participating in sex-segregated sports, and downstream policy views. We note that such socialization can shape the possibilities for policy feedback.

Our conclusions then turn to the future of gender equality in college sports. The fiftieth anniversary of Title IX in 2022 brought with it much public discussion, reflection, and celebration. This included a vastly improved NCAA women's basketball tournament – much more on par with the men's tournament. But Americans should not mistake that event as indicative of fundamental change, a point emphasized by many commentators at the time. There remains an urgent need to move beyond mere improved enforcement of Title IX.

We are not sanguine about this, acknowledging the treasured place that Title IX occupies in the American consciousness and, as we will discuss, its relative (although not absolute) success in postsecondary education more generally. However, the future of gender equality in sports must acknowledge that Title IX, as currently conceived, does little to counteract the hurdles we identify on each pathway toward equality. It promotes sex segregation, remains silent on gendered leadership dispari-ties, and fails to address either the concomitant cultural consequences or market-driven decisions that privilege men's sport. Requiring increased policy compliance would not change such factors and thus will not remove the substantial barriers for equality that our analyses reveal. For these reasons, we argue for more fundamental reforms. These include efforts toward sex desegregation – at the very least involving more shared facilities, training activities, and practice schedules between men's and women's teams. We also demonstrate that there is a reasonable, perhaps surprising, amount of support for coed teams that enable athletically qualified women to participate on men's teams (particularly in noncontact sports).[36] We also argue for reforms that alter the leadership structures of college sports, including affirmative hiring of currently underrepresented candidates (i.e., women or nonbinary people) and efforts to insulate col-lege sports from overreacting to market forces.

We recognize that our reform proposals involve an inferential leap from microlevel data on individuals' opinions to macrolevel institutional processes. The connection between individuals and institutions is far from straightforward. Furthermore, bringing about significant change will require overcoming collective action and mobilization challenges. Such challenges are daunting, but we believe that our results reveal the urgent need to tackle them. Our efforts identify the change needed in hopes that our findings will inspire broader conversation and attention among those best positioned to pursue it.

1.6 THE ROLES OF REVENUE AND INTEREST IN SPORTS

Any contemporary treatment of college athletics requires some discus-sion of sports-generated revenue. We will touch on some relevant history in Chapter 5 when we introduce the role of market pressures. Here, we offer a brief discussion of amateurism, recent related reforms, the role of the so-called "revenue producing sports," and common myths about girls' and women's interest in sports. We do so to explicate, despite

---

[36] As we will note in more detail in Chapter 6, we recognize potential upsides to segrega-tion when one moves beyond a focus of policy preferences. For example, some work suggests negative mental health effects on people from marginalized groups who live in less-segregated areas (e.g., Herbst and Lucio 2016).

common arguments, why revenue sports and interest in sports should not be central to policy discussions about gender equality. We aim to engage readers who may otherwise dismiss our analyses by adopting such tropes.

1.6.1 Revenue Considerations in Public Discourse

Historically, the NCAA actively opposed compensation for college athletes. They even coined the term "student-athlete" to undermine any perception of athletes being employees. Nonetheless, challenges to amateurism persisted, culminating most recently in allowing student-athletes to receive compensation for their name, image, and likeness (NIL).[37] In 2019, California enacted the "Fair Pay to Play Act" that authorized student-athletes in California to earn money when their name, image, or likeness is used for commercial purposes. Further, in 2021 the Supreme Court ruled in *NCAA v. Alston* against any limitations on student-athlete education-related benefits, rejecting NCAA claims that college sports are not "highly profitable" or "professional." In essence, the Court rejected the amateurism doctrine on which the NCAA built its eligibility rules. In response the NCAA itself put forth an NIL policy that largely delegates specific rulemaking authority to the states or the schools themselves.[38] Future evolutions in either enforcement of NIL regulations or the recognition of college athletes as employees remain unclear (as of April 2023).

Additional ambiguity emerged in January 2022 when the NCAA voted to adopt a new, vastly stripped-down constitution that decentralizes control and provides athletic conferences and schools with more independence. This coincided with massive athletic conference realignment with two major football powerhouses (Texas and Oklahoma) joining the Southeastern Conference (SEC) and another two (the University of Southern California and the University of California, Los Angeles) moving to the Big Ten Conference. These moves came about due to substantial revenue opportunities (via television contracts) offered by the

---

[37] The revenue produced by football and men's basketball is highly scrutinized in public discourse. Critics note that such revenue is built on the largely uncompensated, and therefore exploited, athletic performance of Black student-athletes who are disproportionately represented in these sports, sometimes likening the exploited labor to that experienced by enslaved people (e.g., Hawkins 2010; McCants 2018; Rhoden 2006).

[38] The NCAA maintains rules against directly paying student-athletes for playing and outlaws quid pro quo payments based on performance or enrollment at a particular school.

SEC and the Big Ten. The ultimate impact of these changes will depend on the conference movement of other schools and on how conferences and NCAA's division-specific committees proceed.

We do not view these developments, at this point, as directly intersecting with the gender equity initiatives on which we focus. Thus, while they are certainly crucial to understanding college sports writ large, they lie beyond our purview concerning potential futures for gender equality. Whatever changes such forces bring to college sports, they will need to remain compliant with Title IX, not the other way around. Of more explicit relevance are longer-standing questions about the role of money in college sports and, specifically, the role of football in gender equality considerations given football's outsized rosters, expenses, and revenue potential. Women's participation in collegiate football remains scarce and no single "women's sport" rivals the roster size or expenditure profile of many football teams. Public discussions of Title IX and gender equality often become ensnarled in conversations about football and men's basketball since their television contracts, stadium size, and historic legacies enable those two sports to produce the most revenue at many (but not all) colleges and university. Even teams at schools that spend more than they earn from these sports benefit from the perception that football and men's basketball are "revenue producing" sports.[39]

Although revenue streams have become central to the administrative calculus of college athletics, we do not subsequently focus attention on revenue production as a central policy question for several reasons. First, when the OCR adopted the three-part "accommodation of interests and abilities" test of Title IX compliance in 1979, most schools opted to focus on the proportionality criterion rather than satisfying a test of student "interest." In theory, evaluating the nascent "interest" among women on any campus to participate in varsity athletics would require demonstrating that women do not want to play a sport that is not yet available.[40] In some (often high-profile) cases, schools then chose to cut some men's teams as

---

[39] It is also worth noting, although it is largely ancillary for our main analysis, that the language of "revenue producing sports" is owed to debates about the application of Title IX in the mid- to late-seventies (see Suggs 2005). Attempts to frame some sports as revenue producing was related to the failed attempt by those representing the interests of men's football to achieve an exemption from Title IX for some men's sports.

[40] Satisfaction of the second part of the test, which evaluates "historical progress," was meant as a temporary provision insofar as schools (who chose this approach) were also required to develop a long-term plan to accommodate proportionality.

part of a strategy to meet proportionality instead of adding a similarly sized women's team to achieve proportional gender balance. Many of these schools cut men's teams while simultaneously substantially expanding football rosters (see Messner and Solomon 2007; Walton and Helstein 2008). This triggered unsuccessful lawsuits from male athletes (most notably wrestlers, organized through the National Wrestling Coaches Association) claiming that Title IX had harmed men. At the same time, it perpetuated a narrative that "reasserted men's birthright claims to sports and higher education. Men are seen as deserving *all* spots in college sports. Any attempt to provide spots for women is seen as taking something *away* from men" (Hextrum 2021, 103; italics in original). Sex segregation in sports also reaffirmed this perspective that presumes men's interests and capacities in athletics inevitably outpace women's. Moreover, this framing suggests a paternalistic (and legally rejected) argument that men's revenue sports of college football and basketball should be excluded from Title IX requirements since revenues can be used to support a range of other sports. Eckstein (2017, 28) summarizes this perspective:

Despite some popular rhetoric indicting women and Title IX for the precipitous decline in sports such as wrestling and men's gymnastics, it was the explosive, and some might say unnecessary, growth of football squad sizes over the past three decades that forces schools to reduce other male opportunities and still be compliant with Title IX ... this might be less about sports themselves than about securing enrollments that can help a school's 'brand.'

We concur.

Second, we reject the idea of exceptionalizing revenue-generating sports on its face – the revenue sports generally do not make sufficient money to prevent large athletic department deficits, and the evidence demonstrates that most "revenue-producing" sports spend the increased income on their teams rather than holding their spending constant and relinquishing excess revenue to other sports as income grows (Eckstein 2017; Nixon 2014). More importantly, civil rights law does not require oppressed groups to demonstrate their market worth in order to receive civil rights. Nor is the stated mission of college sports, according to the NCAA, to generate profits. The mission is an educational and hence a nonprofit one. In other words, college sports have operated with two simultaneous and competing models – a profit-seeking business model and an educational model. The latter often gives cover to the former to justify not compensating athletes directly (Staurowsky 2018, 105). Ultimately, as long as athletes continue to be treated as students and not employees (and NIL policy does not affect their student status), the relevance of whether particular sports produce revenue is moot from the perspective of civil rights protections. Institutions exercise some choice in how to allocate their resources; however, they lack a moral justification for privileging any athletic teams that bring in revenue given that the mission of higher education is not merely revenue-seeking (e.g., all sports teams could operate on smaller budgets, with less travel, etc. or football teams could shrink their spending etc.).[41] In that sense, we affirm the perspective that institutions cannot disassociate the so-called revenue sports from discussions of gender equity – a view backed by federal law. The relevant protected categories under Title IX assess the relative treatment of men and women, not football players versus gymnastics (or the like).

Third, the forward-thinking policy initiatives on which we focus move beyond participation opportunities and expenditures, including improved protections against sexual harassment and expanded coaching and leadership opportunities. The findings we will present regarding opinion toward these particular items cohere with the findings overall and these are variables on which any distinction over revenue sports has scant direct baring.[42]

In short, we argue that revenue-producing sports invariably enter conversations about Title IX and gender equality freighted with perceptions of their privileged economic status within an unequal system. Yet there is no legal or policy interpretation of Title IX that justifies

---

[41] Nixon (2014) explains that spending on football and men's basketball leads to an athletic trap where schools may operate in deficit but continue to spend due, at least in part, to the perception of intangible benefits of the "brand." Eckstein (2017, 58) captures the essence of the process: "Once this trap becomes entrenched, [college] presidents and other decisionmakers are unable to extricate their schools from intercollegiate athletics' insatiable financial appetite. Because so few intercollegiate athletics programs generate net revenues, almost all schools find themselves diverting increasing general budget resources to athletics or identifying significant external resources to finance the athletics arms race.... presidents have become more concerned with the needs of external constituents (alumni donors, event sponsors, media) than with the internal constituencies focused on scholarship and learning."

[42] Except, of course, due to the extent that many issues of sexual harassment and violence within college sports are related – at least in many high-profile cases – to football players (e.g., Luther 2016). However, the enforcement of sexual misconduct proceedings on college campuses should not be contingent on the extent to which any named student participates in extracurricular programming, athletics or otherwise, revenue-producing team affiliation or not. We included measures of gendered issues beyond mere proportionality, etc. for precisely these reasons.

or rationalizes sex-based inequalities on the basis of revenue calculus. Expanded investment by schools in some sports, particularly football, has been largely responsible for the elimination of men's teams in other sports, even as the so-called revenue producing sports contribute to overall budget deficits.[43] Such choices do not excuse privileging men's sports or entrenching discrimination against women, nor do they justify inequality through the lens of Title IX or under federal civil rights law.

1.6.2 Questions of Women's "Interest" in Public Discourse

At the same time, proponents of increased opportunities for women must contend with perceptions that extant sex inequalities reflect a lack of demand for more equality – that is, the institutions of college sports may be meeting the existing demands of women on their campus for varsity teams (as in the third part of the "three-part test"). For example, Deaner, Balish, and Lombardo (2016) take an evolutionary perspective to argue that "females' underrepresentation generally reflects lesser interest, not merely fewer opportunities for engagement" (73).[44] They attribute this to assumed sex-based differences in motivation, competitiveness, and risk-taking. They also quickly dismiss the role of socialization in shaping interest in sports. We stridently disagree with this perspective as there is clear evidence that lower participation rates reflect societal factors. For one, young girls between the ages of six and eight tend to participate in sports at similar rates to boys in that age group. Gaps subsequently emerge so that by high school boys' participation outpaces girls' by nearly 20 percentage points in some areas (Hopkins et al. 2022; Sabiston 2020). The identified reasons for the decline among girls include low confidence, poor perceptions of belonging/feeling unwelcome, and perceived lack of skill (Hopkins et al. 2022; Sabiston 2020). These findings suggest that low participation rates reflect societal and institutional factors that shape experiences. Indeed, the Women's Sports Foundation (2020), reviewing a quarter century of research, identifies the following reasons why girls and women drop out of sports: lack of access/opportunities, decreased quality of experience, social stigma,

---

[43] In 2016, only 73 of 252 Division 1 football teams earned more than they spent on football (IBA Worldtour 2021).

[44] Additional discussion and debate about this and related perspectives are available in Grasgreen (2012).

and lack of positive role models.[45] These reasons track directly onto the disparities we previously documented: disproportionate participation, less infrastructure investment (e.g., expenditures), and male-dominated culture and leadership. This makes clear that inequalities reflect a failure to meet the expectations of college-aged women. If there is a decline in interest among college-age women, it reflects earlier experiences of inequalities. That said, interestingly, women who participate in high school sports have similar, if not greater, probabilities of participating in college (NCAA 2019a), suggesting no fundamental difference in demand at that acute point.[46]

We also emphasize that inequalities expand beyond participation opportunities. Indeed, Figures 1.2 and 1.3 show substantial disparities when it comes to resources and leadership opportunities. In terms of the former, the differences in quality of experiences come across not only in these objective measures but also in perceptions. As we will discuss further in Chapter 3, we find in our previous work that women student-athletes perceive substantial inequalities across twenty-four measures, including those involving resources, opportunity, personnel, and equipment. At the same time, they believe that there should be more equality – clearly, women student-athletes are not satisfied (Druckman, Rothschild, and Sharrow 2018). This is evident in mass opinion as well, where a Pew survey shows 71 percent of women believe men's and women's college sports should be funded equally: Clearly they are not (Igielnik 2022). In terms of leadership, as mentioned, the number of women coaches has dramatically declined over time, which makes clear that the supply of potential coaches is not lacking. There also are sufficient women working at lower levels of athletic administration to substantiate a sufficient supply of women leaders. In the data we describe in subsequent chapters, 29 percent of department heads are women versus 56 percent of non-heads who are woman.

In sum, extant evidence makes clear that women's demand for opportunities persists, that any decrease in demand stems from the very system that generates the broader inequalities we discuss, and that the other types of inequalities that motivate our inquiry are counter to

---

[45] They also identify safety and transportation issues and individual costs that seem more relevant to younger age groups when socioeconomic status drives participation.

[46] The differences in participation rates we document here stem largely, but not entirely, from men's football spots that are not compensated for with equitable women's opportunities. We have every reason to presume that if women had equitable opportunities to participate in either more sports or expanded rosters, they would do so.

women's preferences or availability. Just as relative revenue production does not justify sex inequalities, these inequalities are *not* a story about demand.

1.7 A NOTE ON THE LANGUAGE OF "MALE" AND "FEMALE"

Before we embark on detailing our data, we want to guide readers through some of the tensions we confront in organizing and discussing our argument. As generations of feminist thought and activism teach, the language and terms we use to discuss gendered identities and oppression matter greatly. Throughout, we employ terms worthy of clarification/ description.

We frequently use the term "sex," the central category named in Title IX, to describe the dominant logic of collegiate athletic team organization (i.e., "sex-segregated teams"). We utilize this language both because it is the terminology used in public policy (i.e., Title IX bans discrimination "on the basis of sex") and because the binary logics commonly connoted in such usage permeate the policy space. Segregated athletic teams are premised on sorting "male athletes" from "female athletes" (Sharrow 2017). However, we employ "sex" as a categorical, sociocultural distinction (e.g., one assigned by medical doctors to infants at birth or used to constitute athletic teams) but not a phenotypical one. Our references to "males" or "females" should not necessarily imply references to individuals' chromosomes, hormones, genitalia, secondary sex traits, and so on.

We are mindful that such binary logics (i.e., male/female or men/ women) are themselves problematic social constructions (see, e.g., Fausto-Sterling 2000; Fine 2010; Jordan-Young 2010). Moreover, ideas about "maleness" and "femaleness" in sport are increasingly used to reinforce androcentric hierarchies and narrow, binary notions of gender (see Karkazis et al. 2012; Sharrow 2021a, 2021b). At the same time, to grapple with the complications we identify in the status quo, we require analyses that rely on the germane categories. We thus employ them somewhat uncomfortably at a time when the research consensus readily notes that "sex is a context-dependent summary of a multidimensional variable space" (Miyagi, Guthman, and Sun 2021, 1569). Although many scholarly and social conventions invoke "gender" as a term to challenge such problematic, biological determinist logics (see for critical discussion Davis 2017; Repo 2016), we attempt throughout to avoid employing "gender" in contexts when policy logics explicitly rely on the language of "sex."

When we refer to "men" and "women," it should be read as referring to those who self-identify as such. Throughout, we use the terms "male" and "female" as adjective modifiers for other group identities (e.g., "female student-athletes," "male coaches"). That is, for descriptive purposes, we employ the salient gendered categories used in sports with some reservation. We are loathe to be misread as authorizing, through language, these forms of gendered oppression. Thus, we encourage readers to engage with these categories critically.

Our analyses nevertheless focus largely on the inequalities between those categorized as women versus men. We do so to evaluate the extant outcomes of sex nondiscrimination policy that operates from such single-axis framing, and doing so gives us purchase on the question of how well Title IX has operated to vitiate inequality for women as an undifferentiated group. However, taking Title IX on its own terms places sex-based categorization in the foreground and obscures intragroup differences among women. This is a tradeoff we do not take lightly and, while not our primary focus, we acknowledge the intersectional critiques of nondiscrimination policy that substantiate how subgroups among women, especially women of color, are particularly underserved by single-axis nondiscrimination policy (i.e., Crenshaw 1989; Hextrum 2021; Hextrum and Sethi 2022).

Likewise, our data do not differentiate cisgender from transgender (nor gender-diverse) status among collegiate athletes, although both retained the right to participate in the women's category during the time of our study (Griffin and Carroll 2010). The consequences of binary categories in sports produce particular harms for gender-diverse athletes, especially transgender girls and women, who do not identify with the sex they were assigned at birth. Numerous state legislators and some national lawmakers have recently targeted the rights of transgender girls and women to participate on athletic teams designated for women and girls, often invoking mere phenotypic notions of sex assigned at birth in order to deny the dignity of self-identification to gender-diverse people (see Sharrow 2021b). This emerging terrain of gendered politics under Title IX is important for the future of policy, in ways that are related to our aims in this book. That is, the notions of "sex" embedded in sex-segregated structures that presume cisgender identities of male/female (i.e., that individuals assigned female at birth will seek participation on a "women's" team) become swift vectors of exclusion and harm for transgender and gender-diverse athletes (Sharrow 2023).

Indeed, rights for transgender girls and women in a sex-segregated system remain tenuous. As we wrote this book, federal-level policy addressing "sex discrimination" itself evolved to increasingly acknowledge gender diversity (i.e., transgender and nonbinary identities) as an important consideration (see DOJ 2021). We assert that any system that presumes sex-based binaries and elevates the status of cisgender men oppresses cisgender women *and* all gender-diverse people in mutually imbricated ways (see also Sharrow 2021a). We delineate the ways in which our critical perspectives on the status quo might create system reform that benefits athletes across the gender spectrum in the concluding chapter.

1.8 CONCLUSION

Our goal in this book is to offer an account of why gender equity initiatives often fail to garner more support and momentum by focusing on how institutions shape policy opinions. This focus on policy and its context provides a crucial assessment of Title IX as we move from its fiftieth anniversary toward the future. Certainly, enacting Title IX forced institutions to change. Even so, women remain a marginalized group that is denied full equality in sports, leaving open questions as to why this persists.

Recently, the stark gender inequalities of the 2021 NCAA basketball tournaments captured the attention of student-athletes, administrators, coaches, and the public, casting a spotlight on problems of gender inequality. While this attention and the more equitable 2022 tournaments may signal a step toward parity, there is reason for caution. The external review of gender equity that followed confirmed that vast disparities will not be easily resolved and likely require structural changes. Indeed, much attention with college sports has shifted away from gender inequities to rules that allow student-athletes to profit from their NIL. The NCAA wrote a new constitution, acknowledging the need for a more decentralized structure. Athletic conferences were realigned, raising questions about how the decentralized system will work. Gender equity initiatives seem fleeting on the agenda.

In what follows, we offer a window into the closed world of sports and the impacts of its totalizing logics. Sex segregation, women's underrepresentation in leadership, socializing experiences, and market demands constitute barriers that sustain an unequal status quo in sports and elsewhere. We will demonstrate how segregation not only structures beneficiary activism and possible coalition formation among student-athletes, it also durably shapes the views of former participants in youth sports (a much larger segment of the population) and suppresses demands for a more equitable future. Institutions foreclose both external and internal coalitions for change. As a result, androcentric cultures and practices remain undisturbed while normalizing marginalization. The findings that follow make clear that the very features built-in (or left out) of gendered policies can become barriers to full equality.

2

Using Survey Data to Study Policy Support

On March 12, 2020, St. John's University went into halftime leading Creighton University 38–35 in a quarterfinal men's basketball game in the Big East conference tournament. At the half, officials announced that the teams would not complete the game due to the emergent COVID-19 pandemic. The National Collegiate Athletic Association (NCAA) subsequently cancelled all remaining winter and spring championships for men's and women's sports, consequently ending athletic competition for the remainder of the academic year. The loss of revenue from the shelved basketball tournaments and other events led many universities to take cost-saving measures by eliminating some varsity athletic teams. Across the country, athletic departments permanently cut more than 350 sports teams (Kumar 2020).

Although financial concerns drove many such cuts, gender equity issues quickly moved to the fore. For example, in July 2020, Dartmouth College announced the elimination of five teams – men's and women's swimming and diving, men's and women's golf, and men's lightweight rowing. At the time, the college claimed it would remain in compliance with federal law despite the cuts, stating that "the percentage of women among varsity athletes will be virtually identical to the percentage of women in the undergraduate student body, ensuring compliance with Title IX" (Dartmouth College 2020). However, the subsequent months revealed that their calculations on proportional opportunities required under Title IX were flawed. In January 2021, the college issued a statement, "We have recently learned that elements of the data that Athletics used to confirm continued Title IX compliance may not have been complete. In light of this discovery, Dartmouth will immediately reinstate all five teams" (Hanlon 2021).

The president of the school also stated, "we will make sure that any future decisions will be based on accurate data" (Hanlon 2021).

This story reveals multiple dynamics, including the vulnerability of women's sports, particularly during periods of economic crisis (Druckman and Sharrow 2020). It also accentuates the role of data in analyses of equality. Title IX's "three-part test" of compliance with the law, which we described in Chapter 1, presents even well-meaning schools with significant data challenges.[1] In the Dartmouth example, administrators confronted the challenges of accurately calculating the key statistics that determine policy compliance, namely the ratio of women enrolled in the undergraduate student body and the relative percentage of women student-athletes. These data were not straightforward given uncertainties over which athletes could be counted as having full "participation opportunities" after the cancellation of many competitions due to COVID-19.

Data problems are rife in the calculations of both quantitative and qualitative measures of Title IX compliance. While quantitative metrics play a key role in the proportionality component of the "three-part" compliance test, calculations for the third part involve "evidence of having accommodated the 'interests and abilities' of the underrepresented sex" – an even more convoluted task. In 2005, the Office for Civil Rights (OCR) in the US Department of Education announced policy clarification guidelines suggesting that a school could assess compliance by employing a survey of enrolled undergraduate students' interests and abilities in athletics, and they initially provided a web-based model survey. The guidelines suggested that a survey of enrolled undergraduates would gauge whether or not women's interest in varsity athletic participation was being met. The proffered survey draft was met with methodological critique because, for example, it suggested that colleges could treat a nonresponse as a qualitative expression of disinterest among women for additional athletic opportunity, rather than merely missing data. Similarly, the clarifying guidelines proposed surveying students after matriculation instead of surveying potential enrollees whose college enrollment decision might be premised on the availability of teams. In short, as Buzuvis (2006, 840) explains, "the survey's flawed methodology virtually guarantees that a school relying on the results will rarely have to increase women's sports opportunities." Ultimately, OCR abandoned the recommendations in 2010.

---

[1] On overall noncompliance with the quantitative measures, see Yanus and O'Connor (2016), and Buzuvis and Newhall (2012). These works discuss the difficulties associated with assessing equality through the "three-part test."

Such examples highlight the role of data in discussions about Title IX and gender equality. It is challenging to collect quality data on these issues. Although our research questions probe different dimensions of equality praxis than those just discussed – that is, we are focused not on data to measure Title IX compliance but rather on data that measure the opinions of key stakeholders on policy issues in college sports – the general point about data limitations applies. There exist scant high-quality data, either scholarly or otherwise, on stakeholders' opinions. This book aims to change that. We investigate opinions about gender equity policies in the chapters that follow. In each, we present our theory concerning the possible route for policy support (and change) among student-athletes, athletic administrators and coaches, and the public and fans. We test predictions from these theories with original surveys administered from 2018 to 2020. As far as we know, ours are the only large-scale survey data that gauge the gender equity policy beliefs across and among the stakeholders of college athletics. That said, given the historic ambiguities of quantitative data in discussions about Title IX, we thought it particularly crucial to detail our research design decisions. As was clear in the Dartmouth case, the collection and analysis of data always involve a set of choices, or what some refer to as researcher "degrees of freedom" – that is, choices that without explanation may seem arbitrary (e.g., Wicherts et al. 2016). In what follows, we explain what we did and why.

2.1 USING SURVEY DATA TO STUDY SUPPORT FOR GENDER EQUITY INITIATIVES

The data presented in the prior chapter make clear that nearly fifty years after the enactment of Title IX, vast gender inequalities persist in college sports. We set out to understand why. As social scientists, we confront an array of possible approaches to tackling this question. For instance, *historical* analyses could identify key moments in policymaking, advocacy, or policy enforcement that, in effect, prevented the possibilities of more equitable outcomes. Alternatively, *case studies* on political discussions of equity initiatives (e.g., equal expenditure requirements, efforts to increase women's professional opportunities), whether ongoing or lacking, could provide crucial insights into structural or leadership barriers. Indeed, a number of studies of gender and sports rely on interviews with stakeholders to reveal the motivations of and challenges faced by key actors (e.g., Eckstein 2017; Hextrum 2021; Markovits and Albertson 2012; Rose 2018). Researchers could also explore comparative analyses of competing policy interventions by contrasting the impacts of actions and inactions by the NCAA and colleges/universities, or state and federal legislatures. They could pair such policy process tracing with public or elite opinion studies that search for feedback effects therein.

We take a different approach. As articulated in Chapter 1, we theorize that inequalities persist because actors who might pursue change – that is, student-athletes from the "bottom up," administrators and coaches from the "top down," or the public and fans from the "outside in" – face prohibitive hurdles to collective action. In each subsequent chapter, we delineate our expectations regarding potential pathways for change, as well as the factors that we predict undermine support for an array of gender equity initiatives within each stakeholder group.

In each chapter, we test our predictions with original survey data ($N \approx$ 7,500 contemporary stakeholders). Specifically, we conduct multiple distinct representative surveys of target populations (i.e., student-athletes, coaches, athletic administrators, and the American public, including college sports fans). Each survey measures opinions on the six policy proposals discussed in Chapter 1: (1) improved enforcement of Title IX, (2) equal participation opportunities for women and men, (3) increased enforcement of sexual harassment laws, (4) equal spending for women's and men's sports, (5) requirements to interview at least one woman in the finalist pool for a women's team head coach position, and (6) requirements to interview at least one woman in the finalist pool for an athletic director job. In addition to eliciting policy opinions, we engage participants in an exercise that requires them to confront inevitable policy trade-offs. Respondents are asked to allocate a fixed budget across funds for gender equity initiatives versus "athlete benefits" initiatives (e.g., proposals to pay college student-athletes beyond athletic scholarships). The array of policy and budget allocation measures allows us to assess the empirical evidence for our theory and to subsequently arrive at generalizable conclusions about the likelihood of policy change.

2.1.1 Why Surveys?

We opt for a large-N quantitative survey approach – in contrast to most extant work on gender equity and college sports that informs our theories – for four reasons. First, this allows us to evaluate possible counterfactuals and understand what might prevent change to the status quo. We accomplish this by (1) identifying concrete equity policy proposals, (2) stipulating the potential institutional factors that impact stakeholders' support, and (3) identifying variation in views among those more or less hampered by the institutional factors. For example, as previewed in Chapter 1, we theorize policy change may emerge from coalitions of student-athletes but that sex segregation vitiates majoritarian support for equity initiatives by depressing cross-sex contact. With our data, we can compare circumstances with low levels of sex segregation against those with high levels of segregation. Even though sex segregation is generally high among student-athletes (albeit with some exceptions among particular teams), our approach provides a view of what could happen if it were not. Similarly, within college sports leadership, we can compare women employed at lower versus higher ranks in the athletic administration hierarchy to isolate the impacts of organizational culture. Given that our argument depends on claims about how institutions alter support for equity, these counterfactual comparisons are essential.

Second, even though we collected our data recently, analyzing large-N data across populations provides insight into the long-term implications of gendered policies. These data provide a "bird's eye view" of the consequences of policy design. Although there are many important scholarly works on Title IX, specifically, we know of no other large-N data like ours.

Third, employing standardized surveys allows us to excavate dynamics of policy opinions both within and across groups. This approach allows us to leverage theories of "policy feedback" that suggest the attitudes of student-athletes and/or the general public should play a role in shaping policy and practice. As primary policy beneficiaries, student-athletes are poised for mobilization to see their rights realized (e.g., Campbell 2003; Druckman, Rothschild, and Sharrow 2018). Likewise, public preferences should bear upon lawmakers charged with allocating taxpayer resources (e.g., via public institutions) and securing civil rights protections. Similarly, coaches and athletic administrators make proximate decisions that determine professional opportunities, policy interpretations, and resource allocation, both within athletic departments and on governing committees of the NCAA. Only a standardized survey approach can directly explore similarities and differences in opinion across relevant groups. In short, our data offer an unparalleled resource for understanding equity beliefs among distinct stakeholder groups in the complex, but powerful, social and cultural institution of collegiate sport.

Fourth, our approach allows us to generalize our findings to understanding the constraints and possibilities for marginalized groups who pursue policy change in other domains. While college sports certainly have idiosyncratic features, our findings about the effects of sex segregation and organizational culture on policy support lend insight into how such factors can influence policy in areas beyond athletics. Marginalized, minority groups confront enduring structures and dominant cultures that inhibit their full inclusion in many realms. Male-dominated workplaces and cultural spaces continue to limit the prospects, potential, and possibilities for women and gender-diverse people. We offer fresh insight into how sex-essentializing logics and androcentric organizational settings contribute to marginalization.

In the remainder of this chapter, we provide a brief overview of the architecture of college sports to contextualize our study. We then discuss and justify our research design – regarding sampling, measurement, and analyses. Doing so in this chapter not only provides efficiency, compared to rehashing our approach in each chapter, it also reveals the underlying connections between each individual data collection effort.

2.2 OVERVIEW OF THE WORLD OF COLLEGE SPORTS

Collegiate athletics in the United States are simultaneously an educational enterprise, a competitive athletic venue, and an economic industry. As we mentioned in Chapter 1, the first intercollegiate athletic competition for men dates back to the 1850s in the sport of rowing (Smith 1990). For women, noncompetitive physical education predated intercollegiate athletic competition (Cahn 1995; Verbrugge 1988, 2012); their first organized competitions took place in 1896 (Gerber 1974). Women's athletics became increasingly institutionalized over the course of the twentieth century, culminating in the creation of the first institutional member organization for women's sport, the Association of Intercollegiate Athletics for Women (AIAW) in 1971 (Bell 2007). During this same era, men's college sports expanded in size and scope. This fueled the power of the NCAA, the central governing body for men's sport since 1910, and increased investment in a profit-seeking model (Chudacoff 2015; Clotfelter 2019). By the early 1980s, models of competition developed by and for men subsumed control of women's intercollegiate sports. Most notably, the NCAA wrested control of governance for women's sports from the AIAW.

Today, athletic competition is organized through several national-level associations and multiple athletic conferences, the most dominant of which is the NCAA.[2] As a private, nonprofit membership association, the NCAA oversees nearly half a million college student-athletes annually at nearly 1,300 institutions, who compete in twenty-four sports across three

---

[2] As noted in Chapter 1, the NCAA does not govern all American college athletics, but it is by far the dominant governing organization.

"divisions."[3] In its current formulation, the NCAA stages ninety national championships and legislates policies that govern collegiate athletics. Each individual school has the latitude to sponsor the sports teams of its choosing; their eligibility to compete at NCAA championships depends on compliance with NCAA rules. Schools may also elect to host club sports or intermural opportunities – these do not involve the NCAA, which only governs varsity intercollegiate competition.

The world of college sports therefore operates on multiple levels. Individual administrators and coaches have purview over decisions about spending on scholarships, coaching salaries, recruitment, facilities, tutors, trainers, and more within their institutions. The NCAA sets the parameters for championship athletic competition but also highly structures elements of collegiate sports including competitive eligibility for athletes (both academic and athletic), amateurism rules (including rules on athlete compensation), equity within their high-profile championship events (including March Madness and the College World Series), and regulations for recruitment of high school athletes. Varsity collegiate athletes (i.e., "student-athletes") who compete in intercollegiate competitions funded by their college or university must comply with many NCAA rules (including on compensation, drug testing, practice schedules, and academic performance) and meet the academic standards of their institution, their athletic conference, and the NCAA.[4] Athletic leadership within each institution (i.e., athletic administrators) conduct oversight of compliance with NCAA rules among student-athletes, coaches, and staff.[5] They also monitor compliance with federal law including Title IX and handle annual federal data reporting of equity practices required by the Equity in Athletics Disclosure Act [34 CFR 668.47]. Finally, student-athletes, administrators, and the NCAA alike are surveilled by fans of college sports who look to these groups for entertainment, alumni-affinity, and the like.[6] This organizational structure produces unique stakeholder communities within and around college athletics.

---

[3] As noted in Chapter 1, Division I includes the programs with the largest budgets; both Divisions I and II are allowed to grant athletic scholarships while Division III is not.

[4] As we explore more extensively in Chapter 3, their lives also are highly regulated by these demands on their time. We focus on "varsity" athletes and not intermural, club, or recreational athletes on college campuses.

[5] As we discuss in Chapter 4, they inhabit a pivotal place in the hierarchy, powering over athletes but available to press for full enforcement of policy on their campuses and with the NCAA.

[6] In Chapter 5, we delineate the contours of the relationships between fans, the general public, and athletic departments on collegiate campuses.

2.3 OUR SAMPLING APPROACH

Researchers collect data to make inferences about a group; in our case, the relevant groups or populations are varsity student-athletes, leaders in college sports (i.e., coaches and administrators such as athletic directors), and the public (as well as college sports fans). As with most populations, it is not logistically feasible to obtain data from every member of the relevant population (e.g., every current student-athlete), and thus, we collect data from a small subset, that is, a "sample" of the given population. Ideally, researchers collect a probability sample where every unit in the population (e.g., a student-athlete) has a known, equal, and nonzero chance of being included in the sample. When data collection is guided by these principles, in all likelihood, the sample will reflect the population and thus researchers can make generalizable statements about the population by studying the smaller, randomly selected group. Data collection of this type is not easy. It entails identifying and locating those chosen to participate in a study at random and then ensuring that they respond to requests for participation. But research that is completed using these standardized methods, even if the sample size is relatively small (e.g., 500), can produce strong inferences about the group.[7]

For our analyses of groups within college sports we employ stratified random sampling. Specifically, we define our populations as each of the aforementioned types of individuals – varsity student-athletes, varsity coaches, and athletic administrators – at NCAA member schools.[8] We identified every college with teams in the NCAA and noted whether the school participates in Division I, II, or III.[9] We then drew a random sample, stratified by NCAA division; that is, we randomly selected sets of schools from Division I member institutions, sets of schools from Division II, and sets of schools from Division III. We oversampled Division I schools for two reasons. First, as discussed, Division I schools typically employ more personnel in their athletics departments and sponsor larger numbers of

---

[7] The larger the sample size, the more precise the inference; however, the gains from larger samples diminish quickly once one approaches several hundred. Also, the size of the population is not relevant here (i.e., the relative size of the sample to the population does not affect the precision of the estimate – what matters is that the sample represents the population on meaningful dimensions).

[8] We thus exclude non-NCAA (e.g., National Association of Intercollegiate Athletics schools). We also excluded sports, notably cheerleading and dance, that do not count in terms of compliance with Title IX or under the Equity in Athletics Disclosure Act.

[9] Some schools have sports that participate at different divisional levels; we grouped a school based on where the plurality of their teams participated.

sports and roster spots for athletes. Oversampling Division I schools thus ensures sufficient sample sizes, particularly when it comes to coaches and administrators. Second, many of gender equity issues (e.g., resource allocation) are discussed most vigorously at the Division I level because of the disproportionate spending on men's football at the Division I level (see Chapter 1's appendix).

For each selected school, we went on the athletic department website and obtained email contact information for every student-athlete, coach, and athletic administrator. (We discuss our precise definition of "athletic administrator" in Chapter 4.) We then sent each individual a personalized invitation inviting them to participate in an anonymous survey (on personalization, see Druckman and Green 2013). We provide other implementation details in this chapter's appendix, which recall can be found at www.cambridge.org/Druckman-Sharrow_EqualityUnfulfilled.

If we would have been able to identify every contact, and if everyone we invited to participate in a survey had responded, the samples would constitute ideal probability samples and allow for direct inferences to the entire relevant populations of student-athletes, coaches, and athletic administrators. Of course, that ideal is never achieved in practice. The two main hurdles in our case were that a small number of sampled schools did not have publicly available email addresses and thus could not be included in the sample, and many people for whom we solicited participation in the study declined. This latter issue refers to nonresponse bias. For example, even very high-quality probability (phone) surveys of the public have response rates of about 9 percent (Keeter et al. 2017). Since such nonresponse (and perhaps the availability of email addresses) is nonrandom – that is, certain individuals may systematically be more or less likely to respond – researchers employ sampling weights.

Sampling weights are applied to the responses to achieve proportionality between the relevant features of the sample and the population. For instance, if the population includes 60 percent men and the sample includes 40 percent men, then each male observation is multiplied to inflate its impact in statistical analyses (and each female observation is down-weighted) so that the sample matches the population on key features. For our samples, we applied poststratification sample weights to ensure we can generalize our results to the populations (e.g., Callegaro et al. 2014). Fortunately, we were able to obtain the population features to aid in constructing our survey weights (e.g., the proportion of male student-athletes in the population) from the NCAA population database. We weighted the student-athlete samples on race, gender, sport played, and division; the coach samples on race, gender, sport coached, division, gender of team coached, and coaching title (i.e., head coach or not); and the athletic administrator sample on race, gender, and division. More details appear in this chapter's appendix. We present the (weighted) demographic details of each sample in subsequent chapters.

In Table 2.1, we provide an overview of our samples. The samples for the first student-athlete study listed in the table and the coach and athletic administrator sample came from the same initial draw of schools (see this chapter's appendix for more discussion).[10] The other student-athlete sample was used for an experiment in an additional study that we will discuss in Chapter 3; for this sample, we included only those schools that had not been included in the first sample. The response rates are between 9 percent and 15 percent, which is in line with typical direct solicitation web surveys (e.g., Van Mol 2017) that have been shown to be sufficient for generalizable inferences (e.g., Nair, Adams, and Mertova 2008). The last column states the purpose of each sample as it relates to the subsequent content of this book and the overview provided in Chapter 1. In each ensuing empirical chapter, we further develop our theoretical approach to studying each group.

Finally, the last row of Table 2.1 describes our sample of the American public. Here we took a different participant recruitment approach. Instead of relying on a probability sample of the public, we hired a survey vendor, Bovitz Inc. (www.bovitzinc.com/). The vendor provides an online panel (called the Forthright panel) of approximately one million respondents recruited through random digit dialing and empanelment of those with internet access. As with most internet survey samples, respondents participate in multiple surveys over time and receive compensation for their participation. Bovitz Inc. draws specific samples – such as ours – by using an algorithm so that the sample matches the US population on key US Census benchmarks.[11] These types of nonprobability but representative samples have become common place in social science research (e.g., Vavreck and Rivers 2008). As we will detail in Chapter 5, we include several questions about fandom on the public survey to isolate the distinct opinions of the "public" versus "college sports fans."

---

[10] As we explain in greater detail in this chapter's appendix, the number of schools differed for student-athletes, administrators, and coaches because fewer schools are respectively required for each group to obtain sufficiently sized samples.
[11] Bovitz Inc. has been used extensively in other political science research (e.g., Druckman and Levendusky 2019; Howat 2021).

TABLE 2.1 *Data collections*

Population	Sample	Date	Number of respondents (response rate)	Chapter(s) used/purpose
Student-athletes	Random sample, stratified by NCAA division of 63 schools	Summer 2018	2,539 (12%)	*Chapters 3, 4* • Identify the correlates of student-athletes' support for gender equity policies. • Test theory of contact with male student-athletes using self-reported measures.
Student-athletes	Random sample, stratified by NCAA division of 53 schools	Spring 2020	2,136 (11.5%)	*Chapter 3* • Test theory of contact with male student-athletes using experimentally manipulated measures.
Coaches	Random sample, stratified by NCAA division of 418 schools	Summer 2018	531 (9%)	*Chapter 4* • Identify the correlates of coaches' support for gender equity policies. • Test theory of institutionally induced preferences with female coaches.
Athletic administrators	Random sample, stratified by NCAA division of 257 schools	Summer 2018	862 (15%)	*Chapter 4* • Identify the correlates of athletic administrators' support for gender equity policies. • Test theory of institutionally induced preferences with female athletic administrators.

(continued)

TABLE 2.1 (continued)

Population	Sample	Date	Number of respondents (response rate)	Chapter(s) used/purpose
Public	Nonprobability representative national sample (based on US Census benchmarks)	Spring 2019	1,508*	*Chapter 5* • Identify the correlates of the public's support for gender equity policies. • Identify impact of prior experience with sex-segregated sports institutions (e.g., high school sports) on support for gender equity policies. • Identify impact of market demanders (for college sports) on support for gender equity policies.

* Response rate for the public sample is not available since solicitations are sent to more potential respondents than are needed and the opportunity to take the survey closes for particular respondents as different sample benchmarks are reached.

2.4 OUR MEASUREMENT STRATEGY

Our sampling approach across populations enables us to draw generalizable inferences about the target populations. Next, we detail how we measure opposition or support for our main measures of gender equity initiatives. As discussed in Chapter 1, we employ measures on six initiatives. Four of them – support for Title IX, equal participation opportunities, increased enforcement of sexual harassment laws, and equal spending – follow straightforwardly from ongoing debates about gender equity and benefits (see, e.g., Brake 2010; Sharrow 2021a).[12]

We develop multiple measures to capture nuance in opinion toward policy issues that remain under public debate. While Title IX is a matter of law, its history is marked by public pushback, particularly from athletes and coaches on certain men's teams who claim that approaches employed by their individual colleges or universities to comply with policy directly led to the elimination of their teams (Messner and Solomon 2007; Simon 2005).[13] This framing that pits men's and women's teams against each other for budgetary decisions became salient again during the early COVID-19 pandemic. Many colleges and universities announced major cuts to their varsity athletics programs, blaming financial losses incurred during the pandemic and suggesting the reductions were attempts at Title IX compliance (as discussed previously) (Druckman and Sharrow 2020).

[12] As shown in Table 2.2, our first item asks about attitudes toward Title IX. This raises the question of whether respondents are sufficiently familiar with Title IX, as applied to college athletics, to answer the question. On our surveys, we also asked respondents whether they had heard of Title IX. Among those involved in college athletics, the percentages are predictably very high – 93.6 percent, 99.25 percent, and 99.8 percent respectively for student-athletes, coaches, and administrators. For members of the public, though, the percentage drops to only 33.6 percent. An April 2022 Pew survey shows, in contrast, that 50 percent of public reports hearing at least a little about Title IX (Igielnik 2022). The discrepancy likely reflects individuals' learning about Title IX due to media attention accompanying the fiftieth anniversary in 2022 (our public survey was in 2019); also, the wording in the Pew survey defined Title IX explicitly, which may have primed people's memory. Regardless, the low level of knowledge in the public sample could be a cause for concern but the other five measures as well as the one we introduce later do not invoke "Title IX" but instead focus strictly on the content of equity initiatives (and thus do not require any prior knowledge). We further confirmed that the results for the public, reported later in the book, are robust to excluding the Title IX item.

[13] Men's sports like gymnastics and wrestling have been particularly hard-hit at schools that have elected to increase their investment in men's football roster spots without simultaneously providing correlate growth in opportunities for women. Advocates in these sports have claimed that Title IX is the reason for a decline in men's opportunities – a claim that the courts rejected in a lawsuit filed (*National Wrestling Coaches Association v. US DOE*). Nevertheless, the critique leveled by these athletes remains salient in public discourse.

Additionally, while equal treatment should follow from Title IX, ambiguous metrics and lackluster enforcement have enabled unequal (and inequitable) opportunities to persist nationwide (i.e., 43 percent of student-athletes are women compared to 57 percent of undergraduates; NCES 2021). We thus include a measure concerning equal athletic participation opportunities as this elicits opinion on the central tenet of existing policy. We also employ a question about increased enforcement of sexual harassment laws to reflect, as discussed in Chapter 1, recent attention to #MeToo activism in sports, reactions to the Larry Nassar sexual abuse and Baylor football sexual assault cases, and the Trump administration announcement of updated draft federal campus sexual misconduct policy guidelines under Title IX in 2018. Research in other contexts shows that poor enforcement of sexual harassment laws undermines equality at work and on college campuses, disproportionately harming women and gender-diverse people (e.g., Dauber and Warner 2019; Edelman and Cabrera 2020; Hirsch and Khan 2020; Saguy and Rees 2021). Finally, we develop a measure to tap into evaluations of resource distributions given that gross inequities in spending are widely recognized (see Chapter 1) but rarely addressed since equal spending is, as we noted, not legally mandated by Title IX.

We also include two measures assessing opinion toward tactics for increasing the number of women in athletic leadership positions given the disparities discussed in Chapter 1, including the downward trend of women employed as head coaches. Moreover, concerns about employment discrimination against women in coaching were salient while we were collecting much of our data. A high-profile legal case concerning the termination of employment for the most successful women's college hockey coach in history concluded in March 2018 with a $3.74 million Title IX settlement from the University of Minnesota Duluth (Zamora 2018; see also Buzuvis 2017).

Our precise items measure opposition or support for requiring a woman to be included (a) on the final interview list for any women's team head coach job and (b) on the final interview list for any athletic director job. These proposals echo the aforementioned Rooney Rule in the National Football League that requires racial or ethnic minority candidates be included in the final interview list for head coaching and senior football operations positions.[14] Not only do these measures pertain to

---

[14] As mentioned in Chapter 1, in 2022, the Rooney Rule added a requirement that all teams must have at least one minority individual on their offensive coaching staff, and "minority" includes women regardless of racial or ethnic background.

the potential solutions to addressing the dearth in women's leadership in college athletics, they also allow us to make connections to the ongoing conversations about methods for increasing women's leadership in political institutions. Researchers in political science argue that policy solutions are required to address women's malapportionment in political leadership because recruitment is insufficient to overcome societal barriers (e.g., sexism, socialization patterns that prioritize men) (e.g., Bos et al. 2022; Dittmar 2015; Hawkesworth 2003; Lawless and Fox 2010). Structural solutions such as gender quotas have, in other contexts, been shown to demonstrably change policy in favor of more gender equal outcomes (Clayton and Zetterberg 2018; Weeks 2022).

Our outcome measures may not constitute a comprehensive set of equity policy initiatives, but they comport with the contemporary gender equality context.[15] Further, because we aim to provide a *forward-looking* assessment of policy change, we employ measures of proposals that, if enacted, would directly increase equality between women and men. Our list though does not include every gendered issue in college sports. For example, we do not include in our analyses questions on policies concerning transgender (or "trans") inclusion. We take up analyses of these questions in distinct but related (later) scholarship for several reasons. First, the NCAA rules for the participation of transgender athletes that were passed in 2010 were in effect during our data collection efforts from 2018 to 2020. Second, the 2010 policy aimed to facilitate inclusion of gender-diverse people in sex segregated collegiate athletics through several pathways which individual schools could adapt during non-championship competitions to meet the needs of their student-athletes (see Griffin 2012). Third, the hyper-politicization of trans inclusion in school-sponsored athletics largely escalated after our data collection. The conservative political forces in American state legislatures were not yet focused on trans athletes during the time in which we fielded our surveys (see Sharrow 2021b). However, we see the fight for trans justice as fundamental to gendered equality (see Sharrow 2021a) and we underscore in our conclusions that trans inclusion in intercollegiate sport is part and parcel of gender equal outcomes, not distinct and outside of them.

---

[15] In one of our student-athlete data collections – that occurred in the early months of the COVID-19 pandemic – we added an outcome variable focused on COVID-19 budget priorities (i.e., gender equity or student-athlete benefits such as sponsorship opportunities). We discuss this further in Chapter 3.

2.5 MAPPING PROPOSALS TO POLICY CHANGE ROUTES

Next, we delineate how we map these policy initiatives to the three policy change routes driven by student-athlete actions (change from the "bottom up"), leadership administration (change from the "top down"), or public pressures (change from the "outside in"). We contemplated competing approaches to guide our survey development across these constituencies. One approach could be to devise distinct survey items for each stakeholder group that match their precise activities in advocating for on enacting policy change. For example, student-athletes can press for change via protesting, athletic administrators through proposing or voting in support of policies, coaches by advocating for policies, and the public by applying pressure though boycotts or buycotts. This tailored approach would require developing distinct questions for each group. Alternatively, we could develop a uniform survey that uses the same measures across all groups, asking about their attitudinal support for each policy proposal.

We opt for the latter approach for two reasons. First, we draw upon our knowledge of history and note that quiescence, not aggressive change, has defined the recent policy environment for women in sports. We suspect that latent factors are impeding nascent but conceivable routes to more sustained progress. Therefore, if we crafted group-specific measures of routes to change we would be asking the relevant stakeholders about rare events (e.g., on the initiatives we study, there have not been nationwide student-athlete protests, explicit policy proposals, or widespread boycotts beyond specific events at individual schools). We are most interested in identifying the structural causes that suppress change. In short, we do not want to ask stakeholders whether they had, in the past, engaged in activities to which most would say "no."

Second, we also considered the downside of crafting a survey of group-specific measures of likely political action. Crafting particular measures for each of our populations would thwart any comparisons *across* the constituent groups. Thus, we employ the same evaluative (attitudinal) items in similar surveys of all constituencies so that we can directly compare levels of support for the initiatives between and among the different groups. This exercise, as will become clear in Chapter 4, is theoretically crucial. In Table 2.2, we detail the initiatives and the precise question wordings. For all items, our survey instrument fully delineated all seven response options to ensure reliable responses (e.g., Krosnick and Berent 1993).

Finally, we address how we handle the long-debated issue of whether attitudinal measures such as ours translate into eventual behaviors (see

TABLE 2.2 *Gender equity initiatives and survey questions*

Initiative	Question
Support for Title IX	Given your knowledge of Title IX, do you disagree or agree with its requirements as applied to college athletics? (7-point scale from definitely disagree to definitely agree)
Equal opportunities	Some people think more should be done to ensure women have the same opportunities as men in college sports. Others think less should be done to ensure equal opportunities. What do you think? (7-point scale from much less should be done to much more should be done)
Increased enforcement of sexual harassment laws	Some people think more should be done to enforce sexual harassment laws in college athletics (e.g., within teams, athletic departments). Others think less should be done. What do you think? (7-point scale from much less should be done to much more should be done)
Equal spending	Do you oppose or support *equal* spending on men's and women's college sports? (7-point scale from strongly oppose to strongly support)
Efforts to increase women head coaches	Do you oppose or support a rule that would require schools to *interview at least one woman* when searching for a new *head coach* for a women's team? (7-point scale from strongly oppose to strongly support)
Efforts to increase women athletic directors	Do you oppose or support a rule that would require schools to *interview at least one woman* when searching for a new *athletic director*? (7-point scale from strongly oppose to strongly support)

Druckman 2022 for discussion). Clearly, these do not necessarily map directly onto each other; however, as Fishbein and Ajzen (2010, 278) explain, "attitudes toward ... policies ... are a central explanatory construct in theories and research on human social behavior ... Work on general attitudes towards psychological objects can therefore provide very useful information. It can help us understand broad behavioral patterns, and it can perhaps also provide a basis for changing such patterns of behavior" (also see O'Keefe 2021). Additionally, in our case, attitudes themselves constitute a meaningful construct: The policies directly affect student-athletes (in particular), and thus whether the policies align with their preferences is relevant from the policy feedback perspective. Similarly, the public's attitudes matter when it comes to public policy in a democratic system; their preferences should be represented in a legitimate policymaking process.

Many of the initiatives on the agenda, such as expanding opportunities, resources, or legal enforcement, come with costs. This introduces inevitable tradeoffs that may attenuate the level of stakeholder commitment to equity initiatives. Thus, we supplement our attitudinal items with a hypothetical exercise that requires respondents to account for budgetary realities. In college sports, the main competing set of initiatives involves those aimed at enhancing financial benefits for college student-athletes above and beyond athletic scholarships, guaranteeing scholarships even if the student ceases participation on their scholarship-granting team, and guaranteeing medical coverage. At the time of our data collections, the NCAA strongly opposed student-athlete compensation beyond athletic scholarships, was considering but not clearly requiring guaranteed scholarships (e.g., if an athlete became injured and could no longer compete), and required student-athletes have some type of medical coverage but did not require that it be from the school (e.g., it could be from parents or the student-athletes themselves) (see, e.g., Commission on College Basketball 2018). In July 2021, the NCAA changed its rules by allowing student-athletes to receive benefits/renumeration beyond athletic scholarships from their name, image, and likeliness – this occurred after our data collections concluded and is notably distinct from schools directly paying salaries or other benefits (i.e., the item in our measure).

To measure how respondents might consider policy tradeoffs as they account for finite budgets, we include an item that asked respondents the following:

Imagine that a fund has been created for college sports initiatives. Your job is to allocate this fund. You can only allocate it to the below items and you must allocate *all* of the fund. Please list what percentage you would give to each initiative. The total must sum to 100 percent.

- Ensuring that men and women student-athletes have equal opportunities.
- Paying salaries to student-athletes, like other employees.
- Infrastructure for the enforcement of sexual harassment laws in college sports.
- Guaranteeing scholarships for as long as student-athletes are enrolled and making progress towards degrees (even if they are no longer participating in sports and thus no longer "student-athletes").
- Training and support (via seminars and events) for women pursuing careers as college coaches.
- Guaranteeing medical coverage for all student-athletes.

We compute a score for gender equity budget allocation by summing the equity initiative percentages (i.e., the sum of percent allocated to ensuring equal opportunities, enforcement of sexual harassment laws, and training and support for women pursuing careers as coaches).

2.6 OUR ANALYSIS STRATEGY

In each subsequent chapter, we derive and test our hypotheses. We also offer details on our explanatory and related (control) variables, as relevant. More details on related variables are available in our in appendices. We focus on two specific outcomes – the first takes the average of the six attitudinal items (for each respondent) to create an aggregate "gender equity support" measure.[16] The second outcome, our "gender equity budget allocation" measure, sums the percentages allocated to the three gender equity items in the budget exercise. Most of our analyses involve statistical models where we analyze the impact of our explanatory variables on our outcome variables, controlling for other factors that might affect the outcomes. For example, we expect levels of sexism to impact support for equity policies, and thus, we need to statistically control for that in our analyses (in addition to many other variables).[17]

We use these statistical models to produce predicted values on the outcome variables for different groups, such as male student-athletes, female student-athletes, male student-athletes who have much contact (a threshold we define in the next chapter) with female student-athletes, male student-athletes who have little contact with female student-athletes, female athletic administrators, female head coaches, and college sports fans (and so on). Each predicted value – since it comes from a statistical model – has a range of uncertainty around it (i.e., a 95 percent confidence interval) that allows us to formally test whether different groups (e.g., male student-athletes and female student-athletes) have distinct levels of support.[18] For instance, we will compare the (predicted) average support for equity initiatives between male student-athletes and female student-athletes or between members of the general public and college sports fans to identify who supports improved equity initiatives and what factors shape their support. More specifically, we will present

---

[16] When taking the average across measures, it is important to ensure the individual items (e.g., the six attitudinal items averaged to produce "gender equity support") are internally consistent or reliable, meaning they closely relate to one another and capture the same underlying construct. To assess this, we use Cronbach's alpha measure of internal consistency. For every data set, we find high values, with alpha scores for student-athletes (2018, 2020), coaches, athletic administrators, and the public being .83, .83, .78, .78, and .81, respectively. Generally, speaking a .70 is the minimum accepted value and scores of .80 and above are seen as very good.

[17] The exception to this approach is in analyzing a survey experiment that we present in the next chapter in which we need not control for other factors.

[18] The uncertainty reflects the reality that our data come from samples of the targeted populations, as discussed, and thus, we are estimating population values (as these are what we ultimately care about) from the samples.

predicted scores on equity support and budget equity allocation for the crucial groups with easy-to-read figures. We will sometimes reference the underlying statistical models when discussing formal tests – the crucial models appear in chapter appendices – but readers will not need to have familiarity with such models to understand what we find. Also, as we will explain, we often truncate some of the axes displayed in our figures with the predicted values to highlight differences, but we always note when we do so in the figures themselves.

2.7 CONCLUSION

Data on gender equity in athletics have played a sizable and often contested role in the implementation of Title IX. The ignominious circumstances previously described at Dartmouth are far from an exceptional case.[19] Such issues underscore that work about gender equity in sports must be carefully devised and transparent. For the reasons articulated above, we opted to use direct solicitation surveys to study stakeholders' attitudes about gender equity initiatives in college sports. We are unaware of any comparable data collection, particularly across stakeholder populations in intercollegiate competitive sports. Our use of representative samples allow for generalizable inferences to student-athletes, coaches, athletic administrators, and the public. Our data allow us to identify the factors that drive attitudes and to compare attitudes across populations.

In what follows, we derive and test hypotheses to answer the question of why actors have not generated more pressure for gender equity policies despite the evidence of abject inequalities. This, in turn, provides an explanation for why such inequalities remain intractable despite fifty years of Title IX's implementation. More generally, our analyses reveal how political, social, and economic institutions condition preferences in ways that undermine the quest for equality, thereby opening new space for conversations about potential interventions.

---

[19] Indeed, COVID-19 cuts led to several Title IX controversies (Hensley-Clancy 2021a).

3

Student-Athlete Contact and Policy Support

In April 2021, dozens of student-athletes from the University of Connecticut varsity women's rowing team marched across campus in protest. School administrators had announced the previous year that financial deficit in their Athletics Department required them to cut the team. The athletes, crying foul, gathered with their teammates to protest the decision and threaten legal action (Lucivero 2021). Across the country, in Minneapolis, similar protests had erupted in the fall of 2020. The University of Minnesota announced deficit-driven cuts to their intercollegiate programs as well, ending their support for varsity men's gymnastics, track and field, and tennis. The next week, 400 athletes from the men's *and* women's programs gathered on campus to protest the cuts in a march organized by the women's track team (Blount 2020).

Such instances of athlete protest are woven through the history of battles for equality in sports. From the 1976 Yale University women's rowing team, who stripped in the athletic director's office to reveal "Title IX" written on their bodies to demand a locker room like the men enjoyed at their off-campus boathouse (Sharrow 2017), to the lawsuits pursuing equal pay in women's professional tennis and soccer (Murray 2019; Ware 2011), there is a long history of policy advocacy by athletes on issues of gender inequality.[1] Even so, activism among athletes has

[1] Women's sports history contains many such examples (Aswell 2018; Goldman 2012; McCoy 2020; Mervosh and Caron 2019). Sports annals are also rife with examples of racial protests (e.g., Epstein and Kisska-Schulze 2016). These include University of Michigan football players threatening to boycott play when one of their Black teammates was asked not to participate in 1934 (Epstein and Kisska-Schulze 2016, 83–84) and the 1968 Olympic podium Black Power salute by two Black sprinters (Bass 2002; Hartmann 2003), among others.

grown exponentially in the last decade, with attempts to unionize college athletics, scores of athletes kneeling during the national anthem to protest police brutality, movements on behalf of transgender athletes, and political gestures on the Olympic medal stands. It is clear that "the era of the 'apolitical' athlete appears to be drawing to a close as a 'new era of athlete awareness and advocacy' has emerged" (Cooky 2017, 4).

The success of these efforts depends on an array of factors such as momentum from historic legacies, media coverage, public interest, and judicial decisions on relevant lawsuits. It also depends on the level of contextual support received by the activists – the broader their support and coalitions, the more likely their success (e.g., English 2021; van Dyke and Amos 2017). Indeed, the Connecticut women's rowing team was eventually reinstated, a full year later, but only after a federal judge issued a temporary restraining order that prevented the dissolution of the team. In contrast, the Minnesota men's track team regained its status only one month later, following the public outcry and protests organized by the women's team. The two cases highlight the potential power of coalitional responses. While both ended with reinstatement, the distinct processes accentuate how a coalition of support across men and women can expedite success without intervention from entities outside college sports.

Garnering a broad coalition often plays a crucial role for groups seeking change. This is particularly the case for marginalized groups whose minority status often leaves them without institutional power. A sizable body of work makes clear that advocacy from marginalized groups (and from those in coalition with them) is often critical to creating successful movements for social and political change (Han, McKenna, and Oyakawa 2021; Strolovitch 2007; Weldon 2011). Research on how such coalitions emerge and when distinct institutional structures influence their formation remains more challenging. In the domain of college athletics, we know of limited scholarship that explores how coalitions might impact change from the "bottom up." Among student-athletes, what leads men to support the push for gender equality in coalition with women? Why have such coalitions not been more prevalent?

We address these questions in this chapter. Our interest is in understanding the potential for bottom-up change, which, for marginalized groups, often occurs only with the support of more empowered allies. In so doing, we also seek to identify why male student-athletes have not expressed greater support for gender equality, which, in turn, provides insight into the persistent inequalities documented in Chapter 1. To be clear, fully explaining the complex array of factors that ultimately lead to the failure or success of advocacy efforts is beyond our purview. Cross-sex coalitions – that is, men and women in coalition together – may or may not have played a pivotal difference in the Connecticut or Minnesota examples.[2] Yet majoritarian coalitions are better positioned to push for change than are minority groups on their own (e.g., Lee 2002), so investigations into what prevents their formation remain crucial.

In the next section, we begin by discussing the persistent marginalization of female student-athletes and how this status creates a barrier to achieving equality. We then advance a new theory of coalition formation that engages work on interpersonal contact. We extend prior work by arguing that interpersonal contact between "male" and "female" student-athletes is a key to coalition emergence but that it also requires that male student-athletes trust that policymakers will not act against men's own interests.[3] We test our hypotheses with two representative sample data collections of student-athletes – one a survey and one an experiment. The results strongly support our hypotheses, revealing the attitudinal opportunity for coalitions on gender equity policy change.

However, we also consider the realities of status quo structures on student-athlete life. Namely, we study and analyze the consequences of sex-segregated athletics. Our data reveal a key barrier: The amount of contact between male and female student-athletes is notably low. Sex-based segregation of training, competition, and athlete social life that organize most (but not all) teams prevents significant cross-sex contact. Those male student-athletes who experience limited contact with female student-athletes are less likely to express support for gender equity policies. It is not surprising, for example, that the Minnesota track and field

---

[2] As noted, the Minnesota case involved efforts to reinstate the men's track and field team, raising related by distinct equity issues. At Minnesota, it is notable that the administration, under simultaneous financial pressures and Title IX mandates, voted to eliminate men's indoor track, gymnastics, and tennis rather than expand opportunity for women to achieve parity (see longer history in Kihl, Schull, and Shaw 2016). So, while women's equality issues were certainly relevant, the coalitions emerged to support men.

[3] As discussed in Chapter 1, the language around sex and gender identities is complicated. The reliance on sex-based terminology for "male" versus "female" athletes frequently falsely suggests that all participants on "men's" versus "women's" teams participate in the competitive category aligned with their sex assigned at birth. Our terminology choice is imperfect but descriptively aligns with the categories imposed by sex-segregated sports. It is a system that forces people with gender-diverse identities to select what could be a misaligned category (Sharrow 2021a). It also problematically reifies socially constructed binary identity classifications. We employ male/female designations here with skepticism and discuss them carefully to demonstrate another perverse impact of building institutions around false gendered binaries.

team – one of the few sports with (relatively) high levels of coed training – saw the emergence of a cross-sex coalition, whereas the Connecticut rowing team – a highly segregated, single-sex sport – did not. More generally, we argue that sex segregation suppresses possible coalition formation between women and men, thereby rendering change based on demands from the bottom up unlikely. We conclude the chapter by discussing how institutionalized constraints can undermine efforts aimed at equality.

3.1 PURSUING POLICY AS A MARGINALIZED GROUP

A marginalized social group is one that faces systemic exclusion from a given social, economic, and/or political system (Cohen 1999; Young 2000). Such groups occupy a minority status and face the persistent challenge of enacting change to improve their condition within and despite systems in which they lack power (Bedolla 2007; Proctor 2022; Wong 2008). In the case of sports, women have long been a marginalized group: "In general, sport is considered a male domain ... despite the exploding athletic participation rates of females observed these latter decades, the sport domain continues its long-time conservative role in gender relations" (Chalabaev et al. 2013, 138). The evidence presented in Chapter 1 substantiates that in college sports competitive opportunities and leadership positions still disproportionally favor men. Men enjoy 15 percentage points more participation opportunities, 16 percentage points more in annual athletic expenditures, and 46 percentage points more of the coaching opportunities (and hold 59 percent of head coaching positions for women's teams) (also see Cahn 1995 for the historical context). Even nearly fifty years after Title IX's edict to end discrimination based on sex, women face persistent subordination compared to men. Much like women's persistent minority status within elected positions at all levels of American government (CAWP 2021), decades of focused attention on increasing their representation in other historically male-dominated spheres has only rendered partial and uneven success. They constitute a marginalized group while male student-athletes enjoy the benefits of the resource and opportunity gaps of an advantaged group.[4]

---

[4] We recognize that women of color constitute an intersectionally, secondarily marginalized group who face additional challenges within college sport. Indeed, Hextrum (2021) makes a strong case that college sports recruitment favors White suburban athletes in ways that foundationally shape the demographic pool of athletes. At the same time, race introduces complex dynamics that are salient in college sports given the disproportionate demographic representation of Black student-athletes in some sports and not others (e.g., basketball and track and field), the role of athletics in ameliorating other forms of educational racial

To understand how marginalized group status impacts women's opinions toward gendered policies, consider scholarship on policy feedback. Work on policy feedback suggests (among other things) that the experiences of individuals affected by policies shape their preferences (Bruch, Ferree, and Soss 2010; Jacobs and Mettler 2018; Lerman and McCabe 2017; Mettler and Soss 2004).[5] For instance, Lerman and McCabe (2017) show those with direct interest in the Affordable Care Act (ACA) and Medicare (e.g., those with public health insurance, in poor health) exhibit greater support for these policies even if it goes against their partisan leanings (e.g., the Republican Party stands against the ACA but beneficiaries in their base tend to support it). Our first hypothesis applies these findings to female student-athletes who are policy beneficiaries directly impacted by inequalities in sports (e.g., they have fewer participation opportunities, lower quality facilities and events, and fewer athletic leadership appointments). Further, research suggests that they likely notice and identify these disparate practices as inequalities, given the prominence of gender as an identity that often shapes political reasoning (e.g., Burns and Kinder 2012; Strolovitch 1998). As Norton (2004, 58) notes, "decisions on equal protection and Title [IX] have encouraged, and in some cases created, populations of female athletes and have given more salience to that identity." In short, the policy context of Title IX, having educated women on their gendered political rights (Mettler and Soss 2004, 61), functions as a catalyst that enables women to recognize inequalities and support ameliorating them. Thus:

Relative to male student-athletes, female student-athletes will be more likely to support gender equity policies, all else constant. (Hypothesis 3–1)

Of course, in their pursuit of equity initiatives, women face clear challenges.[6] First, they constitute a marginalized numeric minority among the

exclusions, and concerns about the exploitation of Black athletes in high-profile sports (e.g., Hawkins 2010). Without minimizing the relevance of such considerations for the functioning of contemporary college sport (see Simien, Arinze, and McGarry 2019), we foreground the gendered dimensions of coalition formation in our study.

[5] The general theory of policy feedback posits that policies reshape the political environment – by affecting the public and/or elite actors – and hence subsequent policies in a cyclical manner (Béland, Campbell, and Weaver 2022). Among the findings in this field is that policies, in their implementation and/or design, can affect individuals and their concomitant attitudes about those and other policies. Such attitudes can then play important roles in shaping policy futures (e.g., Campbell 2003).

[6] The premise of Hypothesis 3–1 is not that gender equity policies always entail a zero-sum tradeoff with men's sports. Some of the policies we explore (as described in Chapters 1 and 2), such as better enforcement of sexual harassment laws and expanding

cohort of collegiate student-athletes. In order to pursue durable change to an historically exclusionary institution, they likely require support from a coalition of empowered allies (Katzenstein 1998; Minta and Brown 2014; Swers 2002). Second, several of the policies on which we focus – those that would increase support for Title IX, equal opportunities, enforcement of sexual harassment laws, equal spending, and obligatory consideration of women for head coaching and athletic director positions (see Chapter 2) – could destabilize the material standing of male student-athletes due to the reallocation of resources. Third, pursuing any policy change, including mere improved enforcement of Title IX, requires overcoming decades of inertia that has naturalized women's subordination in athletics and left women perpetually seeking expanded resource and leadership opportunities. The history of male domination and cultures of masculinism in collegiate sports can make control by the advantaged group seem like a natural order, rather than contested terrain. Furthermore, the erasure of persistent androcentrism is reinforced by the common celebratory narratives concerning Title IX and athletics, as described in Chapter 1.

Despite this uphill battle, female student-athletes have long pursued advocacy via protest, federal-level complaints to the Office for Civil Rights, or/and lawsuits to force institutions to fulfill the promise of Title IX (e.g., Belanger 2016; Brake 2010; Reynolds 2019). The preceding decade of college sports also makes clear that student-athletes can alter the system or, at the very least, shift the policy agenda. College athletes have pursued efforts to unionize (Druckman et al. 2014b; Druckman, Howat, and Rodheim 2016), receive compensation (Druckman et al. 2014b), and avoid COVID-19 pandemic-related reductions to their athletic opportunities (Druckman and Sharrow 2020). With these recent histories in mind, the question then becomes, how can female student-athletes who support improved equity initiatives pursue them?

3.1.1 Forming Coalitions

A marginalized group can press for change by working with those in power to create beneficial policies or by organizing through social

---

opportunities for women leadership, do not have to be zero-sum since resources for such initiatives need not come from men's sports. For instance, the aforementioned updated (2022) Rooney Rule regulations in the National Football League provide league-based salary supplements for minority hires. That said, in other instances, there is a zero-sum aspect to policy decisions given finite budgets and it is for this reason that we also include the budget allocation task (described in Chapter 2) as an outcome variable.

movements.[7] Ultimately, most policy proposals designed to improve a marginalized group's (i.e., female student-athletes') circumstances need to garner the support of those outside the policy's targeted population (i.e., male student-athletes). Similarly, much research on women's activities as lawmakers in elected bodies emphasizes the need for coalition-building to achieve their aims (e.g., Dittmar et al. 2017; Dodson 2006; Reingold 2000). In the absence of broad-based support, movements for change are vulnerable, with the potential for success often hinging on support from beneficent others. In essence, marginalized groups need to build coalitions through sometimes ephemeral political dialogue. As Mutz, Sniderman, and Brody (1996, 1) explain, political change "hinges not just on whether citizens at any one moment in time tend to favor one side of an issue over another, but on the numbers of them that can be brought, when push comes to shove, from one side to the other."

When advocating for policy change on gender equality issues, we theorize that female student-athletes could benefit from forming a coalition with the advantaged group: male student-athletes. How do men in sports think about issues of gender equality? To address this question, we conducted a survey in 2016 (distinct from the main surveys described in Chapter 2) that included a representative sample of 1,615 student-athletes from a major National Collegiate Athletic Association (NCAA) Division I conference (the Big Ten).[8] We asked respondents to evaluate how they felt resources and opportunities *should* be distributed between women and men. They rated twenty-four distinct items (e.g., finances, athletic scholarships, and coaches) on 5-point scales ranging from "women should be extremely advantaged" (1) to "men should be extremely advantaged" (5), with the midpoint of 3 indicating "neither men nor women advantaged." We found an average male student-athlete's score of 3.10 (standard deviation = .38) with 62 percent of men expressing an average across all items of exactly 3.0 (i.e., preferences for equal distribution) (Druckman, Rothschild, and Sharrow 2018).[9]

---

[7] Scholars point to many examples of these processes in the literatures on gender justice in politics (Htun and Weldon 2018), social movements (Goss 2012; Weldon 2002, 2011), lawmaking (Minta and Brown 2014; Swers 2002), and other nongovernmental contexts (Katzenstein 1998).

[8] We weight the data based on gender, sport, and university. The full study is published elsewhere (Druckman, Rothschild, and Sharrow 2018).

[9] The mean for female student-athletes is 3.00 (.19), which is statistically significantly lower ($p < .01$).

These results make clear that most male student-athletes support an abstract norm of gender equality in college athletics, with scant variation among men.

Yet we also find that male student-athletes have an impoverished sense of objective gender inequalities in resource and opportunities. We asked respondents for their perceptions of how each of the twenty-four items is *actually distributed* between men and women in collegiate sports. While the average score for female student-athletes is 3.42 (.44) – indicating their clear perception that distributions skew toward men – the average male student-athlete score is 3.07 (.47) ($p < .01$) (which is closer to equality than their normative assessment). This study provides evidence that male student-athletes may value gender equality but do not – given the objective metrics documented in Chapter 1 – grasp the extent of inequalities in the status quo. This finding aligns with well-established literature regarding disparities between individuals' abstract values and their applied perceptions (e.g., Sullivan and Transue 1999). It also raises questions about how male student-athletes' abstract values might be translated to concrete support for equality, thereby making them viable coalition partners. We theorize a feasible pathway by turning to the literature on interpersonal contact.

3.1.2 Contact, Trust, and Policy Attitudes

What is required to sway members of an advantaged group (male student-athletes) to support policies that benefit a marginalized group (female student-athletes)? First, in addition to holding the aforementioned abstract equality values, male student-athletes must recognize the marginalization of female student-athletes (i.e., they must have concrete knowledge of disparate conditions) and the potential role of policies in redressing the inequalities. The absence of such knowledge disconnects support for abstract equality from applied policy support: Male student-athletes must be aware of marginalization to support addressing it.[10] Second, they must trust the entity charged with policymaking and implementation. The advantaged male student-athletes need to believe that the new policies, as implemented by their schools and/or the NCAA, will not ultimately have an adverse impact on them. As trust increases, so

---

[10] This is reflected in the well-documented relationship between education and tolerance, which partially comes about from learning about other groups (van Doorn 2014; Vogt 1997, 103).

does comfort in delegating policymaking power (Lupia and McCubbins 1998, 85). Hetherington and Rudolph (2015, 36) explain that "if people perceive the architect of policies as untrustworthy, they will reject its policies; if they consider it trustworthy, they will be more inclined to embrace them" (also see Hetherington 2005, 51).

The bedrock of our theory is that interpersonal contact between male and female student-athletes can play a crucial role in building a policy coalition to support gender equity policies. Most of the considerable literature on intergroup contact focuses on how increased contact leads to diminished prejudice (e.g., as contact with Black people increases, White people's racial prejudice decreases) (e.g., Allport 1954; Paluck, Green, and Green 2019; Pettigrew and Tropp 2006, 2011, Paolini et al. 2021).[11] Several recent studies from educational and workplace settings – areas similar to our focus – provide evidence for positive contact effects. For instance, contact through education-based national service settings (i.e., Teach for America) between economically advantaged and disadvantaged individuals leads the former to adopt beliefs closer to those of the latter (Mo and Conn 2018). Likewise contact in the workplace between native-born citizens and immigrants decreases natives' support for an anti-immigrant party (Andersson and Dehdari 2021), and White individuals who interact more with Black coworkers exhibit significantly less pro-White bias than those who do not (Darling-Hammond, Lee, and Mendoza-Denton 2021).[12]

Contact often induces these types of effects by actuating understanding of others.[13] For instance, it can "facilitate understanding of the structural disadvantages faced by the minority group" (Kim, Fishkin, and Luskin

[11] Contact typically reduces prejudice, although there is substantial variation based on the groups involved (Paluck, Green, and Green 2019); it is also unclear whether decline in prejudice builds more societal cohesion in general (Mousa 2020) and what conditions are required for prejudice reduction (Paluck et al. 2021; Paluck, Green, and Green 2019).

[12] In a slightly less relevant but intriguing context, recent evidence also suggests that cross-partisan contact in canvassing reduces out-party animosity (Kalla and Broockman 2022).

[13] Allport (1954) poses four conditions under which contact works best: equal status in the contact situation, common goals shared among groups, cooperation, and support of authorities or customs. While these conditions have not been systematically tested (Paluck, Green, and Green 2019), student-athlete interactions likely approach them. Even if they have distinct resources, student-athletes share a similar status in each contact situation. They also likely have a shared goal of improving student-athlete life and have no reason to conflict per se when in contact. Support of authorities may vary and aligns with our argument about the role of trust.

2018, 1034).[14] Wiley et al. (2021, 700) find this occurs with cross-sex contact acutely: "positive contact with feminist women may make issues of gender inequality more salient for men, calling attention to men's moral imperative to address these issues as perpetrators and beneficiaries of sexism." They find that men who have more contact with feminist women report increased feminist solidarity and awareness of their gender privilege; however, they find mixed results when it comes to the impact on support for gender equality in the public and domestic spheres.

In the context of college sports, then, interpersonal contact can satisfy the condition of helping male student-athletes recognize the need for policies to rectify gender inequalities through increased knowledge.[15] Our argument aligns with research documenting the effectiveness of sharing narratives by or about group members to alter attitudes (including policy support) concerning marginalized groups (Kalla and Broockman 2020).[16]

Of course, this understanding need not necessarily lead to support for policy changes (as indicated by Wiley et al.'s 2021 mixed results); Hässler et al. (2020, 381) explain, "contact may improve advantaged group members' feelings towards disadvantaged groups while having little impact on their support for policies or actions designed to redress group-based inequalities." These authors nonetheless show that intergroup contact leads to support for social changes among the advantaged group. However, they do not explore policies that could directly threaten

---

[14] Kim, Fishkin, and Luskin (2018) focus on deliberative contexts, pointing out that many day-to-day interpersonal interactions do not offer the context to exchange such personal details. This occurs, in part, because they minimize the likelihood of political discussions. In situations where discussion of the relevant topic likely occurs with frequency (such as the one we study), interpersonal contact can suffice. Of related relevance is work showing that heterogeneous interactions affect an understanding of other's views (Huckfeldt, Mendez, and Osborn 2004; Mutz 2006, 74–87).

[15] Other work shows that heterogeneous interaction can lead people to change their policy views (Druckman, Levendusky, and McLain 2018; Druckman and Nelson 2003; Ugarriza and Caluwaerts 2014). Tropp, Ulug, and Uysal (2021) show that contact stimulates action by the advantaged group via communication about group differences in power.

[16] Nonjudgmental narratives facilitate persuasion because – compared to direct argumentation – they are perceived to be less manipulative, produce less counterarguing, and cause less threat to the receiver. Kalla and Broockman (2020) offer evidence that a key to impactful contact is invoking the listener to engage in perspective-giving – that is, hearing about the experiences of an out-group member (from group members or others). It seems likely that the interactions among student-athletes involve personal narratives. Most of the contact occurs in the context of day-to-day athletic participation, rather than a setting where deliberative argumentation about public policy occurs.

the material standing of the advantaged group.[17] As Dixon et al. (2010) point out, the positive outcomes of contact may not carry over to policies that directly threaten advantaged groups in such ways.[18] This is a crucial point as male student-athletes who abstractly support gender equality may balk at concrete support if they worry that the advancement of women will undercut their material (e.g., resources) or symbolic (e.g., media or fan attention) standing. Thus we argue that trust becomes relevant: If members of the advantaged male student-athlete group trust policymakers – namely, within their schools and/or the NCAA – it will reduce the perceived threat of a new policy. This argument aligns with work on group threat that finds that people with power are more willing to support those without if they feel their relative material standing will remain stable (e.g., Meuleman et al. 2020). To be clear, our focus is on general trust in the policymaking entities to do "what is right." That is, we focus on assessing the belief among individuals in the advantaged group that such entities will not make decisions that substantially undermine their interests. We thus arrive at the following hypothesis:

As the amount of contact with female student-athletes increases, male student-athletes who trust their schools (and/or the NCAA) will become more supportive of gender equity policies, all else constant. (Hypothesis 3–2)

Trust provides male student-athletes with confidence that gender equity policies will not wholly undermine their own standing. Put another way, contact facilitates male student-athletes learning about the plight of female student-athletes and the need for policy change, while trust can reassure them that new policies will not unduly subvert their interests. We theorize that these could, in turn, create pressure for change from the bottom up. We recognize that even supportive male student-athletes may not necessarily join active coalition efforts given collective action challenges. Here we put such considerations aside, focusing on the necessary first step to coalition formation of garnering policy support. Even so, our recognition of the role of trust constitutes a novel insight given

---

[17] Hässler et al. (2020) show increase in support for low-cost collective actions (e.g., signing an online petition), high-cost collective actions (demonstrating), empowering policies (e.g., ensuring the disadvantaged group has more decision-making power), raising in-group awareness, and working in solidarity.

[18] Dixon et al. (2010) show that contact produces policy support by altering perceptions of the marginalized group's plight/injustice and by reducing threat of the other group. A reduction of threat means the advantaged group worries less about adverse consequences that benefit the marginalized group. We focus on trust in policymakers instead of threat although it captures a similar idea.

the vast prior literature on contact has not explicitly identified conditions under which contact shifts support for policies (rather than group-related attitudes) that benefit the marginalized group at the potential material expense of the advantaged group.

3.1.3 Summary of Theorizing Change from the Bottom Up

Female student-athletes face substantial hurdles for equality in college sport. Although institutions have evolved to better facilitate their inclusion due to the on-going implementation of sex nondiscrimination policy (i.e., Title IX), women continue to confront substantial participation and resource gaps. The policy agenda contains a number of proposals to address these inequities. We argue that female student-athletes are more likely than male student-athletes to support these proposals, but their ability to see such proposals realized as policy change may be contingent on building a coalition with male student-athlete allies. This requires that male student-athletes support the policy proposals. In what follows, we present two studies to explore whether increased contact, in tandem with high levels of trust, leads male student-athletes to support equity policies.

3.2 STUDY I

As described in Chapter 2, we test our hypotheses on a random sample of 2,539 student-athletes, weighted by race, sex, NCAA division, and sport. The data were collected in summer 2018; further details about sampling and implementation appear in Chapter 2 (and that chapter's appendix; recall all appendices are available at www.cambridge.org/ Druckman-Sharrow_EqualityUnfulfilled).[19] We present a weighted demographic profile of the sample in Tables 3.1 and 3.2. All question wordings for these and other variables used in this chapter appear in the chapter's appendix. Due to our poststratification weights, our student-athlete sample perfectly matches the population on sex, race, and NCAA division. (We do not have access to population figures on the other features displayed in Table 3.1.) The percentages in Table 3.2 show some disparities between the weighted sample and the population by sport, reflecting that the weighting process constrains particular observations from having too large of an impact in our analyses (see Chapter 2's appendix). The most

---

[19] We preregistered our data collection at: https://aspredicted.org/hy5ks.pdf.

TABLE 3.1 *Weighted student-athlete sample description, Study 1*

Variable	Mean/Percentage
Sex (self-identified by respondent)	Male: 57%; female: 43%
Race (that best describes the respondent as self-identified)	White: 65%; Black: 16%; Hispanic/Latino: 8%; Asian/Pacific Islander: 6%; other: 5%[1]
Religion	Protestant: 42%; Catholic: 23%; Jewish: 2%; other religion: 5%[2]; not religious: 28%
Parent with a college degree	78%
Familial income	< $30,000: 7%; $30,000–$69,999: 16%; $70,000–$99,999: 22%; $100,000–$200,000: 35%: >$200,000: 21%[3]
Year in school	First year: 32%; sophomore: 25%; junior: 26%; senior: 17%; postgraduate: 1%[4]
Athletic scholarship (full or partial)	41%
Academic scholarship (full or partial)	51%
Coed team (self-reported)	9%
NCAA division	Division I: 36%; Division II: 24%; Division III: 40%
Political ideology, mean (1–7 scale, with higher scores indicating more conservative)	3.76 (std. dev.: 1.49)
Racial conservativism, mean (1–7 scale, with higher scores indicating more racial conservatism)	2.95 (std. dev.: 1.27)
Hostile sexism, mean (1–7 scale, with higher scores indicating more sexism)	3.17 (std. dev.: 1.60)
Average percentage time of male student-athlete contact with female student-athletes	32% (std. dev.: 16%)
Average trust in school (1–5 scale, with higher scores indicating more trust)	3.32 (std. dev.: .98)

[1] Less than 1 percent classified themselves as Middle Eastern/North African; less than 1 percent classified themselves as Native American; 4 percent classified themselves as "other."

[2] Less than 1 percent classified themselves as Muslim; less than 1 percent classified themselves as Hindu; 4 percent classified themselves as "other."

[3] The total exceeds 100 percent due to rounding error.

[4] The total exceeds 100 percent due to rounding error.

TABLE 3.2 *Weighted student-athlete sports participation, Study 1*

Sport	Weighted sample percentage	Population percentage
Baseball	7.59	7.91
Basketball	7.39	7.91
Beach volleyball	0.05	0.26
Bowling	0.02	0.17
Cross-country	6.14	6.69
Equestrian	0.32	0.32
Fencing	0.22	0.31
Field hockey	1.41	1.38
Football	15.59	16.49
Golf	1.96	3.13
Gymnastics	0.69	0.43
Ice hockey	1.58	1.50
Lacrosse	5.52	5.90
Rifle	0.23	0.08
Rowing	3.65	2.15
Rugby	0.09	0.14
Sailing	0.15	0.13
Skiing	0.19	0.14
Soccer	11.09	11.79
Softball	4.25	4.55
Squash	0.60	0.21
Swimming	5.05	5.07
Tennis	3.10	3.68
Track and field	18.20	13.16
Volleyball	3.26	4.38
Water polo	0.25	0.51
Wrestling	1.19	1.61
Other	0.22	0.02

* Our survey separated diving and swimming, lightweight rowing and rowing, and acrobatics and gymnastics but we merge them here to compare with the population figures. Our sample percentages also are normalized to 100 percent (i.e., otherwise they sum to more than 100 percent since about 9 percent of our weighted sample participated in multiple sports). The population percentages sum to slightly over 100 percent due to rounding error.

notable disparity concerns respondents who compete in track and field who are slightly overrepresented in our weighted sample by about 5 percent compared to their proportion in the population.

The survey contained our six main measures for gender equity policy, as described in Chapter 2 – that is, opposition or support for: Title IX,

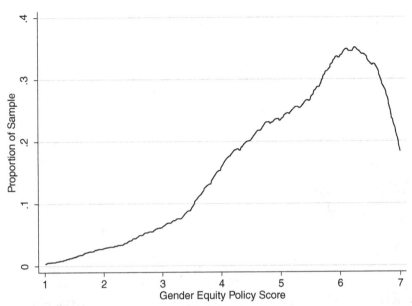

FIGURE 3.1 Sample distribution for gender equity policy (scaled), student-athletes (Study 1)

more equitable opportunities, greater enforcement of sexual harassment laws, equal athletic spending, requiring schools to interview women for head coaching jobs, and requiring schools to interview women for the athletic director job (each measured on a 7-point scale where higher scores indicate greater support). As discussed in Chapter 2, these items scaled into a single average scale gender equity policy score. We display the distribution of the scale in Figure 3.1 with the x-axis showing the gender equity policy score that ranges from 1 to 7 and the y-axis displaying the proportion of the sample that reported the given score. It reveals a clear skew toward support among student-athletes – indeed the weighted mean is 5.09 (1.29).[20] We also examine responses to the budget allocation exercise that required respondents to allocate funds across gender equity initiatives relative to student-athlete benefits proposals. Recall, as described in Chapter 2, the measure is the sum of the percent of a budget that respondents allocate to three gender equity initiatives (ensuring

---

[20] The distribution in Figure 3.1 is unweighted but looks similar when weighted, although with slightly fewer high values – e.g., the unweighted mean is 5.29 (1.26).

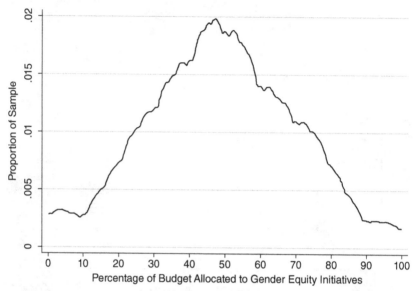

FIGURE 3.2 Sample distribution for gender equity budget allocation, student-athletes (Study 1)

equal opportunities, enforcement of sexual harassment laws, and training and support for women pursuing careers as coaches) as opposed to three initiatives that focus on benefits (paying salaries to student-athletes, guaranteeing scholarships regardless of participation in the sport, and guaranteeing medical coverage). Figure 3.2 displays that distribution, again with the x-axis showing the score that ranges from 0 percent to 100 percent and y-axis showing the proportion of the sample reporting that score. It reveals that when faced with explicit tradeoffs support for gender equity is diminished.[21] It is somewhat normally distributed (i.e., the distribution of responses takes on a bell shape) with a weighted mean of 46.23 (21.59).[22]

As illustrated in Table 3.1, the survey included independent measures that allow us to test our hypotheses. We asked individuals to report their gender (using categories male, female, other), and we created a dummy

[21] The y-axes in Figures 3.1 and 3.2 differ so much because the gender equity policy score scale takes on 7 values whereas the gender equity budget allocation scale takes on 101 values (and thus the proportion allocated to each specific value for the budget allocation scores is much smaller than for the gender equity policy scores).

[22] The distribution in Figure 3.2 is unweighted but looks similar when weighted; the unweighted mean is 48.71 (21.51).

variable to indicate "female."[23] Hypothesis 3–1 straightforwardly pre-dicts that identifying as a woman should be positively related to sup-port for gender equity initiatives and gender equity budget allocation. In Hypothesis 3–2, we posit that support is related to measures of cross-sex contact and trust in schools and/or the NCAA. For contact, we asked individuals to report – of the total amount of time they spend with fel-low student-athletes – what percentage is spent with each of four demo-graphic groups: White men, Black men, White women, and Black women (Amsalem and Nir 2021; Druckman et al. 2018; Paluck, Shepherd, and Aronow 2016, 567). We then compute a variable for percent contact that a male respondent has with female student-athletes. While our key vari-able is the amount of contact male student-athletes have with women, we also include a variable that assesses percent male contact among female student-athletes (see Hässler et al. 2020).[24] In order to assess the role of trust, we focus here on trust in the student-athletes' college or univer-sity since decisions about how to allocate resources and whom to hire are made at the school level (within the broad confines of policies lev-ied by the NCAA that dictate the number of allowable coaches for each sport and the roster size caps for individual sports).[25] We asked respon-dents how often they trust their school to do what is right on a 5-point scale from "never" (1) to "always" (5).[26] Hypothesis 3–2 posits a sig-nificant positive effect of the "male student-athlete contact with female

[23] As discussed in detail in Chapter 1, we note that the available gendered categories in a sex-segregated system are both hyperscripted and restricted. As explained in Chapter 2's appendix, a small number of respondents self-identified as neither "male" nor "female." Moreover, we cannot discount the possibility that some transgender respondents selected the "male" or "female" response category, given sex-segregated sports make narrow sex-based categories so salient in their lives as student-athletes even if their sense of self is more gender-expansive. That said, the limited number of self-identified gender-diverse respondents in our sample is not unexpected. Although public attention in recent years has become more pronounced on issues of transgender inclusion in sport, and the NCAA passed initial trans inclusion policies in 2010, the number of out transgender athletes competing at the collegiate level is negligible.

[24] Hässler et al. (2020) find that for members of a marginalized group, contact with the advantaged group (i.e., female student-athlete contact with male student-athletes) can (with some outcomes) decrease support for social change (i.e., the inverse effect of what we predict for male student-athlete contact with female student-athletes).

[25] Study 1 did not include a measure of NCAA trust; we explore this more in Study 2.

[26] A 2020 Gallup report revealed that compared to non-student-athletes, student-athletes are more likely to graduate in four years, less likely to transfer, and more likely to feel attached to and donate to their school (Gallup 2020). Roughly, 50 percent report strong agreement that their undergraduate education was a good investment. While this does not directly measure trust, it suggests that student-athletes have relatively positive expe-riences but also substantial variance (e.g., 50 percent did not report strong agreement).

student-athletes X trust" interaction, on support for gender equity initiatives and on the gender equity budget allocation (our dependent variables). That is, we expect that male student-athletes with more female student-athlete contact will express higher equity policy support *contingent* on having a high trust score.

As explained in Chapter 2, we test our hypotheses by using statistical analyses where we control for various other factors that could impact equity attitudes. This includes the variables listed in Table 3.1. An explanation of the variables included as well as the analyses themselves appear in the chapter's appendix. (Generally, the regression analyses that undergird every relevant figure in the book appear in the appendix.) In presenting the results, also as noted in Chapter 2, we will use figures that display the predicted levels of support for gender equity policy and the percentage of the budget allocated to gender equity initiatives for key groups (to assess our hypotheses), along with the uncertainty around these predictions (i.e., confidence intervals).

Before doing so, however, we acknowledge potential concerns about causality since we measure the amount of contact and policy attitudes at the same point in time on a single survey. Thus, the amount of contact could be a product of policy views if those who hold certain opinions (e.g., support gender equity policies) seek out particular discussion partners (e.g., more interactions with female student-athletes among predisposed men). If so, then, policy preferences may drive discussion and not vice versa.[27] Our response is threefold. First, the interpersonal contact items do not contain political content – they are purely demographic measures.[28] Moreover, student-athletes' lives are highly structured with notable time commitments to their sport, travel for competition, and studying, and so they have constrained choices about with whom they spend time (and thus have limited choice about contact) (e.g., NCAA 2019b). Second, if policy concerns drive choices in discussion partners, we would likely see strong negative correlations between sexism and the

---

[27] A distinct, albeit related, issue concerns the self-selection of student-athletes themselves. That is, it is possible that those who participate in college sports are socialized into a segregated participatory environment and may even prefer it. Regardless, they also are the beneficiary population, and thus understanding their preferences, even if they differ from other individuals, is crucial.

[28] This differs from the measures typically used in political science to study discussion networks – those focus on the partisan nature of one's network with the question of whether the nature of the networks moderate issue positions. There is good reason to be concerned in that case that political considerations affect choices about with whom to interact (Mutz 2006, 46–48).

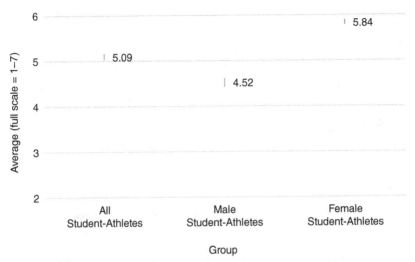

FIGURE 3.3 Gender equity policy support averages for student-athletes (Study 1)

frequency of interactions between women and men. Individuals with sexist views would probably avoid interactions with groups they tend to dislike and with whom they likely disagree on policy. Yet we find a small negative correlation between these measures (-.07). Third, even with these reassurances, we cannot entirely rule out endogeneity concerns or omitted variables, and so in our second study, we employ an experiment to offer a stronger causal test. Next, we turn to the results from the survey.

3.2.1 Results

We start by presenting graphs, Figures 3.3 and 3.4, of the raw mean scores (and 95 percent confidence intervals) of equity policy support and gender equity budget allocation (i.e., these are not predicted values from statistical models that control for other variables but rather just basic averages). Importantly, the y-axes on these figures are truncated to be between, respectively, 2 and 6 (even though the full scale is between 1 and 7) and 30 percent and 70 percent (even though the full scale is between 0 percent and 100 percent). We follow this truncation approach throughout the chapters of the book, always noting the full scale on the figures when appropriate. We do so to accentuate the areas of difference, while also being transparent by explicitly stating the full scale.

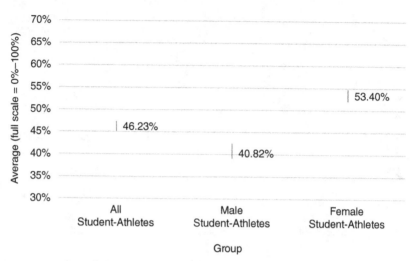

FIGURE 3.4 Gender equity budget allocation averages for student-athletes (Study 1)

The equity score graph – Figure 3.3 – shows high support with an overall mean of 5.09 and a substantial gender disparity of 4.52 for men and 5.84 for women ($p < .01$ for a two-tailed test, meaning, roughly, that the probability of there being no difference between the two values in the population is lower than .01). As stated earlier, the budget allocation graph – Figure 3.4 – shows a middling overall score that skews slightly away from gender equity toward more allocation to benefit policies (i.e., 46.23 percent is allocated to gender equity initiatives). We again see a large gender disparity from 40.82 percent among men to 53.40 percent among women ($p < .01$). Consistent with Hypothesis 3–1, this shows that the gendered nature of these policies leads women (the marginalized group) to express more support.

We next turn to the results from the statistical models that appear in the chapter's appendix. We gauge the effects of sex-based identity and cross-sex contact by plotting the predicted values (from the regressions in the online appendix) and 95 percent confidence intervals – setting all other variables at their mean values – for the average woman and for a man with low contact/low trust, low contact/high trust, high contact/low trust, and high contact/high trust. For low contact, we use the first quartile score (that represents a man who spends 20 percent of his time interacting with female student-athletes) and for high contact we use the third quartile (that represents a man who spends 45 percent of his time

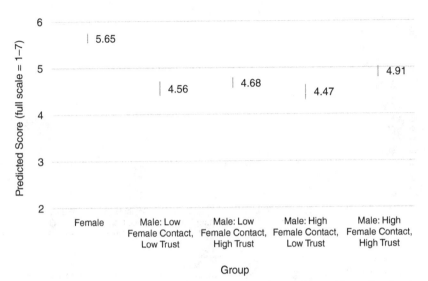

FIGURE 3.5 Predicted gender equity policy scores for student-athletes (Study 1)

interacting with female student-athletes). (We discuss the full distribution in greater detail later.) For low trust, we use the second score (i.e., answer option) on the 5-point scale that indicates trusting the school "some of the time," and for high trust, we use the fourth score (i.e., answer option) that indicates trusting the school "most of the time." (We find the same results if we use other operationalizations; see this chapter's appendix for statistical models.)

In Figure 3.5, we display the predicted values for equity policy support. When controlling for all other factors, we see the predicted score for a female student-athlete is 5.65 (down from the raw mean reported in Figure 3.3 that does not control for other variables). Further, in all cases, male student-athletes exhibit significantly lower scores at a statistically significant level ($p < .01$), consistent with Hypothesis 3–1. We also find that support among men with low contact and low trust drops precipitously to 4.56 and remains low (in fact lower) with high contact and low trust (4.47). We see some increased support when men have low contact and high trust (4.68), reflecting that our low contact scenario still has some contact (i.e., 20 percent). Clearly though, without trust contact has little effect, and without contact trust has little effect. Yet when there is both high contact and high trust, the score substantially increases to 4.91 – a 5.8 percent increase from low contact–low trust ($p < .01$). This

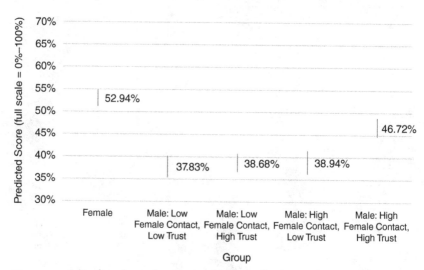

FIGURE 3.6 Predicted gender equity budget allocation for student-athletes (Study 1)

size of the effect is in line with other recent work on contact and marginalized groups (e.g., Kalla and Broockman 2020).[29] It also clearly supports Hypothesis 3–2: *Interpersonal contact with the marginalized group increases support when there are high levels of trust in the policymaking institution.*

In Figure 3.6, we find a more dramatic impact of trust–contact: With high levels of both, the score jumps to nearly 47 percent, nearly 10 percentage points higher than low contact/low trust. We also see that without trust or contact, allocation to gender equity initiatives is substantially lower ($p < .01$), confirming Hypothesis 3–2 again.[30] Indeed, we see male student-athletes moving from clearly favoring allocation to benefit initiatives (in the absence of contact and/or trust) to being nearly equally supportive of benefit and gender equity spending under conditions of high trust and high contact. The models underlying Figures 3.5 and 3.6, which appear in the appendix, confirm the statistical necessity of both

[29] To formalize the size of the effect of high contact and high trust, we computed a Cohen's D score, which produces a standardized difference score between two means. In this case, we find that moving from the lowest score (4.47) to the highest score (4.91) leads to a Cohen's D of .12. This is a "small" effect size (i.e., a small impact of moving from the lowest to the highest score on support for gender equity policy) but, as mentioned, consistent with related work on contact.

[30] The effect size here is also on the small side, with a Cohen's D of .15.

high contact and high trust (i.e., the interaction between the two variables is significant and positive for both outcomes).

In sum, we find that interpersonal contact with a marginalized group
can increase the extent to which members of the advantaged group support policies that benefit the marginalized group. However, this occurs
only in the presence of institutional trust. Trust likely appeases feelings
of threat among members of the advantaged group. The finding speaks
to Allport's (1954) condition of institutional supports, albeit in a distinct
way since what matters is not having the contact sanctioned by institutions but rather having those involved trusting the institutions to act in
their interests. Although male student-athletes do not approach the level
of support exhibited by female student-athletes, the effects reveal a path
to a potential policy coalition in support of gender equity policies – or
at least meeting the initial condition to garner male student-athlete support. This suggests that if levels of contact were increased in the presence
of institutional trust, coalition formation would become more possible.

3.3 STUDY 2

We next sought to replicate the contact–trust results of Study 1 using an
experiment. While the structure of college athletics gives us confidence in
the direction of Study 1's results, we cannot entirely put aside concerns
about omitted variables (e.g., those that may otherwise explain contact–
trust and policy views). Thus, we rely on the imagined contact approach.
This entails having individuals "imagine" contact with those from the
other group. This is a distinct construct, not a direct substitute, for actual
contact. As Miles and Crisp (2014, 3) explain, it is the "concept of contact,
mentally articulated in the form of an imagined interaction." Even so, we
use the paradigm as a way to isolate causal processes and document policy
attitudes immediately after priming male student-athletes to think of interactions with female student-athletes, as well as institutional trust.[31] Here,
because we randomly assign individuals to different scenarios – which we

---

[31] Miles and Crisp (2014) meta-analyze seventy-one tests of imagined contact and report
evidence of a small to medium effect size on attitudes, emotions, intended behaviors, and
actual behaviors toward the out-group. That said, there is debate about the robustness
of the imagined contact paradigm. For example, Bigler and Hughes (2010) raise various
concerns such as demand effects where participants express more favorable out-group
attitudes since they anticipate that is what the experimenter desires. That is less of a concern for us given our focus on policy and not out-group attitudes; however, we directly
address this concern by assessing the possibility of demand effects.

explain in detail in the next section – groups of participants can be assumed to be, on average, the same. Any average differences we find between groups likely reflect (i.e., are caused by) the experimental manipulations we employ, which puts us on strong causal footing.

3.3.1 Participants and Design

As explained in Chapter 2, we drew a unique sample of 2,136 student-athletes for this study in spring 2020. We present a weighted demographic profile of the sample in Tables 3.3 and 3.4. The weighting again means our sample matches the population on sex, race, and NCAA division.[32] Otherwise, the sample is similar to the one from Study 1, with the most notable difference being that this sample is slightly less racially conservative. Table 3.4 shows that we again oversample track and field.

To test the hypotheses, we use an experiment that randomly assigns male respondents to (1) imagine in-group or out-group contact and (2) be primed to have low or high trust.[33] For the in-group contact conditions, we matched the demographic of the respondent; for example, we asked White men to imagine a White male, while we asked Black men to imagine a Black male. We operationalized race by describing the race in the (imagined) vignette as well as with previously tested names that tend to be perceived as indicative of the given race (e.g., research shows that Jabari and Eboni are often perceived as a Black names while Dalton are Shelbi are often perceived as White names) (see Druckman et al. 2018; Druckman and Shafranek 2020). For the male respondents, the crucial out-group involved imagining a female student-athlete of the same race (we kept race constant between respondent and the manipulation to avoid potential confounds). For example, Black men were asked to imagine a Black woman, and White men were asked to imagine a

---

[32] The percentages of Hispanics/Latinos, Asian/Pacific Islanders, and other racial identities differ from the first study because we did not directly weight on them. (We anticipated Black identity to matter regarding student-athlete benefits, which was our main motivation for weighting on race.)

[33] We exclude control conditions – such as no contact or not trust manipulations – to ensure sufficient statistical power. Moreover, they are not necessary for testing our prediction. Miles and Crisp (2014) find that inclusion of a noncontact control group does not differ from the in-group contact condition (which is likely a more conservative baseline given the possibility of conformity effects; also see Kuchenbrandt, Eyssel, and Seidel 2013; Stathi and Crisp 2008). Excluding a trust control prevents us from isolating the "natural" level of trust; however, we already have a gauge on that from Study 1, where we find a relatively high level, with more than half the sample having a score of 4 or 5 on a 5-point scale.

TABLE 3.3 *Weighted student-athlete sample description, Study 2*

Variable	Mean/Percentage
Sex (self-identified by respondent)	Male: 57%; female: 43%
Race (that best describes the respondent, as self-identified)	White: 65%; Black: 16%; Hispanic/Latino: 7%; Asian/Pacific Islander: 7%; other: 6%[1]
Religion	Protestant: 42%; Catholic: 24%; Jewish: 4%; other religion: 4%[2]; not religious: 26%
Parent with a college degree	81%
Familial income	< $30,000: 6%; $30,000–$69,999: 12%; $70,000–$99,999: 19%; $100,000–$200,000: 38%: >$200,000: 25%
Year in school	First year: 29%; sophomore: 27%; junior: 24%; senior: 19%; postgraduate: 2%[3]
Athletic scholarship (full or partial)	42%
Academic scholarship (full or partial)	44%
Coed team (self-reported)	7%
NCAA division	Division I: 36%; Division II: 24%; Division III: 40%
Political ideology, mean (1–7 scale, with higher scores indicating more conservative)	3.69 (std. dev.: 1.51)
Racial conservativism, mean (1–7 scale, with higher scores indicating more racial conservatism)	2.57 (std. dev.: 1.17)
Hostile sexism, mean (1–7 scale, with higher scores indicating more sexism)	3.11 (std. dev.: 1.64)

[1] The total exceeds 100 percent due to rounding error; 1 percent classified themselves as Middle Eastern/North African; 1 percent classified themselves as Native American; 4 percent classified themselves as "other."

[2] 1 percent classified themselves as Muslim; less than 1 percent classified themselves as Hindu; 3 percent classified themselves as "other."

[3] The total exceeds 100 percent due to rounding error.

White woman. We present the design in Figure 3.7 (focusing on male respondents).[34] Hypothesis 3–2 straightforwardly suggests that, for male respondents, the "female student-athlete contact X high trust" condition

[34] We treated those who did not identify as White or Black as White in terms of assignment – that is, they were assigned contact with a White named individual. Including or excluding these participants from the analyses does not change the results.

TABLE 3.4 *Weighted student-athlete sports participation, Study 2*

Sport	Weighted sample percentage	Population percentage
Baseball	7.24%	7.91%
Basketball	7.42%	7.91%
Beach volleyball	0.36%	0.26%
Bowling	0.06%	0.17%
Cross-country	6.74%	6.69%
Equestrian	0.08%	0.32%
Fencing	0.86%	0.31%
Field hockey	1.13%	1.38%
Football	16.02%	16.49%
Golf	2.40%	3.13%
Gymnastics	0.73%	0.43%
Ice hockey	0.78%	1.50%
Lacrosse	5.48%	5.90%
Rifle	0.00%	0.08%
Rowing	2.48%	2.15%
Rugby	0.00%	0.14%
Sailing	0.29%	0.13%
Skiing	0.61%	0.14%
Soccer	10.89%	11.79%
Softball	4.18%	4.55%
Squash	0.26%	0.21%
Swimming	4.63%	5.07%
Tennis	3.46%	3.68%
Track and field	18.21%	13.16%
Volleyball	4.06%	4.38%
Water polo	0.41%	0.51%
Wrestling	0.94%	1.61%
Other	0.28%	0.02%

* Our survey separated diving and swimming, lightweight rowing and rowing, and acrobatics and gymnastics but we merge them here to compare with the population figures. Our sample percentages also are normalized to 100 percent (i.e., otherwise they sum to more than 100 percent since about 9 percent of our weighted sample, again, participated in multiple sports). The population percentages sum to slightly over 100 percent due to rounding error.

should lead to higher levels of support for gender equity policies and gender equity budget allocations than for all the other conditions.[35] Our

[35] We preregistered this prediction at: https://aspredicted.org/ua67j.pdf. The design has two notable extensions not relevant to testing Hypothesis 3–2. First, for White male

	Low trust	High trust
Male student-athlete (in-group) contact	1	2
Female student-athlete (out-group) contact	3	4

FIGURE 3.7 Experimental design (for male respondents, Study 2)

contact manipulation read as follows, with the inserted names for White and Black respondents (as well as the respective race of the imagined contact inserted), respectively:

We would like you to take a minute to imagine yourself meeting with another student-athlete (in person; not during the COVID-19 pandemic). To help you imagine the meeting, we are going to provide some details about the other person and the encounter.

Imagine you are meeting a [race] [male/female] student-athlete named [Dalton Wood/Shelbi Wood][Jabari Washington /Eboni Washington]. He/She is discussing [his/her] life as a student-athlete. The interaction with [Dalton/Shelbi][Jabari/Eboni] is positive, relaxed, and comfortable. You learn some interesting things about [his/her] experiences in sports.

While imagining this think specifically of *when* (e.g., after a workout) and *where* (e.g., at a training facility, tutoring center) this conversation with [Dalton/Shelbi] [Jabari/Eboni] might occur. Finally, please make sure that you imagine the scenario with your eyes closed for a minute or so.

In the text box below, please describe some aspects of the scenario as you just imagined it.

We included substantial detail in the imagined scenarios (e.g., where the interaction takes place and what it is about) and instructed participants to elaborate to increase ecological validity and better mimic our construct of contact frequency (i.e., many interactions with more lasting impacts). Instructing participants to close their eyes during the imagined encounter also prompts greater elaboration (Crisp et al. 2009; Husnu and Crisp 2011). Finally, as mentioned, we add realism by not just describing the gender identity of the imagined contact, as is typical, but also supplying a gendered name (e.g., Shelbi Dalton, Eboni

---

respondents, it also included conditions that involved contact with Black male student-athletes. Second, Black women did a distinct exercise to gauge how they juggle gender equity policy support with benefit policy support. We do not present these race-based contact results since they are orthogonal to our interests here.

Washington), similar to practices in audit studies (e.g., Butler and Crabtree 2021).[36]

To manipulate trust, we focused on how the policymaking bodies, in this case the school and the NCAA, either help (high trust) or hurt (low trust) student-athletes' success. Specifically, for the low trust manipulation, we explained that policymaking committees include fewer than 5 percent student-athletes. We also mentioned a survey that found that 75 percent of student-athletes who start in preprofessional majors – such as premed or engineering – change to more "manageable majors" (Adler and Adler 1985). For the high trust manipulation, we pointed to school and NCAA student-athlete advisory committees that provide policy input, as well as a survey that shows that 56 percent of former student-athletes report having strong "purpose" and well-being (Gallup 2016). We implemented the trust manipulations relaying the information (for the given condition) and then asking what the respondent thinks using asymmetric scales (see Petrocelli, Martin, and Li 2010). Precise wording appears in this chapter's appendix.[37]

After reading the relevant stimuli, participants answered the same outcome variables as in Study 1 regarding gender equity policies and budget allocation. Since the study was conducted during a period when substantial financial cuts to collegiate athletics were being made due to the COVID-19 pandemic, we added another outcome variable that asks about the relative priority of ensuring gender equity (e.g., equal resources and leadership opportunities) or ensuring student-athlete benefits (e.g., sponsorship opportunities and guaranteed scholarships) in light of the current financial situation (see also Druckman and Sharrow 2020). Answers are on a 5-point scale from "definitely ensure benefits" (1) to "definitely ensure gender equity" (5). We included a set of manipulation checks to ensure that our trust manipulation succeeded and that people envisioned a positive interaction (as instructed). We evaluated demand effects by asking respondents why they thought we asked them to imagine the encounter and whether they imagine that we, the researchers, support gender equity policies (e.g., Mummolo and Peterson 2019).

---

[36] Druckman et al. (2018) provide data on the equivalence of names in terms of perceived class and familiarity.

[37] We piloted the trust items to ensure they had the intended effect; as discussed below, we also included manipulation checks in the experiment.

3.3.2 Results

We begin with our manipulation checks.[38] When asked about the positivity of the interaction, respondents reported an average score of 4.43 (std. dev.: .80) on a 5-point scale, with higher scores indicating great positivity. Eighty-six percent of the sample provided a score of 4 or 5. As instructed, respondents viewed the interaction positively. Also, relative to those assigned to a low trust condition, those assigned to a high trust condition reported significantly higher levels of trust in their school with respective means of 3.53 (.92) and 3.66 (.88) (on a 5-point scale; a difference of means score of $t_{1,915} = 2.40$; $p < .05$ for a two-tailed test).[39] Only 15 percent of respondents answered that the purpose of the imagined interaction was to alter their policy views (from six options; the most frequent answers included "to recognize comradery" and "to think of the person's demographic group"). Finally, when asked whether the researchers advocate for greater gender equity, the average score is 3.49 (.70) on a 4-point scale, with higher scores indicating they believe that the researchers harbor greater support. However, this variable does not correlate with the respondent's experimental condition assignment, and thus male student-athletes in the female student-athlete imagined contact conditions are no more likely to respond to potential demand expectations than those in other conditions. All of these checks give us confidence in our manipulations and minimize concern about demand effects.

In presenting the results, we focus on male respondents since they constitute the relevant population for our main hypothesis.[40] In this chapter's appendix, we present results for women. We present the primary results with figures of the mean values (and 95 percent confidence intervals) for each randomly assigned experimental condition for each outcome variable. As mentioned, the random assignment to experimental conditions means that, on average, the groups are comparable to one another other than exposure to the given treatments (e.g., the type of contact they imagine is uncorrelated with prior attitudes or sensibilities). We thus do

[38] We do not include the male respondents assigned to the Black male contact conditions or Black female respondents in these analyses given they are not included in the main analyses (see prior note).

[39] We also asked about trust in the student-athlete's athletic department and in the NCAA. For both these measures, those in the high-trust condition reported higher scores (with respective p-values of .07 and .02).

[40] We also combine all men, regardless of race, since our hypothesis does not depend on race – even though the exact experimental stimuli depended on race (as discussed earlier). In this chapter's appendix, we break out the results by race.

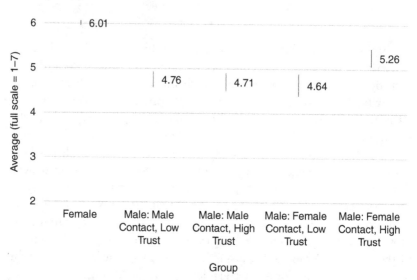

FIGURE 3.8 Gender equity policy support averages for student-athletes (Study 2)

not need to rely on predicted values from statistical models that control for other variables. Nonetheless, in the chapter's appendix, we present models analogous to those used in Study 1, all of which mimic the results we next present. (We also discuss what the model shows in terms of the impact of other variables [e.g., sexism].)

Figure 3.8 shows a remarkably high (6.01) average score among female student-athletes, merged across conditions (with little variance – a small confidence interval). In contrast, the average scores among men who do not imagine interactions with a female student-athlete register roughly 1.25 points lower (4.76, 4.71). This coheres with Hypothesis 3–1 that female student-athletes are significantly more supportive of equity policies than male student-athletes. We also see that even when male student-athletes imagine contact with a female student-athlete but have low institutional trust they become slightly less supportive relative to imagined male student-athlete contact (i.e., 4.64). Female student-athlete imagined contact on its own is not sufficient. Yet, as predicted, imagined contact with a female student-athlete along with high institutional trust (i.e., female student-athlete contact and high trust) leads to a significant increase, 5.26 ($p < .01$ versus all-male conditions). While this increase does not rival support for policies among female student-athletes, the roughly 9 percent increase (versus male student-athlete contact and low trust) reveals clear potential

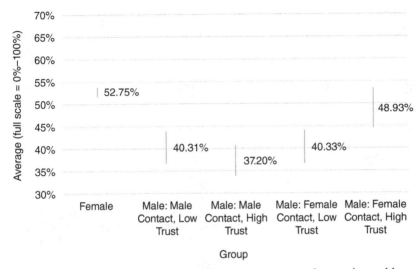

FIGURE 3.9 Gender equity budget allocation averages for student-athletes (Study 2)

for policy coalitions.[41] This substantiates Hypothesis 3–2, complementing Study 1 in showing that the intersection of contact and institutional trust is needed to form supportive equity coalitions.

We find the same patterns for both the budget allocation, displayed in Figure 3.9, and COVID-19 gender equity prioritization, displayed in Figure 3.10. For the budget allocation task, we see that male student-athlete imagined contact or female student-athlete imagined contact but low trust leaves male student-athletes 10 percentage points or more below female student-athletes who register an average score of 52.75 percent ($p < .01$). Yet when male student-athletes imagine contact with a female student-athlete in the presence of high trust, they nearly split the budget between gender equity and athlete benefits (i.e., approaching 50 percent). Again, they do not match the score of female student-athletes generally, but the increase compared with the other conditions is substantial, around 10 percentage points.[42]

Turning to gender equity prioritization during COVID-19, men's imagined contact with women, along with high trust actually leads to a higher, albeit not significantly so, average score (3.24) versus the score

[41] This registers as a medium effect size; for example, comparing the lowest score (4.64; female student-athlete contact, low trust) with the highest (5.26; female student-athlete contact, high trust) produces a Cohen's D of .52.

[42] This is medium effect size; for example, comparing the smallest score (37.20) to the largest (48.93) produces a Cohen's D of .56.

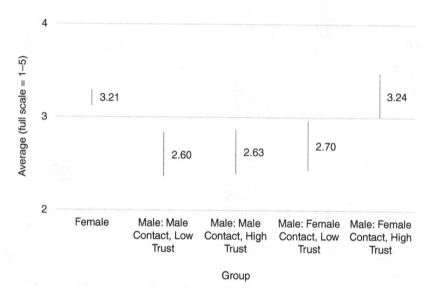

FIGURE 3.10 COVID gender equity prioritization averages for student-athletes (Study 2)

among female student-athletes (3.21). And again, we see such movement only with the mix of female student-athlete imagined contact and trust ($p < .01$).[43] In sum, the experiment provides consistent results with the survey and shows that the dynamic holds for a gender equity prioritization measure during the COVID-19 pandemic.

3.4 THE ROLE OF SEX SEGREGATION

Our results appear promising for those interested in gender equality. They reveal a way that a marginalized group can build a coalition of support for gender equity initiatives. Further, they reveal that student-athletes maintain reasonably high levels of institutional trust (e.g., Study 1's average of 3.32 on a 5-point scale), meaning that a critical condition to coalition formation can be met. However, the more pressing hurdle concerns the lack of interpersonal contact between women and men in college sports. Even though most other social domains now outlaw sex segregation, it defines the training and competition environments of collegiate athletics.

---

[43] This is a medium effect size, with Cohen's D = .58 for the smallest (2.60) versus the largest (3.24) contact conditions.

Both single-sex education and women's exclusion from higher education (e.g., medical and law schools) have largely, though certainly not entirely, diminished because of Title IX's implementation and concomittant shifting social norms (Rose 2018). Likewise, women's inclusion in many long-standing, male-exclusive occupations such as firefighting, policing, and the military have integrated areas of the historically androcentric workforce over recent decades (Grossman 2016). But within sports in general and college athletics specifically, sex segregation remains profoundly entrenched. College sports are built on overt segregation based on participant sex that hyperstructures the training, competition, and social experiences of athletes. Rather than integrating women into historically "men's" athletic programs, women remain incorporated into American college sports under an ethos of "separate, but equal" (McDonagh and Pappano 2007; Sharrow 2017, 2021a). Title IX's policy guidelines coerce institutions to cement segregated approaches to sex equity in sports by incentivizing the expansion of women's-only teams to address past discrimination. This has substantial consequences for student-athletes who have highly structured lives with notable time commitments organized overwhelmingly around athletic obligations. Their social networks generally reflect their athletic existence (e.g., NCAA 2016); the median NCAA Division I student-athlete reports that they spend thirty-three hours a week on their sport (NCAA 2019b).[44] The amount of cross-sex interaction thus varies based mostly on factors orthogonal to policy preferences, such as whether one's sport shares training facilities with the team for the opposite sex. In short, the institutions that determine intergroup contact appear unusually rigid in collegiate athletics.

In Figure 3.11, we present a density plot – based on data from our first study – of the self-reported percentage of time male student-athletes spend interacting with female student-athletes (as a proportion of time spent interacting with student-athletes).[45] The x-axis reports the percentage of time while the y-axis reveals the proportion of the sample for the given times. While contact plateaus around 50 percent, the more important aspect of the figure is the dramatic drop-off after 50 percent. The median male student-athlete reports spending only 31 percent of his time interacting with female student-athletes, with a first quartile score of

---

[44] The medians for NCAA Division II and Division III respectively are 31 and 28.
[45] Figures 3.11 and 3.12 are based on unweighted data but weighted histograms offer the same picture.

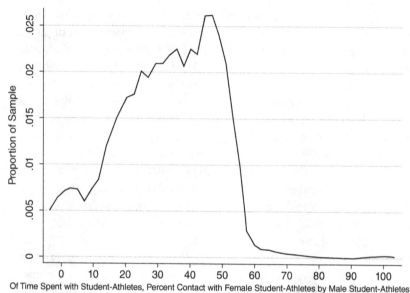

FIGURE 3.11 Percentage of female student-athlete contact by male student-athletes (Study 1)

20 percent and a third quartile score of 45 percent.[46] Given that women comprise 43 percent of the student-athlete population, the artificially deflated 31 percent median reflects the impact of sex-segregated institutions and accompanying homophily.

Other institutionalized features are also relevant. Not surprisingly, the amount of cross-gender contact increases among those who report participating in coed sports that share training facilities, coaches, and so on, even if they compete in sex-specific divisions (90 percent of those reporting coed teams are track and field/cross-country and swimming/diving). In Figure 3.12, we plot the analogous densities separately for coed and not coed sports.[47] It reveals the substantial difference between the two. The median score for the non-coed athletes is 30 percent while the median score for the coed athletes is 40 percent. Among the non-coed athletes, less than a quarter

---

[46] The mean is 32 percent. Recall we employed the first and third quartile scores in Study 1's result figures.

[47] The y-axis for Figure 3.12 differs from that for Figure 3.11 because Figure 3.12 splits the sample and thus each value becomes a larger proportion of the relevant (coed or not coed) group. Interestingly, we see in Figure 3.12 that the non-coed proportions disappear at about 80 percent; no male student-athletes, in non-coed sports, spent more than 80 percent of their time interacting with female student-athletes.

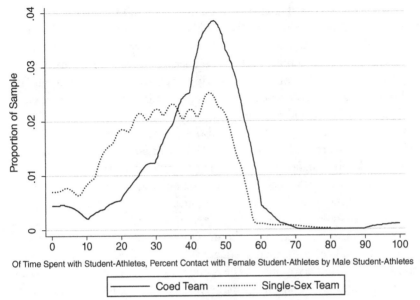

Of Time Spent with Student-Athletes, Percent Contact with Female Student-Athletes by Male Student-Athletes

|——— Coed Team   ············· Single-Sex Team |

FIGURE 3.12 Percentage of female student-athlete contact by male student-athletes (participants on coed/not coed teams) (Study 1)

of the sample register a "high contact" score as shown in Figures 3.5 and 3.6 versus 43 percent of the sample for the coed sports. This suggests that an additional 18 percent of male student-athletes could conceivably find cause to join a coalition for gender equity policies if rigid structures did not preclude their interactions with women. Although we recognize the artificial nature of this exercise given our "high" contact score, the point remains clear – the amount of cross-sex contact among men is dramatically higher in coed sports and that higher level of contact substantially affects their support for gender equity initiatives, increasing the potential for coalitions. To make our point bluntly – only 7 percent of male student-athletes report being on a coed team and thus the increased contact that affects coalitional possibilities occurs among only a tiny part of the population.[48]

These results suggest several possible responses. Although our primary conclusion suggests the need to center critique of sex-segregated sports among those concerned with gender equality, others may reasonably argue that persuading male student-athletes to support equity initiatives does not require integration. Instead, more education could suffice as our imagined

---

[48] In Table 3.1, we report 9 percent but this is because in our data more women report being on coed teams, pushing up the overall average.

contact result shows that merely thinking about contact has effects and thus actual contact is unnecessary. While we view the imagined contact experiment as crucial confirmatory evidence for Hypothesis 3–2 about the intersection of high contact and trust rendering greater support for gender equity policy, we do not believe this approach suffices as a solution. We asked our main outcome measures immediately after the imagination exercise, and, as Bigler and Hughes (2010) articulate, the effects of imagined contact exercises rarely endure (see also Miles and Crisp 2014, 20–21).[49] More telling is a related experiment by Dahl, Kotsadam, and Rooth (2021). They randomly assigned Norwegian female military recruits to some boot camp squads but not others. They find integrated squads cause men to have substantially more egalitarian attitudes, such as believing household work should be shared equally and that mixed-gender teams perform well. Yet the effects do not endure once the integration concludes; the attitudes of men who had been integrated in squads with women converge with nonintegrated men after six months. The authors explain that "even in a highly gender-skewed environment, gender stereotypes are malleable and can be altered by integrating members of the opposite sex. But ... without continuing intensive exposure, effects are unlikely to persist" (Dahl, Kotsadam, and Rooth 2021, 987). They further explain that "intensive contact with women needs to continue or the gains are likely to disappear" (1026).[50] We interpret these results as suggesting that any stable coalitions poised to embark on policy changes require enduring integrated teams.

In sum, sex-segregated institutions dramatically shape coalitional possibilities – the status quo of overwhelming segregation exemplifies the significant hurdles while the sex-integrated exceptions reveal the possibilities. The results also accentuate the relevance of student-athlete life. Student-athletes spend an inordinate amount of time with and among their teammates while they train, travel, compete, study, and often eat and live (Ottaway 2018). Thus, sex-segregated team structures (and the impacts they have on athletes' social time and networks) have major ramifications for who athletes spend their time among outside of training and competition; this, in turn, has downstream effects on gender equality.

[49] We did not pursue a follow-up survey to assess durability because we felt it important to maintain participant anonymity to encourage respondents' initial survey response.

[50] Dhar, Jain, and Jayachandran (2022) show that a classroom intervention (in India) that engaged students to discuss gender equality caused participants to become substantially more supportive of gender equality and the effects persisted for at least two years. The durability of effects likely reflects the intensive treatment aimed to intentionally change preferences and the notably young age of the intervention, with it occurring among those with an average age of fifteen. (We return to analysis of the durable impacts of youth experiences in Chapter 5, albeit in a different light.)

3.5 CONCLUSION

In our introductory chapter, we detailed the inequalities during the 2021 NCAA women's and men's basketball tournaments, including facilities, catering, gift bags, and more. One of the primary sources of initial documentation came from a viral tweet by University of Oregon player Sedona Prince that showed images of a single stack of weights in the women's training room versus expansive equipment for the men. She stated, "If you're not upset about this problem, then you're part of it." This example highlights the power of student-athletes in the contemporary era of social media technology and evolving norms where advocacy has become commonplace. Social media served as a mechanism for sharing information about marginalized status. However, the social media environment is fast moving, so what happens in the aftermath of viral tweets matters most. As detailed in Chapter 1, despite the NCAA's apology, the same types of inequalities appeared shortly thereafter during the NCAA's men's baseball and women's softball tournaments. The next year's basketball tournament was vastly improved but, as we explained in Chapter 1, there is reason to be cautious about interpreting this as evidence of systematic improvement. Thus, we see clear need for more sustained pressure toward change from below, motivated by a robust coalition to press for change. We have seen evidence of such coalitional success in recent years: Student-athletes played a crucial role in pressing for additional athlete benefits policies, such as the right to earn money by signing sponsorship contracts during their collegiate careers (thereby challenging the basis of amateurism in college sports). Likewise, other examples include the unsuccessful but widely scrutinized bid by Northwestern football players to unionize in 2013–15, as well as the (related) formation of various organizations led by current and former student-athletes to push for change (e.g., All Players United, the College Athletes Players Association, and the Coalition for College Athletes Advocacy).

Yet female student-athletes such as Prince face the challenge of being a numeric and subordinated minority in a system long defined by gendered inequalities and rationalized by logics that value revenue streams generated by men's basketball and football over civil rights protections (Nixon 2014). While social media protests can go "viral," durable change requires more than public attention. In our earlier example of the Minnesota men's track team, protests played a vital role in the team's reinstatement: protests initially organized by the women on the track team who train with the men. It highlights how cross-sex contact can engender coalitions that make a difference. In contrast, the path to reinstatement for the Connecticut women's rowing team was much longer and more tedious; perhaps if they had the power of a cross-sex coalition advocating for them, they would not have had to rely on the legal system. The reality though is that most women's teams find themselves in situations akin to the Connecticut rowing team with fewer allies and longer, more contentious routes to achieve their aims.

Overall, we have shown that female student-athletes strongly support more progressive equity policies. Male student-athletes also express moderate levels of support – but lasting change from below likely requires transforming those moderate levels to high levels. We identified a way forward via coalition-building that requires interpersonal contact and institutional trust. Contact has long been seen as a route to increased tolerance and understanding. Less work considers policy support that can be vital for sustainable changes. Ours is a novel theory with substantial evidence demonstrating how contact can alter policy beliefs in support of a marginalized group.

Regrettably, as we have explained, rather than integrating women into "men's" athletic programs, women have been incorporated into American college sports under an ethos of "separate, but equal." These circumstances diminish contact across gendered identity groups that, in turn, undercuts potential coalitions and ultimately policy reform. Two partial solutions could entail the promotion of shared coaching staffs and coed practices and training, as well as allowing athletically qualified women to participate on men's teams. These are possibilities to which we will return in the concluding chapter.

The larger lesson is that understanding change from below requires considering the institutional settings in which that change would come. This point is often assumed by scholars of power and group politics but less often theorized and investigated in terms of its policy implications in discussions of marginalized groups. In arenas where institutional practices were originally targeted for change intended to benefit subordinated groups, structures initially established to provide opportunities – that is, expanded offerings for female athletes on women's teams – can have unanticipated downstream consequences that *sustain* marginalization. Separate but purportedly equal systems remain problematic not only because they are unlikely to be fully "equal" but also because such separation undermines the likelihood of coalitions that work in the interest of the marginalized group. These problems suggest the need to entertain other mechanisms for change. In the next chapter, we explore the potential role of athletic leadership and the possibilities for change from the top down.

4

Organizational Culture and Policy Support

When the media turned their attention to inequalities between the 2021 men's and women's NCAA basketball tournaments, women's coaches had plenty to say. Reflecting on the evidence of disparate facilities and support for the women's teams, former Notre Dame coach Muffet McGraw tweeted that she was "tired of having to preface everything we do with the word 'women's' which would be fine if men had to do the same, but they don't, and when they don't it makes us look like the JV tournament to their event. The fact that there are inequities … is not what bothers me. What bothers me is that no one on the NCAA's leadership team even noticed" (Hill, Bieler, and Boren 2021). Stanford coach Tara VanDerveer later added, "a lot of what we've seen this week is evidence of blatant sexism. This is purposeful and hurtful. I feel betrayed by the NCAA" (Hill, Bieler, and Boren 2021). The leadership, both coaches implied, was responsible for falling short of full equality. The history of college athletics provides multiple examples of coaches speaking out on inequalities in women's sports (e.g., Borzi 2014), often with limited administrative response. Even in the aftermath of events in 2021, beyond admitting that the NCAA "dropped the ball," the most the organization's president Mark Emmert would commit to was an external review of NCAA tournament practices.

Who has the power to lead college sports toward full equality? Since the mid-1970s, policymakers in intercollegiate athletics departments have been concerned with the implementation of Title IX. Indeed, the most direct way to pursue gender equity initiatives is through a top-down process where those in policymaking positions act. However, despite actions from select lawmakers and those in the bureaucracy who work on Title IX implementation, movement to full gender equality remains stalled.

This chapter grapples with the question of why, scrutinizing the role of athletic leadership. In it, we consider a possible source of gender equity initiatives beyond mere government oversight, namely among those who directly oversee and govern college athletics: athletic administrators and, less directly, coaches. Because these actors have the proximate power to decide on opportunity and resource allocation as well as hiring, we focus on them as possible sources of "top-down" policy change.

We begin in the next section by discussing extant gender equity efforts by the NCAA and its member institutions. We consider how athletic administrators and coaches can and do act as policymakers. We then synthesize work on policy feedback, organizational culture, and women in college sports to argue that women leaders face institutional pressures that impact their preferences.[1] They work in a culture where "gender equity" is defined by Title IX compliance, where progress (at its best) is demarcated by modest incremental changes that improve upon an historically exclusionary status quo, and where avoiding federal investigations or Title IX lawsuits is prioritized over pursuing full equality (see Staurowsky and Rhoads 2020). Women leaders face additional hurdles as a numeric minority in a male-dominated environment. We argue that this culture depresses women's support for novel, more progressive equity initiatives. Consequently, change from the top down – via collegiate sports leaders – becomes unlikely.

We test this prediction with representative samples of college athletic administrators and coaches who we compare with the student-athletes. The results reveal that those better positioned to push for change – that is, women leaders compared to student-athletes and, even more so, women who head athletic departments or teams compared to those who do not – are *less* likely to do so. Organizational culture acts to institutionally induce preferences counter to gender equity initiatives.

4.1 MAKING GENDER EQUITY POLICIES

Policymaking on gender equity takes two major forms: federal-level policies and NCAA policies. Thus, the relevant policymakers include both lawmakers and college athletic leadership. Historically, federal

---

[1] We again rely on self-reported gender categories in our analyses and the language used throughout the chapter. Although leadership identities are not as hyperscripted by sex-segregated teams as are athletes' identities, notions of identity narrowly tied to sex assigned at birth permeate the world of college sport. They thus often erase and/or exclude gender-diverse people.

lawmakers have played a direct role in crafting and implementing Title IX (Wu and Mink 2022). Although the NCAA is a non-governmental association that therefore does not enforce Title IX, "it does support its member schools in their efforts to work toward equity, diversity and inclusion goals in their athletics departments" through policies, programming, and educational resources (NCAA 2017a, 5).

In principle, the NCAA affirms that gender equity is an essential element of intercollegiate athletics. It maintains an office of inclusion that "is committed to supporting the membership as it strives to comply with federal and state laws regarding gender equity, to adopting legislation that augments gender equity and to establishing an environment that is free of gender bias" (NCAA 2021a).[2] On its website, it offers its own definition of gender equity, based on a 1992 task force (NCAA 1993), stating, "An athletics program can be considered gender equitable when the participants in both the men's and women's sports programs would accept as fair and equitable the overall program of the other gender. No individual should be discriminated against on the basis of gender, institutionally or nationally, in intercollegiate athletics."

In contrast to elements of federal policy (detailed in Chapter 1), NCAA stances on equity remain ambiguous. They evade specific metrics regarding gender bias or assessing whether member institution student-athletes view available athletic programs as "fair and equitable."[3] More importantly, the NCAA Constitution mentions that while it is the "responsibility of each member institution to comply with federal and state laws regarding gender equity" (2.3.1.), the "Association should not adopt legislation that would prevent member institutions from complying with applicable gender-equity laws, and should adopt legislation to enhance member institutions' compliance with applicable gender-equity laws" (2.3.2, see NCAA 2017a, 5). The NCAA expects member schools to maintain active gender equity plans that guide the evaluation of and initiatives for gender equity performance (NCAA 2021c).[4] Despite

---

[2] The NCAA Office for Inclusion focuses on multiple dimensions of inclusion including those related to race, disability, international student-athlete participation, and LGBTQ concerns.

[3] They also fail to recognize how a history of exclusion and inequality can condition perceptions of students.

[4] The NCAA requires Division I schools to maintain five-year gender equity plans that demonstrate commitment to fair and equitable treatment of student-athletes and department personnel. They require Division II and III schools to conduct self-studies at least once every five years (see NCAA 2021a). Also, relevant, when it comes to female coaches and administrators, is Title VII of the Civil Rights Act of 1964, which prohibits employment discrimination based on sex, race, color, religion, and national origin.

ambiguity in their stated commitments to what other "legislation that augments gender equity" entails, the NCAA promulgates guidance on a number of equity initiatives. These include the creation of a "Senior Woman Administrator" designation within each member institution athletic department (intended to vest authority in the senior-most female athletic director within a school), the maintenance of both standing and ad hoc committees and task forces on diversity and equity (e.g., the NCAA Committee on Women's Athletics), and the publication of reports and primers on diversity and inclusion. They also conduct internal research on women in college sports and provide grant opportunities and support for women's athletic leadership development (e.g., the NCAA Women's Coaches Academy) (NCAA 2017a).[5]

However, there is a notable absence of concrete policies designed to close the gaps documented in Chapter 1 – including those in participation opportunities, resources, and leadership. Such policymaking may appear to be beyond the purview of the NCAA since it does not directly enforce Title IX. But the NCAA has significant latitude to create policies aimed at supporting its implementation at member institutions. In other realms, they maintain policy manuals that are hundreds of pages long that dictate rules and regulations for athlete eligibility, high school recruitment, cross-institutional athlete transfers, financial aid, practice and training limits, and consequences for rule infractions. They also hold the capacity to ban schools from NCAA championships, a tool frequently used for other violations of NCAA recruiting or academic eligibility policies. Yet despite their stated commitment to "increase opportunities for female student-athletes, coaches, administration and officiating personnel," we are aware of no serious efforts by the NCAA to pursue the more aggressive equity policies on which we have focused.[6]

---

[5] The Committee on Women's Athletics "study and make policy recommendations concerning opportunities for women in athletics at the institutional, conference, and national levels" (NCAA Bylaw 21.2.10.2). The Women's Coaches Academy (WCA) is "a 4-day educational training available to NCAA coaches of all experience levels. The WCA is designed for women coaches who are ready and willing to increase their individual effectiveness by learning advanced skills and strategies that directly affect their personal and team success" (WeCOACH Inc. 2021).

[6] Nixon (2014: 36) explains that the NCAA's focus has been on "fostering growth and commercialization." Of relevance (as noted) is the 1999 US Supreme Court decision in *National Collegiate Athletic Association v. Smith* (525 U.S. 459) that ruled the NCAA cannot be sued under Title IX, only the schools (who may be NCAA member institutions) can be sued.

4.2 WHO GOVERNS?

We seek to explain why leaders have not advocated for more gender equity initiatives. Our first task entails identifying our population. On campuses, this constitutes readily identifiable individuals who work in athletic administration and coaching. What is their relationship to NCAA policy? Policymaking and governance in the NCAA occur through an elaborate committee structure populated by approximately 1,300 elected individuals from member institutions.[7] The NCAA (2021d) refers to these committees as "legislative bodies" tasked with "upholding and advancing the Association's core values of fairness, safety and equal opportunity for all student-athletes." Four types of actors serve on committees: academic personnel (e.g., college presidents, faculty known as "faculty athletic representatives"), student-athletes, athletic administrators, and coaches. We identified the members of each group among the 2018–19 committees by accessing the NCAA website and downloading the membership list of all committees (which included names and affiliations). We then located all individuals on the relevant school's websites and recorded their jobs and demographic information (N = 1,227).[8]

In Figure 4.1, we display the composition of committee membership based on job type. Athletic administrators populate a majority of the positions at nearly 55 percent. The bulk of these individuals work in the athletic director's office at their institution; however, some also come from appointments in athletic training, academic services, medicine, and so on.[9] Coaches, nearly all of whom are head coaches, hold about 23.02 percent of the committee positions. Moreover, 13.70 percent of academic representatives are mostly college and university presidents (and some faculty athletic representatives). This percentage is highly concentrated on three committees composed largely of presidents.[10] Similarly, student-athletes serve on very few

[7] These committees are distinct types: association-wide, common (academic-oriented), division-specific, and sport-specific.

[8] We checked the reliability of the coding by having a second coder recode 25 percent and had nearly 100 percent agreement on position and gender and above 95 percent for race (adjusted for chance agreement). Also, there are fifteen committee members who were classified as "other" – largely because of an inability to identify their exact positions. They are not included in Figure 4.1.

[9] We coded for forty-two different administrative jobs; however, in our survey data described later in this chapter, we designate jobs as falling into one of five categories: athletic administration, athletic medicine, academic services, athletic performance/strength and conditioning, and other.

[10] These include the NCAA board of directors, board of governors, and each division's presidential council.

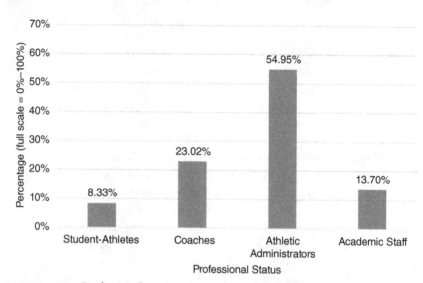

FIGURE 4.1 Professional status among NCAA committee members, 2018–19
Source: Authors' calculations of data from the National Collegiate Athletic Association, 2019.

committees – mostly, on each division's student-athlete advisory committee. Overall, more than three-quarters of those involved with policymaking within the NCAA are athletic administrators and coaches – and we focus on these actors for our empirical inquiry. These individuals also play vital roles at their individual institutions in making hiring and resource allocation decisions (including how resources are distributed across men's and women's teams) and in creating the policy culture in which student-athletes live.

4.3 WHO ARE THE POLICYMAKERS?

Before exploring the equity policy preferences of athletic administrators and coaches – that is, the policymakers – we briefly profile their demographics. In Figure 4.2, we present the demographic breakdown of NCAA committee membership (i.e., the actors from Figure 4.1). It reveals a stark gender imbalance as nearly 60 percent of the members are men. This gender imbalance on committee representation reflects the vast underrepresentation of women in athletics, particularly as coaches and administrators. The industry as a whole and the NCAA committees are overwhelmingly White male-dominated.

Our own survey data mirror this committee distribution. As explained in Chapter 2, we conducted representative surveys of collegiate athletic

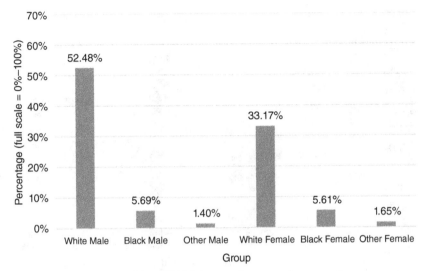

FIGURE 4.2 Demographics of NCAA committee members, 2018–19
Source: Authors' calculations of data from National Collegiate Athletic Association, 2019.

administrators and coaches in 2018 (more details appear in the next section). In Figure 4.3, we present the percentages of women and men among head coaches, other coaches (e.g., associate and assistant), athletic administrators who head departments (e.g., director of athletics), and other administrators within our respondent pool.[11] An overwhelming 79.08 percent of head coaches are men.[12] Among coaches of lower ranks, we see smaller, but still substantial, gender differences. As mentioned in Chapter 1, during the post-Title IX period of growth for women's collegiate athletic teams, women experienced a perversely declining trajectory in employment as collegiate coaches (LaVoi and Baeth 2018). Our data illustrate the consequence of these trends: the vast underrepresentation of women within all coaching positions but particularly among head coaches.

[11] The coach percentages strongly resemble those found in the population since we weighted on gender and coach position in our analyses. For administrators, we weight the sample on gender (and hence we match the population) but not head of department (since our survey designations of administrator level do not map directly on what is available in the population data). However, our estimates look like those found in other work that generally focuses on athletic directors (e.g., Lapchick 2020).

[12] This differs from the number reported in Chapter 1 since there we focused on any type of coach; moreover, the data there came from the NCAA database whereas the data in this chapter comes from our survey (which will generate some discrepancies).

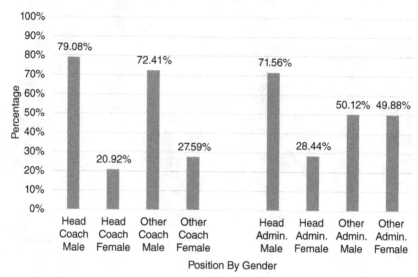

FIGURE 4.3 Coaching and athletic administrator positions by gender, 2018–19 *Source: Authors' study of NCAA Coaches and Athletic Administrators, Summer, 2018.*

We also note a substantial gender disparity among administrators who head athletic departments, with 71.56 percent being men. In contrast, we see near equality in the distribution of women and men among other administrative positions (e.g., lower-rank athletic administrators tasked with midlevel leadership and management of college sports). All of these data tell the same story – women constitute a clear minority within athletic leadership, particularly among the senior levels.

4.4 DESCRIPTIVE REPRESENTATION AND ORGANIZATIONALLY-INDUCED PREFERENCES

The potential for change from the top down stems from administrators and coaches being vested with the power to pursue gender equity policies. Much as the implementation of workplace nondiscrimination laws depend on leadership from corporate personnel (Dobbin 2009; Edelman 2016), equity initiatives in college sports require athletic leadership. Although either women *or* men could initiate and support such policy efforts, we expect greater support from women leaders. This expectation comes from work on descriptive representation: Those who are descriptively representative of the beneficiary population typically pursue or enact more substantive changes on behalf of the group, particularly when they have shared experiences (e.g., in this case, a majority of athletic coaches and a near majority of athletic administrators were previously student-athletes) (Mansbridge 1999).[13] As Lowande, Ritchie, and Lauterbach (2019, 644) state, women "are more likely to work on behalf of constituents with whom they share identities."[14] For our purposes, female administrators and coaches ascriptively represent female student-athletes, and thus, we expect them to exhibit more support for equity policies (relative to male administrators and coaches). Moreover, they would directly benefit from the proposed policies to increase women coaches and administrators included in our policy measure, so there also exist substantive reasons for their support.

Female coaches/athletic administrators will exhibit more support for equity policies than their male counterparts, all else constant. (Hypothesis 4–1)

Descriptive-substantive representation – that is, women serving as representatives of both women as a group and "women's interests" (e.g., Cowell-Meyers and Langbein 2009; Jones 2014) – plays a particularly crucial role since the NCAA is not a democratic organization. Women policymakers (i.e., athletic administrators/coaches) are not held accountable to those most directly affected by the policies (i.e., student-athletes) (Nixon 2014). Even so, women in positions of power could work to enact change on behalf of women's interests using their institutionalized power (notwithstanding their minority status) and/or in coalition with empowered men. Such representative processes can successfully elevate minority interests in policymaking contexts (Dittmar, Sanbonmatsu, and Carroll 2018; Reingold 2000). Moreover, across many colleges and universities, aggressive implementation of Title IX has often resulted from activism by women leaders (e.g., Belanger 2016; Boschert 2022; LeBlanc and Swanson 2016). The reactions of coaches McGraw and VanDerveer to the 2021 NCAA basketball tournaments, quoted at the start of this chapter, exemplify this type of advocacy, as well as the frustration that often occurs from chronic institutional inaction and persistent inequalities.

We track the inaction, at least in part, to the reality that administrators and coaches work within institutions – the NCAA and their schools – that shape their behavior. The context is conditioned by the historical

---

[13] The data we use in this chapter show 85 percent of coaches and 41 percent of athletic administrators participated in varsity college sports.

[14] Our usage of the descriptive and substantive representation concepts should be thought of heuristically. We recognize that we are evading more profound conceptualizations of representation that are beyond our purview.

development of gender equity policy, as defined by Title IX. Here, we invoke Mettler's idea of a policyscape: "a landscape densely laden with policies created in the past that have themselves become established institutions" (2016, 369). She argues that a substantial challenge for extant policies comes from policymakers failing to maintain them, as is the case with several higher education policies (e.g., student aid). This concept applies to Title IX given that a substantial number of colleges remain noncompliant with Title IX, yet none have ever faced full enforcement by having their federal funding revoked (which is the ultimate noncompliance penalty) (Staurowsky et al. 2020; Yanus and O'Connor 2016).[15]

For these reasons, much of the discussion around gender equity focuses on compliance enacted by athletic leadership. This reflects a policy feedback process where "policy once enacted, restructures subsequent political processes" (Skocpol 1992, 58; see also Mettler and Soss 2004; Pierson 1993, 2004). The policy feedback literature demonstrates how past policies influence the capacities, interests, and preferences of relevant actors, including policymakers and citizens (Campbell 2012). What receives less attention is how feedback also conditions organizational culture, that is, the patterns of behaviors and beliefs imparted to members of the organization (Schein 2004). We argue that the legacy of Title IX and compliance debates establish such a cultural context. Women in collegiate sports leadership enter a culture that normalizes numeric gender inequality and views progress through the lens of mere Title IX compliance as opposed to more sweeping notions of equality.[16] Consequently, they are more apt to foreground the fifty-year-old point of comparison defined by women's exclusion from athletics rather than a contemporary counterfactual of equality, and to benchmark the status quo against historic constraints rather than more expansive ideas about potential future progress.[17]

---

[15] The federal Office for Civil Rights in the US Department of Education investigates Title IX complaints at individual institutions, but its findings are based on interpreting policy guidance now decades old (i.e., the "three-part test").

[16] And, as intimated, whether compliance has even been fully endorsed remains unclear at best. Staurowsky and Rhoads (2020, 387) note, "In a regulatory environment where those being asked to comply see little downside in not complying, the approach is more about managing perceptions than actual compliance."

[17] This is exemplified within extant Title IX debates concerning compliance via meeting the "interests" of women students. Indeed, interests themselves depend on past opportunities (such as participating in youth and high school athletic opportunities and envisioning competitive opportunities in college during youth athletic development). Pape (2020) finds similar dynamics in her study of the International Olympic Committee, where archaic conceptions of gender equity limit organizational changes and hierarchical gendered logic continue to shape informal norms and procedures.

More acutely, work on the organizational culture of college sports reveals numerous challenges faced by women in athletic leadership. Both blatant and subtle sexism are endemic. Researchers track women's experiences of differential treatment and tokenization, revealing how women are sometimes even misidentified and belittled (e.g., being mistaken for parents) at work (e.g., Siegele et al. 2020; see also Hindman and Walker 2020). As a numeric minority, women in leadership have fewer role models and mentors (Taylor and Hardin 2016) and often labor at the periphery of male-dominated networks (Katz, Walker, and Hindman 2018).[18] More than two-thirds (65 percent) of coaches believe it is easier for men to obtain top-level coaching jobs and more than half (54 percent) believe men are more likely to be promoted (Sabo, Veliz, and Staurowsky 2016). Many women resist even discussing these challenges – a third of women coaches express reluctance in asking for help with gender bias for fear of retaliation (Sabo, Veliz, and Staurowsky 2016). More generally, Staurowsky et al. (2020) report that college athletic leaders view "the perception that women are less competent than men at doing their jobs" as the most salient workplace climate issue. Men in college sports often fail to recognize gender bias despite clear evidence (presented in Chapter 1) that it defines the collegiate sports environment (Darvin, Hancock, and Williams 2021; Sabo, Veliz, and Staurowsky 2016). Darvin, Hancock, and Williams (2021, 3) characterize the general nature of the culture:

The "win at all costs" culture within intercollegiate athletics lends itself to unethical and destructive organizational practices that largely do not align with women employees resulting in their voluntary departure from the field prior to reaching a leadership role (Darvin 2020). Overall, these barriers and socialized cultural norms have not been improved by the symbolic structures/policies that intercollegiate sport organizations have developed in order to increase diversity. The critical aspect of such shortcomings rests within the assertion that organizations have a social, moral, and ethical responsibility to be inclusive (Cunningham 2015; Humberstone 2009) ... The presence of a sport leadership labyrinth suggests that women, in comparison to men, will experience additional obstacles throughout their leadership quests (Burton and Leberman 2017; Darvin 2020; Eagly and Carli 2007).

Thus, women who pursue careers to become athletic administrators and coaches grapple with a workplace unwelcoming to women, and they

---

[18] Such role models are found to be crucial for women's leadership in business and politics (Campbell and Wolbrecht 2006; Wolbrecht and Campbell 2017). The absence of both mentorship and critical mass further suppresses women's influence and participation in the workplace (Karpowitz and Mendelberg 2014).

confront perennial challenges including struggling to advance in a male-dominated structure (Walker and Bopp 2011) or to overcome sex-based stereotypes and stigma (Cunningham, Wicker, and Walker 2021; Wells et al. 2021), and operating in a cultural context designed to naturalize and reproduce male authority (Schull, Shaw, and Kihl 2012). This underscores a climate and cultural milieu that suggests incremental change is sufficient on gender issues, thereby undermining the possibility of targeting full equality for women. Consequently, the research suggests that contemporary organizational practices are at odds with visionary leadership aimed at disrupting the status quo. Women leaders who may be highly motivated to enact gender equity initiatives, as representatives and in the interests of women student-athletes, operate in a workplace setting that at best fails to prioritize such efforts and at worst actively discourages them.

Such an organizational culture, in turn, influences the values, beliefs, and identities of those who work in it (e.g., Flamholtz and Randle 2014). As Miscenko and Day (2016, 216) explain, "[p]eople spend a considerable portion of their lives at work or otherwise engaged in work-related activities. Correspondingly, organizations are often crucial in shaping a person's identity ... occupational environments can also motivate change in personal traits and identity" (also see Wille and De Fruyt 2014). When a work identity conflicts with a social identity (e.g., gender or race), individuals engage in coping strategies that often involve altering their personal perspectives to better assimilate. Evidence of such adaptation for women in college sports comes from Staurowsky and Weight (2013), who find that women administrators fear backlash for speaking about Title IX noncompliance (see also Sabo, Veliz, and Staurowsky 2016). Among female coaches, Walker and Bopp (2011) point to a double standard where women face fierce competition for women's team coaching jobs and are almost entirely excluded from men's sport coaching jobs; the authors suggest this stems from organizationally entrenched structural beliefs biased against women (see also Kane 2016). Likewise, most coaches work on limited employment contracts with renewal at the discretion of athletic administrators. Attempts to contest the existing organizational culture can be subtly or dramatically discouraged (see Zamora 2018).

Organizational culture thus forces women who do become leaders to confront an identity conflict. While their gender identity and representational imperatives may align them with the cause to pursue equity policy innovation, their professional identities push them toward authorizing and assimilating into the status quo where even advocating for enforcement of Title IX within their work environment can be difficult. Extant work suggests that organizational culture exerts particular pressure on those with subordinated social status groups, including women, who feel pressured to align with the majoritarian perspectives of the institutions (e.g., Chattopadhyay, Tluchowska, and George 2004; Derks, Van Laar, and Ellemers 2006). In college sports, this assimilation may be a necessary strategy for advancement due to the history of attributing the lack of women in leadership rules to individual qualities (e.g., qualifications or family obligations) rather than organizational or structural factors (Kane and LaVoi 2018; see also Stangl and Kane 1991). Scholars of gender and the workplace identify an adaptive strategy known as the "queen bee" phenomenon wherein women in leadership within organizations traditionally dominated by men distance themselves from more disadvantaged women in the organization and legitimize gender inequality (Derks, Van Laar, and Ellemers 2016, 459).[19] This leads us to the expectation that women coaches and administrators will moderate their support for equity policies.[20] They do so in an effort to cope with the cultural conflict and overwhelming pressures to naturalize the status quo as sufficient.[21]

To assess this expectation, and due to our interest in representation, we compare female athletic leaders to female student-athletes. Female student-athletes are the other core female stakeholder group in college athletics and are the group whose interests could be descriptively represented by the actions of women leaders. While female student-athletes also find themselves in a particular cultural milieu, it is one not as strictly defined by persistent biases and the need for assimilation to an androcentric culture.

---

[19] The queen bee effect is conditional on individuals, contexts, and dynamics (e.g., Arvate, Galilea, and Todescat 2018). Here, we suspect it may have some explanatory power given that sports are a traditional male domain that relegates women as a numeric minority in an historically counter-stereotypic situation.

[20] Some works suggest that adaptation might lead to opinion reversal (e.g., women administrators become even less supportive of equity policies) due to pressures to prove loyalty to the organization (e.g., Brown and Frank 2006). We argue that the organizational pressures in college sports (on these issues) are not sufficiently strong for this to occur. Afterall, many women leaders remain the primary stakeholders tasked with overseeing Title IX implementation and equity reporting to the US Department of Education (i.e., as designated senior woman administrators). As such, expectations produced by organizational culture versus those of federal civil rights law create cross-pressures on women leaders to walk the line without rocking the proverbial boat.

[21] Another relevant framework is role congruity theory (see Darvin, Hancock, and Williams 2021 for an application to college sports). This suggests that the "potential for prejudice exists when social perceivers hold a stereotype about a social group that is incongruent

Likewise, their employment status does not potentially rely on acquies-
cence with organizational norms.

Specifically, we do not expect a conservatizing organizational culture
effect on female student-athletes for two reasons. First, the teams of student-
athletes do not constitute a workplace per se and women on teams (versus
women at work) are less likely to feel compelled to support an organizational status quo. Second, female student-athletes, due to sex segregation,
do not experience an overtly gender-subordinated status within the immediate surroundings of their teams (as the other deleterious effects of segregation, discussed in Chapter 3, are easily obscured by segregation itself). In
short, our theory of potential change from the top down suggests that we
use opinions of female student-athletes as a critical comparison point. We
theorize that female coaches and athletic administrators could act as representatives of women's interests in policymaking circles. However, they
inhabit a distinct institutional space where disruptive representation is possible but substantially cross-pressured, and thus, they shift their opinions in
the direction of the cross-pressure.[22] Our precise prediction is as follows:

The effect of being a woman will have a smaller impact on support for equity
policies among coaches and athletic administrators relative to its effect among
student-athletes, all else constant. (Hypothesis 4–2)

with the attributes that are thought to be required for success in certain classes of social
roles. When a stereotyped group member and an incongruent social role become joined in
the mind of the perceiver, this inconsistency lowers the evaluation of the group member
as an actual or potential occupant of the role" (Eagly and Karau 2002, 574). This could
apply when women hold positions that they are not expected to hold – this includes,
for women, leadership positions in many jobs in college sports where male-domination
persists. Role congruity can alter the behavior of such individuals and, in many cases,
might cause them to behave in gender-stereotypic ways, such as women acting in a more
communal style (see LaVoi and Dutove 2012). This perspective could suggest the opposite dynamic of what we predict – for example, that women administrators and coaches
would become even stronger supporters of gender equity policy to avoid incongruence
with gendered expectations. We do not expect this, however, because the theory seems
more applicable to behaviors (within structured hierarchies) than beliefs. Neither do we
suspect that holding stronger equity beliefs would be a straightforward "reflexive" display of gender identity per se, nor one that would ease external social expectations where
androcentric practices are normalized. In short, we theorize that the pressures to conform
and adapt to the "most advantageous identity in a given situation" would dictate a moderation of equity policy beliefs among women in athletic leadership (Miscenko and Day
2016, 235). To be clear, though, while our prediction suggests a moderation of the policy
views of women, we do not mean to suggest there will be any tempering of their gender
identities directly – just that their perspectives on these issues will be less attached to those
identities due to workplace expectations.

[22] As we will discuss, we recognize age and experience are potential confounds in these
comparisons.

This prediction echoes Galvin's (2012, 54) point regarding the relationship between culture and leader assimilation, that "[t]hough individuals enter with their own beliefs, values, interests, and goals, their behavior becomes more or less structured once they are assigned a formal role." Those who advance through the ranks and obtain increasingly defined formal roles adapt most strongly to the organizational culture. Indeed, they become leaders of the organizations. Along these lines, Kane and LaVoi (2018) report that female athletic directors (i.e., at the top of the athletic administration), more intensely than their male counterparts, attribute the decline of women in leadership positions to women's failure to apply for jobs (rather than, for example, structural forces like the so-called "sticky floor" that makes upward career mobility difficult for women; Siegele et al. 2020). However inaccurate this belief is, we note that it reveals a system-justifying (rather than critical) perspective among those who the system rewards with promotion up the hierarchy. This leads us to the following hypothesis:

Female head coaches/women athletic administrators who head departments will be less supportive of gender equity politics than their coach/administrator counterparts in lower-level positions, all else constant. (Hypothesis 4–3)[23]

Testing these hypotheses about how organizational culture shapes women's preferences is tricky. Researchers would ideally compare identically situated women who enter the organizational structure of college sports to those who do not. In parallel contexts, Enemark et al. (2016), for instance, study the impact of holding public office by comparing those who narrowly won election to those who narrowly lost. They had the individuals participate in the same set of economic games, where they find officeholders display more reciprocity than non-officeholders. Since narrowly winning or losing elected office is near-random, the authors safely conjecture that the groups are, on average, equivalent, and thus the difference in reciprocity stems from the causal effect of institutions on political behavior.[24] Unfortunately, we do not have access to a similar discontinuity or randomization mechanism, such as comparing those finalists who were hired for high-level administrator positions to those who were not, amid a highly competitive process.

---

[23] This hypothesis also coheres with parts of Michels' (1911) iron law of oligarchy that posits the emergence of a ruling class in organizations where the leaders become "detached from the mass ... [and develop] their own way of thinking" (66–67).

[24] Similarly, Lawless and Fox (2005) evaluate the emergence of women as political candidates using a design that examined the broader pool of likely female candidates, not merely those who started political campaigns.

As explained, we instead compare coaches and athletic administrators to student-athletes. Admittedly, this comparison comes with a host of confounds, most notably age and professional experience. Consequently, we cannot directly claim that organizational culture causes female coaches and administrators to become less supportive of equity policies (relative to student-athletes). If we find that they do express less support than female student-athletes, an equally compelling possibility is that the collegiate athletic departments *select* women with weaker preferences for gender equality. The same is true when it comes to our head coach/ department head hypothesis – our research design does not allow us to disentangle what could be a socialization or a selection process.[25] While our theory suggests socialization, ultimately, the mechanism is less crucial to us than the empirical pattern. Lower levels of support, regardless of the underlying process, would suggest an institutional/cultural hurdle for gender equity policy: that those in policymaking positions (i.e., female coaches and athletic administrators) have relatively lower levels of support for such initiatives.

4.5 DATA

We test our hypotheses with a survey of coaches and athletic administrators conducted at the same time as our 2018 student-athlete survey (see Chapter 2 for an overview).[26] We identified coaches for our sampled schools by accessing each athletic team webpage and identifying all coaches (e.g., head coach, associate, assistant, or graduate assistant). For athletic administrators, we included individuals who have the potential to influence policy via the NCAA rulemaking committees or within individual school decisions and who have regular contact with student-athletes. We included this latter designation since they comprise potential "representatives" of student-athletes in the policymaking process (e.g., they interact with student-athletes, as do coaches). Examples of athletic administrators include those employed in the athletic director's office, medical personnel (e.g., athletic trainers), athletic performance staff, and academic services staff (see discussion in Chapter 2's appendix). We identified these individuals through staff directories catalogued on

---

[25] Another possibility for which we cannot test is a "rite of passage" effect where people are expected to have particular experiences at a given life stage (Janusz and Walkiewicz 2018). In this case, it could mean that women leaders expect others to share their own experiences, including those challenges that they encountered or avoided.

[26] We preregistered our data collection at: https://aspredicted.org/hy5ks.pdf.

each school's athletic department website. On the athletic administrator survey, we asked how many hours in a typical week they spend working directly with student-athletes; we find athletic administrators report interacting with student-athletes, on average, 31.24 (std. dev. = 21.28) hours a week.[27] Thus they do engage with and could act as representatives of student-athletes.

As noted in Chapter 2, we obtained a sample of 862 athletic administrators and a sample of 531 coaches by soliciting their participation in our online survey. We collected respondent sex (again, self-reported) and whether they are a head coach/head of department as key explanatory variables to test our hypotheses. We also measured a host of descriptive variables that serve as controls in our analyses; many of these are the same as those employed for the survey of student-athletes in Chapter 3.

We present the weighted portrait of our samples in Tables 4.1 and 4.2 (all question wordings appear in the appendix).[28] Table 4.1 reiterates the striking gender disparity documented in Chapter 1 – only 26 percent of coaches overall are women.[29] We also assess women's representation in coaching of women's teams where women also remain a minority, occupying just 41 percent of positions (not shown in the table). Among men's teams, only 9 percent of coaches are women. Otherwise, we find coaches are well-educated, with more than half holding advanced degrees, and are very experienced, with an average of nearly seventeen years in the field. As mentioned, most also played a varsity sport in college (85 percent).

As shown in Table 4.2, among athletic administrators, 42 percent are women, a substantially higher number relative to coaches. We again see a highly educated population, as nearly 85 percent hold an advanced degree, and a professionally experienced group, with an average of nearly fourteen years in the field. Compared to coaches, fewer administrators played a varsity sport in college – 41 percent. Further, 38 percent head their unit, which is greater than the percent of head coaches (29 percent). This is the case because athletic administration can be quite decentralized, broken down into constituent units (e.g., finance, training and athletic medicine), each of which has a designated head. We also find gender disparities across the administrative areas. In Figure 4.4, we present the percentage of women by the main employment domains (see Table 4.2); it shows vast disproportionalities with women overrepresented among

---

[27] Only 3 percent reported 0.

[28] For details on weighting, see Chapter 2's appendix.

[29] This number comes from our survey data but aligns with the percentage reported in Chapter 1 from NCAA data (partially due to our use of sample survey weights here).

TABLE 4.1 *Weighted coach sample description*

Variable	Mean/percentage
Sex (self-identified by respondent)	Male: 74%; female: 26%
Race (that best describes the respondent, as self-identified)	White: 79%; Black: 13%; Hispanic/Latino: 2%; Asian/Pacific Islander: 3%; other: 2%[1]
Religion	Protestant: 49%; Catholic: 21%; Jewish: 2%; other religion: 4%[2]; not religious: 24%
Highest level of education	Less than high school: 0%; high school: <1%; some college: 1%; 4-year college degree: 42%; master's: 53%; PhD: 5%[3]
Income	< $30,000: 5%; $30,000–$69,999: 29%; $70,000–$99,999: 21%; $100,000–$200,000: 37%: >$200,000: 9%[3]
Age	Under 18: 0%; 18–24: 8%; 25–34: 35%; 35–50: 30%; 51–65: 21%; over 65: 6%
Years employed in the field	16.75 (std. dev.: 12.47)
Head coach	29%
Employed as both a coach and administrator	12%
Played varsity sport in college	85%
Gender of teams coached	Men's: 52%; women's: 57%; coed: 13%[4]
NCAA division	Division I: 38%; Division II: 23%; Division III: 39%
Political ideology, mean (1–7 scale, with higher scores indicating more conservative)	3.73 (std. dev.: 1.41)
Racial conservativism, mean (1–7 scale, with higher scores indicating more racial conservatism)	2.75 (std. dev.: 1.10)
Hostile sexism, mean (1–7 scale, with higher scores indicating more sexism)	2.81 (std. dev.: 1.43)
Average percentage time of male coach contact with female student-athletes	40% (std. dev.: 32%)

[1] Less than 1 percent classified themselves as Middle Eastern/North African; 0 percent classified themselves as Native American; 2 percent classified themselves as "other." The total does not sum to 100 percent due to rounding error.
[2] Less than 1 percent classified themselves as Muslim; 0 percent classified themselves as Hindu; 4 percent classified themselves as "other."
[3] The total exceeds 100 percent due to rounding error.
[4] This does not sum to 100 percent because individuals coached multiple types of teams.

TABLE 4.2 *Weighted athletic administrator sample description*

Variable	Mean/percentage
Sex (self-identified by respondent)	Male: 58%; female: 42%
Race (that best describes the respondent, as self-identified)	White: 79%; Black: 11%; Hispanic/Latino: 6%; Asian/Pacific Islander: 3%; other: 1%[1]
Religion	Protestant: 53%; Catholic: 24%; Jewish: 1%; other religion: 3%[2]; not religious: 19%
Highest level of education	Less than high school: 0%; high school: <1%; some college: 1%; 4-year college degree: 16%; master's: 74%; PhD: 7%; MD: 3%; PhD and MD: <1%[3]
Income	< $30,000: 2%; $30,000–$69,999: 28%; $70,000–$99,999: 24%; $100,000–$200,000: 34%: >$200,000: 12%
Age	Under 18: 0%; 18–24: 8%; 25–34: 36%; 35–50: 35%; 51–65: 19%; over 65: 3%[4]
Years employed in the field	13.93 (std. dev.: 10.58)
Director/head of department	38%
Played varsity sport in college	41%
Gender of teams with which respondent works	Men's: 69%; women's: 66%; coed: 18%; none directly: 14%[5]
NCAA division	Division I: 67%; Division II: 16%; Division III: 17%
Political ideology, mean (1–7 scale, with higher scores indicating more conservative)	3.81 (std. dev.: 1.39)
Racial conservativism, mean (1–7 scale, with higher scores indicating more racial conservatism)	2.76 (std. dev.: 1.14)
Hostile sexism, mean (1–7 scale, with higher scores indicating more sexism)	2.66 (std. dev.: 1.35)
Average percentage time of male administrator contact with female student-athletes	38% (std. dev.: 22%)
Area of athletics	Athletic administration: 37%; athletic medicine: 37%; academic services: 16%; athletic performance/strength and conditioning: 9%; other: 19%[6]

[1] Less than 1 percent classified themselves as Middle Eastern/North African; less than 1 percent classified themselves as Native American; less than 1 percent classified themselves as "other."

[2] Less than 1 percent classified themselves as Muslim; 0 percent classified themselves as Hindu; 3 percent classified themselves as "other."

[3] The total exceeds 100 percent due to rounding error.

[4] The total exceeds 100 percent due to rounding error.

[5] This does not sum to 100 percent because individuals worked with multiple types of teams.

[6] This does not sum to 100 percent because individuals worked in multiple areas. The "other" area includes compliance, finance, Title IX coordinator, and "other" (those who did not choose an option offered).

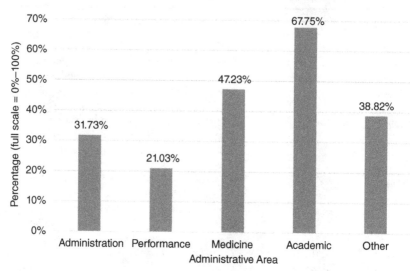

FIGURE 4.4 Percentage of women in athletic administrative positions (in weighted sample)

those in academic services and underrepresented in athletic performance (e.g., strength and conditioning staff) and, more importantly, among "athletic administration" (e.g., director of athletics, associate athletic director) (also see Staurowsky et al. 2020).

This latter point – that only 32 percent of those in general "athletic administration" (i.e., athletic directors at all ranks) are women – reveals a subtle but highly impactful gendered inequality. Actors in these roles have the final say on policymaking, particularly within individual schools as this group includes the designated overall athletic director and proximate subordinates (e.g., associate or assistant athletic directors). Further, while we previously demonstrated that women compose about 40 percent of NCAA committee members, roughly resembling their presence among athletic administrators, women are underrepresented on the most powerful committees that draw from those in athletic administration.

4.6 RESULTS

We next turn to testing our hypotheses where we again focus on our two main outcomes of support for gender equity policies and the budget allocation exercise. Figure 4.5 displays the distributions for gender equity policy (scaled) attitudes with scores on the x-axis (where 7 = strong support) and the proportion of the sample exhibiting a given score on the

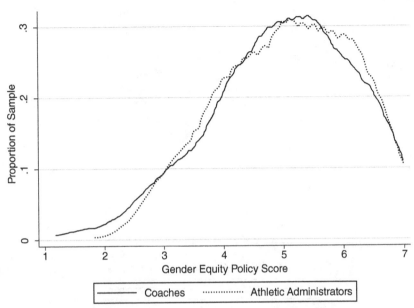

FIGURE 4.5 Sample distribution for gender equity policy (scaled), coaches and athletic administrators

y-axis.[30] It shows relatively high scores, with the mode plateauing over 5 on a 7-point scale for both samples. The means are 5.07 (std. dev.: 1.22) for the coach sample and 5.02 (1.11) for the athletic administrator sample. Turning to the gender equity budget allocation, Figure 4.6 shows normal distributions centered around 50 for the percentage of the budget each sample allocates to gender equity initiatives.[31] The respective means for the coach and athletic administrator samples are 52.85 (23.05) and 51.64 (22.82). These descriptive results suggest that, on average, there is support for gender equity initiatives among coaches and athletic administrators but also notable variance among the populations best poised to either fully implement Title IX or enact change from the top down.

We next look at each sample independently to test hypotheses 4–1 and 4–3: Women express more support (than men) for gender equity policies and budget, but less so when they are head coaches or administrative athletic department heads. As in Chapter 3, we present the results with figures of predicted values (holding all other variables at their mean values) for

---

[30] The distribution is unweighted but looks similar when weighted.
[31] The distribution is unweighted but looks similar when weighted. As was noted in Chapter 3, the y-axis for the gender equity policy figure (Figure 4.5) differs from the y-axis for

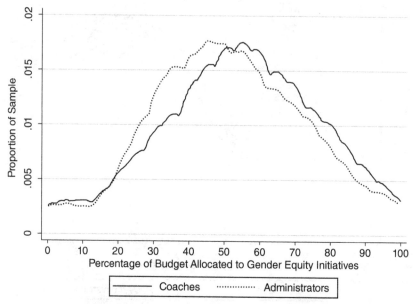

FIGURE 4.6 Sample distribution for gender equity budget allocation, coaches and athletic administrators

gender equity policy support and equity budget allocation, drawn from statistical models (with control variables) that appear in the chapter's appendix. Figure 4.7 displays scores on gender equity policies for women versus men. It reveals that women, regardless of their employment position, show substantially greater support for these policies than do men ($p < .01$), in line with Hypothesis 4–1.[32] However, the drop in support due to being a female head coach (compared to being a female non-head coach) is notable, accounting for more than a full point on a 7-point scale – women who are not head coaches register a 6.06 whereas head coaches score a 5.05 ($p < .01$).[33] This coheres with Hypothesis 4–3, which posits that movement into leadership roles – via socialization or selection – undercuts support for equity policies among women coaches. Given that women often receive encouragement to pursue leadership roles to advance women's issues, it is a troubling finding. Because our data provide only a

the gender equity budget allocation figure (Figure 4.6) since the former is a 7-point scale while the latter is a 101-point scale.

[32] In terms of substantive sizes, if we compare male non-head coaches to female non-head coaches, the Cohen D's effect size is medium .34; comparing male head coaches to female head coaches provides a smaller effect size of .09.

[33] The Cohen D's effect size is .23, which is a small (but nearly a medium) effect.

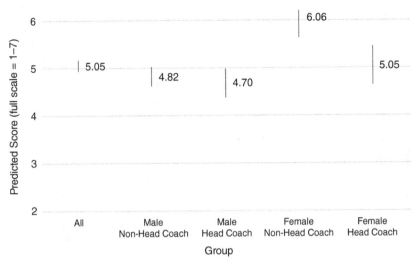

FIGURE 4.7 Predicted gender equity policy scores for coaches

snapshot, we cannot know whether women shift their commitments away from gender equity as they advance in their careers (in essence, to better align with attitudes of their male colleagues) or if those with lower levels of commitment are more likely to be promoted, but the data suggest that the roles themselves do not seem conducive to pursuing gender equity.

The findings are not as stark when we turn to the budget allocation values in Figure 4.8. Here, we again see notable gender effects, aligned with Hypothesis 4–1, with women allocating much more of the budget (more than 60 percent) to gender equity initiatives ($p < .01$).[34] The impact of being a female head coach (compared to being a female non-head coach) again decreases the gender effect but only by about 3 percentage points in this case.[35] We thus see women in higher-level coaching positions allocate less of the budget to gender equity initiatives, relative to those women below them in the hierarchy. This is consistent with Hypothesis 4–3, but the effect is small.[36]

---

[34] For male non-head coaches compared to female non-head coaches, the effect size is .23, while male head coaches versus female head coaches gives an effect size of .06.

[35] The effect size is a mere .02.

[36] We also see that male head coaches score 55.60, which substantially exceeds male non-head coaches who score 46.64. More generally, the regression model that underlies Figure 4.8 shows that being a head coach (generally) significantly increases gender equity budget allocation ($p < .05$). This partially explains the smaller female head coach effect – the magnitude of the impact is small since it is counteracted by the positive general head coach effect.

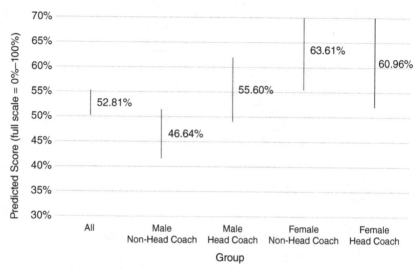

FIGURE 4.8 Predicted gender equity budget allocation for coaches

While we present findings regarding other variables with coaches in the chapter's appendix, one such result is worth pointing out here. Specifically, male coaches who have more contact with female student-athletes, relative to those who have less, exhibit significantly more support for equity policies and equity budget allocations. This finding holds even when controlling for the gender of the team coached. In other words, the finding does not stem merely from men who coach women's teams. Instead, it aligns with the contact finding reported among our student-athletes in Chapter 3.

We next turn to the athletic administrators, with the statistical models again in the chapter's appendix. We plot the predicted values from these models in Figures 4.9 and 4.10 (holding all other variables at their mean values). We find that, all else constant, female athletic administrators, compared to men, exhibit significantly more support for both gender equity policy and budget allocation ($p < .01$), consistent with Hypothesis 4–1. For equity policy, for instance, male non-heads register 4.88. Among female non-head athletic administrators, the equity policy score increases to 5.43 (Figure 4.9). The analogous shifts for budget allocation are from 51.16 to 56.94 (Figure 4.10).

Yet there is nuance to the results. The scores among female head administrators for both outcomes notably drop (but recall that few women are employed at the top of athletic administration, hence the overall effect of gender). We interpret this diversion from the dominant trends as strong

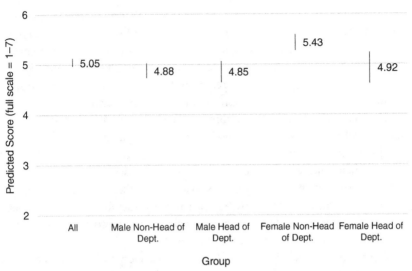

FIGURE 4.9 Predicted gender equity policy scores for athletic administrators

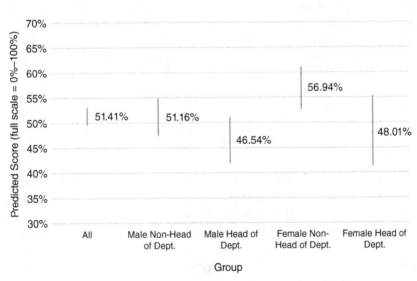

FIGURE 4.10 Predicted gender equity budget allocation for athletic administrators

evidence for Hypothesis 4–3. For example, Figure 4.9 makes clear that women who are not heads of departments are the most supportive of equity policy and that support dramatically diminishes among department heads – dropping from 5.43 to 4.92 ($p < .01$).[37] In fact, their responses largely resemble those of men once they become heads of departments; being a female head of department virtually eliminates the positive impact of gender on support for gender equity policies, all else constant. Figure 4.10 offers a similar portrait with regard to budget allocation; even though the impact of being a female department head is not statistically significant (see the chapter's appendix), the substantive movement is nontrivial (from 56.94 to 48.01).[38] As an additional aside, the statistical model results in the appendix show, like coaches, male administrators' support for both equity policies and equity budget allocation increases as they have more contact with female student-athletes. Taken together, we have compelling evidence that women in roles with more leadership responsibilities (among coaches and athletic administrators), relative to those without, are less likely to push gender equity policies.

Overall, the results show that the levels of coach and athletic administrator support for gender equity policies and budget are nominally substantial. We interpret this as a promising result, suggesting latent support for the premise of equity among those in a position to lead. These findings suggest principled possibilities for substantive representation of women's interests among athlete leadership. Yet, at the same time, institutionalized features of college athletics constrain the potential impact of such support on policy change. While women, all else constant, express substantially greater support for gender equity than their similarly situated male colleagues, their notable underrepresentation, particularly among coaches and administrators who work in the main athletic administrative domain, suppresses the likelihood of them successfully generating and implementing policy change. Much like women in minorities of legislative bodies can struggle to successfully push for policies that support women's interests, women in minoritized positions among athletic leadership are limited by their lack of critical mass.[39] While women's presence in policymaking institutions may not be sufficient to achieve policy change (e.g., Beckwith and Cowell-Meyers 2007; Carroll 2002), their ability to make change without effective collaborators is significantly

---

[37] The effect size is .14. As for the substantive effect for gender, if we compare male non-heads of departments versus female non-heads, the effect size is .25; the comparison between male heads and female heads is .02 (i.e., nonexistent).

[38] The effect size is .11. If we compare male non-heads versus female non-heads, the effect size is .10, while comparing heads gives an effect size of .02 (i.e., nonexistent).

[39] Scholarly debate remains unsettled about whether critical mass alone is sufficient for better representation of women's interests (e.g., Dahlerup 2006).

hampered (e.g., Holman, Mahoney, and Hurler 2021). In college sports, there remain extremely low proportions of women head coaches and heads of departments (under 30 percent for both), where there exists more concentrated power over policymaking.

Thus, the lack of women in these positions constitutes an undeniable hurdle for gender equality since their underrepresentation enables those in power to pursue other objectives. At the same time, the lack of parity in leadership subtly creates and reinforces expectations – the absence of a fulsome cohort of women in top leadership positions suppresses both critical mass for policymaking and possible role model impacts on the future of equity issues. Instead, and most notably, the women who currently fill these jobs, on average, express less support for equity initiatives than those lower in the athletic leadership hierarchy. In other words, those women with the most power to press for full equality express the least support for policies that might achieve it.[40] We suggest this reflects pressure to conform to an organizational culture that does not strongly embrace such equity efforts through socialization nor pursue such equity efforts through selection. One might hope that increasing the number of women in top-level leadership (i.e., "heads" of departments or teams) would counteract the ostensible cultural pressures to conform to the status quo, but that would require increased and active recruitment of women (indeed, such policy shift is among the initiatives we study in our policy outcome variable).

This leads to our next set of analyses. Regardless of their positions, women constitute a minority of coaches and athletic administrators and thus, even those who are not heads, face a culture that may be less supportive of equity initiatives. Would women's support for equity initiatives be even higher if not for such a culture? This is the question we next explore.

4.6.1 Comparing Samples

Hypothesis 4–2 suggests that, due to organizational culture, female coaches and athletic administrators express lower support for equity initiatives and budget allocation than female student-athletes. To evaluate

---

[40] Here, a key difference from literatures on women in elected office is clear: Policymaking in college sports exists in an employment hierarchy in which individuals can advance their status through promotion presumably achieved by receiving favor from higher-level leaders in the same organization. Women in elected office sustain their careers as representatives through democratic elections that fulfill the preferences of those from the mass public. Thus, comparisons to policymaking in electoral institutions are provisionally analogous.

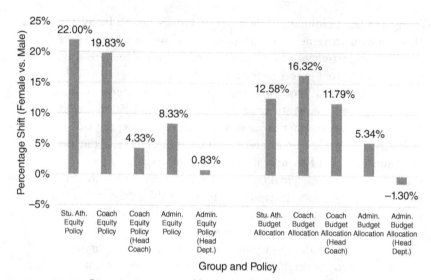

FIGURE 4.11 Percentage impact of being female, across stakeholder groups, on support for gender equity policy and budget allocation

this prediction, we isolate the impact, all else constant, of being a woman (versus being a man) in each population on both outcome variables. That is, we ask: What is the percentage change in support for equity policies among women relative to men?[41] We present these results in Figure 4.11.

The left-most bar shows, for example, that among student-athletes, women exhibit 22 percent more support for gender equity policy than men (on average). While the impact of gender among (all) coaches is similar, 19.83 percent, we see that its effect shrinks dramatically among female head coaches (versus male head coaches) to 4.33 percent. Moreover, being a woman (compared to being a man) has a much smaller effect on gender equity policy support among athletic administrators, regardless of their position (as head of the department or not). The right half of Figure 4.11 displays the results for the gender budget allocation. Here the impact of gender is not smaller for coaches (and is in fact even larger for all coaches, merged, than for student-athletes); however, we again see that its effect declines among athletic administrators.

---

[41] We compute these values by generating predicted values based on Study 1 in Chapter 3, and the two regression tables presented in this chapter's appendix (holding other variables at their mean values). We then calculate the percentage change in the predicted value for switching from male to woman.

In the chapter's appendix, we offer a statistical test of this hypothesis with the results echoing those presented in the figure. Female coaches do not exhibit significantly less support than female student-athletes, except for female head coaches when it comes to gender equity policies ($p < .01$).[42] Thus, we find only partial support for Hypothesis 4–2 with regard to coaches. Reflecting on this, we note that on budgeting concerns, female coaches may be uniquely positioned to understand the need for and impact of funding for women's teams. Since nearly all of the female coaches coach women's teams, they are the stakeholders most apt to respond to equity budgeting task with both full information on the importance of funding (compared to female student-athletes who are not forced to balance team budgets) and who have a vested self-interest in funding for women's teams (compared to athletic administrators whose job it is to weigh competing concerns across the athletic department).[43]

However, evidence in support of Hypothesis 4–2 is very strong among athletic administrators; female administrators exhibit greater support for equity policies compared to male administrators but that difference is dwarfed compared to the gender impact among student-athletes ($p < .01$). The same is true for our test of the hypothesis with the gender equity budget allocation ($p < .05$) (here female head administrators are even less supportive than male head administrators). The incongruent results among athletic administrators and coaches, particularly non-head coaches, likely reflect their respective places in the organizational culture. Women coaches appear more similar to student-athletes than are women athletic administrators. This may reflect women coaches spending more time with female student-athletes, given that nearly all of them coach women's teams. They also have fewer administrative duties and obligations than those whose primary jobs are in athletic administration. Moreover, our finding that women head coaches become less supportive of gender equity policies suggests that they assimilate more to the organizational culture: Relative to non-head coaches, head coaches serve as conduits between their teams and the athletic administration, hold more responsibilities to enforce rules, and have greater expectations placed upon them from athletic administrators.

---

[42] The head coach effect on budget allocation is, as mentioned, complicated by the positive impact of being a head coach, regardless of sex.

[43] In our (weighted) data, 92 percent of female coaches (head or assistant) coach women's teams; 89 percent of female head coaches coach women's teams.

Taken all together, the results provide evidence that the identity basis of stakeholder preferences depends on their position within the landscape of college sports. Entering an organizational culture with leadership responsibilities can depress the impact of a social identity in this context, leading to lower support for gender equity initiatives.[44]

4.7 CONCLUSION

Athletic administrators and coaches have substantial responsibility when it comes to college sports. They create the environment in which student-athletes live; they also design and implement policy. As such, they constitute crucial actors who could pursue gender equity initiatives. Episodically, leaders in college sports emerge as strident advocates for equal treatment. Amid public scrutiny of the inequalities between the men's and women's 2021 college basketball tournaments, high-profile female coaches made powerful statements about the disparate treatment they have long endured in their work with women's teams. Notably, these statements referenced the history of unequal treatment and a failure of institutional leadership to rectify the inequalities. The quotes with which we opened the chapter came from two of the most successful coaches in women's basketball history, with eighty years of combined experience between them.[45] Their frustrations reflected a lifetime of marginalization and continued organizational nonchalance.

However, significant change in gender equity initiatives has not come to college athletics from the top down. Theoretically, we offer an account

---

[44] As noted, we recognize two alternative explanations to our theory that institutions drive preferences: age and experience. First, the smaller effects may arise from an "aging" process since coaches and athletic administrators are older than student-athletes and may therefore evaluate potential policy changes through a different lens. This explanation is unlikely, given the centrality of these issues in the world in which coaches and athletic administrators work and live (e.g., the issues are on their radar given their prominence in college sports and the legal imperative of all athletic departments to seek compliance with Title IX). In our data, we find no main effect of respondent age. Second, some coaches and athletic administrators differ from student-athletes in that they did not experience competing for a varsity college team. To test this possibility, we reran our analyses including only coaches and athletic administrators who reported having played a varsity sport in college. The substantive results are unchanged.

[45] VanDerveer is the winningest coach and McGraw the seventh most winningest coach in NCAA Division I women's basketball history (statistics which hold through the conclusion of the 2023 season). Their standing may have put them in a position where, counter to our findings regarding female head coaches, they felt emboldened to take a stand, perhaps because doing so was unlikely to threaten their employment (in the case of VanDerveer; McGraw retired in 2020 and therefore could presumably speak without constraint).

in which we argue that women leaders are most likely to take leadership in pursuing such policies due to the salience of their gender identity and as representatives of women' interests. However, their position in the contemporary world of college sports leaves them entrenched in an organizational culture that remains male-dominated and defined by a policyscape that undermines progressive gender equality initiatives.

Much of the contemporary equity discussion revolves around compliance with Title IX, and perspectives are weighed against expectations from the past. Organizational structures in collegiate sports are dominantly focused on the maintenance of opportunities generated in past decades, rather than the strident pursuit of full equality through equalizing funding for women's teams or increasing and diversifying women's leadership. The limited policyscape generates a feedback process informing lowered expectations for future possibilities that constrains equity initiatives. As a numeric minority, women leaders, as individuals, may encounter a conflict between their gender and professional identities, intensified by a culture that retains vestiges of overt sexism. Our evidence suggests that, at a minimum, the culture contributes to vitiating support for equity initiatives among the women best poised to operate as top-down representatives of women's interests. The impacts of this culture and the pressures for leaders to assimilate to androcentric perspectives on equity conversations are particularly striking among those in head positions. To be clear, absolute levels of support for more progressive gender policies are high, but they remain relatively low compared to those whose interests (and fates) they might represent – student-athletes. And those with the most power over policymaking and ability to lead – heads – exhibit the least support.

This leads us to conclude that those concerned with the future of gender equality in college sports must attend to the significant hurdles within organizational culture. Quiescence instead of change is highly valued among those who advance in the athletic leadership hierarchy. We posited that such impacts could stem from the socializing effect of culture, while recognizing the possibility that selection effects could (also) be at work. Either way, attention to the fallacy of hoping for unilateral change emerging from the current array of college athletic leadership will be needed in future scholarship and policy work.

Attending to this concern will require multiple shifts to current practice. Certainly the absence of a gender-balanced leadership structure should alarm those who understand the problems associated with women's underrepresentation in leadership in politics, business, and elsewhere (e.g., Dittmar, Sanbonmatsu, and Carroll 2018; Lawless 2015). Absent role models and diverse perspectives from women, male-dominated structures and interests are unlikely to evolve. Without strong enforcement of existing policy from the federal government, campus-level leaders possess significant leeway thereby exacerbating the consequences of organizational cultures. Thus, one modest solution would be to pursue one of the policies we study: increasing the number of women leaders by requiring interviews of women for head positions. While women's increased presence in leadership is not itself sufficient to end sex discrimination, it likely would contribute to organizational change and counteract pressures that favor homophily or homologous hiring of men, by men. The presence of more female leaders could also embolden other women to act in policymaking bodies (e.g., Beckwith and Cowell-Meyers 2007; Wahman, Frantzeskakis, and Yildirim 2021) and generate positive feedback effects that support women's leadership over time (McDonagh 2010). At a minimum, our results suggest that installing more women as coaches of women's teams would likely increase the demand for gender equitable budgeting, given the notably large gendered effect on budget preferences.

This stepwise approach to addressing the occlusion of women's leadership depends on maintaining a pipeline for those lower in the hierarchy (i.e., female student-athletes) so that they can envision a pathway to advancement. The gender equality views from that population are more progressive and therefore more likely to enable change from below to bubble "up." Ensuring a robust pipeline with structures to support and advance women as leaders – as well as to provide role models for future generations to envision inhabiting these roles – are among the recommendation from gendered literatures on women in politics (e.g., Campbell and Wolbrecht 2006; Lawless and Fox 2010; Sanbonmatsu 2006). Pressing to ensure access to leadership for women in sports is a step schools and/or the NCAA could take, as well; instead of apologies and platitudes, progressive policies are needed. The NCAA has barely tapped its potential to incentivize women's leadership, or to enact robust equity policies. It expends far more time and resources to explore minor recruiting violations than to pursue gender equality.

More generally, our analyses show an underappreciated dynamic of policy feedback. Prior policies not only shape capacities and preferences, but they also alter (or entrench) organizational culture. They condition how policymakers think of policies – often constraining them to view possibilities through the lens of extant policies, thereby contributing to drift (Galvin and Hacker 2020). This makes it difficult to institute changes, especially when it comes to civil rights policies. Although these policies aim to empower marginalized populations, they rarely lead to full enfranchisement. Limited institutional leadership and mere symbolic measures addressing race and sex discrimination in workplace policies illustrate similar limitations of civil rights policies elsewhere (see Dobbin 2009; Edelman 2016; Edelman and Cabrera 2020). As societal expectations evolve, the status quo policy remains in place, subtly undermining more progressive approaches. The case of Title IX exemplifies this: In 1972, it was reasonable for the policy implementation goal to be expanded women's opportunities versus the historic practice of offering very few teams or opportunities for girls or women. Yet, fifty years later, a more appropriate standard is actual equality – a reality that faces an uphill battle because of a policymaking culture "stuck" in debates about piecemeal Title IX compliance with scant attention to escalating additional support for women's sports. A culture that has never been fundamentally challenged by existing civil rights policies has undermined the possibilities for future equality.

5

The Public, Fans, and Policy Support

In June 2021, the US Department of Education's (DOE) Office for Civil Rights (OCR) hosted a virtual public hearing on the future of Title IX. Two hundred and eighty students, parents, teachers, professors, administrators, and members of the general public provided direct testimony regarding the future of equity under the status quo. During the hearings, Americans offered perspectives on an array of issues including sexual harassment and the participation of transgender athletes in school-sponsored athletics. They also discussed the status of equality between men's and women's sports. For instance, one speaker explained:

Virtually all federally funded schools across the country are not yet making good on the requirements of Title IX, despite the nearly 50 years since the law was passed ... The girls that are playing sports face obviously inferior or nonexistent locker rooms, team rooms, scheduling, publicity, and coaching, in violation of Title IX. As OCR assesses the current regulations and approaches regarding Title IX and its implementation, athletic equity must be a key pillar to OCR's work, regulations, updates, and strategies. (US DOE 2021b, 126–27)

Another participant stated:

There are many real threats to women and girls receiving equitable access and opportunity in sports such as the lack of Title IX awareness and compliance, girls in underserved communities facing inequity in sport access, resources, and opportunity. The fight for equal pay, the lack of sponsorship support and media coverage, and the harassment and abuse of girls and women who work or play in sports. These real threats are well known and well documented yet they have become tolerated or worse ignored. (DOE 2021b, 889)

Such comments seek change to the system from the outside in. That is, in addition to the insider pressures investigated in previous chapters, the push for change in college sports can emerge from those outside of the college sports infrastructure. Major reform can occur through various mechanisms, and examples abound. On a number of occasions, the US government has acted to shift both practice and policy. Indeed, an impetus for the formation of the Intercollegiate Athletic Association, the precursor to the National Collegiate Athletic Association (NCAA), came from President Theodore Roosevelt's call for athletic conferences to address injuries in college sports. The implementation of Title IX of the Education Amendments of 1972, of course, expanded athletic participation opportunities for women. A 1978 US Congressional investigation scrutinized the NCAA's enforcement of amateurism rules. A 1984 US Supreme Court (*NCAA v. Board of Regents of the University of Oklahoma*) ruling allowed individual schools and conferences to negotiate their own television contracts, vastly increasing television exposure for college sports. And, most recently, lawsuits (e.g., *O'Bannon v. NCAA*), state legislation, and federal congressional hearings paved the way for college student-athletes to profit from sponsorship and endorsement deals. All of these examples make clear that the government – which, in a democratic society, is ultimately responsible to its citizens – can instigate change.

In other instances, the marketplace drives reform. In 1991, Notre Dame signed an exclusive television deal that sparked the rise of the modern era of college sports broadcasting. It led to conference realignment, collegiate football games throughout the week (instead of the traditional Saturday game days), and significant shifts in the flow of money to collegiate athletic departments competing at the NCAA Division I level. College coaches make external endorsement deals with apparel and shoe companies, allowing them to earn salaries that sometimes surpass those of professional coaches. These external forces have long contributed to frustrations with the rules that govern collegiate athlete amateurism (i.e., those that until recently precluded student-athletes from compensation beyond their athletic scholarships).

Increasingly, public discourse has placed the practices of college athletics under substantial scrutiny (e.g., Branch 2011). This was evident in the public outcry about the 2021 NCAA women's basketball tournament – fan reaction appeared to play a substantial role in pushing the NCAA to review its equity practices. The equity report referenced fan reaction to the video displaying inequities: "That video was quickly picked up and shared by professional athletes and thousands of other basketball fans. Other reports quickly followed, raising questions about everything from

disparities in COVID-19 testing and food, to the NCAA's unequal promotion of the men's and women's events" (KHF 2021a, 17).

This all suggests two possible paths to reform from the outside in:
governmental oversight and market-driven pressures. These pathways
foreground perspectives from the American public; in this chapter, we
explore the opportunities and challenges of relying on the public to press
for change. We begin by discussing the public's role and its relationship to
public policy – here, the opinions of the entire public matter (as opposed
to the policy constituent publics we explored in previous chapters). We
derive a set of hypotheses about factors that affect opposition or support
for gender equity initiatives. Notably, these include the socializing effects
of family structure and of adolescent competitive sports experiences on
individual opinions. We next describe how those who financially invest
in college sports (i.e., fans) can affect change via "private politics." That
is, if fans of college sports pressured the NCAA toward stronger gender equity policies, the NCAA would likely respond. However, we also
explain why we expect such fans to be relatively opposed to novel equity
initiatives, leaving the status quo unchallenged.

We then turn to our data, collected from a nationally representative
sample of the American public, first explaining our measure of "market
fandom." We next explore the correlates of support for gender equity
policies and women's college sports more generally among the public
and fans of college sports. We find support for our expectations that
factors embedded in lived experiences of the general public suppress support for policy change. We identify two specific barriers to change: the
long-term impacts of sex-segregating institutions of high school sports
and the market-driven nature of college sports within an androcentric
sporting culture. Both of these factors vitiate support. While the negative
impacts are somewhat countered by other forces, such as parenting a
daughter who plays sports, the bottom line is that athletic institutions –
even through their impacts on the general public – work against efforts
to achieve gender equality in college sports.

5.1 PUBLIC ATTITUDES AND GENDER EQUITY INITIATIVES

On issues of gender equity in college sports, the American public has
long played a key role. In the years after the passage of Title IX, public
commentary during the development of enforcement provisions was significant. Interest groups and average Americans filed over 9,700 letters
during the initial phase of public comments on the June 1974 proposed

regulations; the vast majority of comments came from individuals (Fishel 1976; Fishel and Pottker 1977).[1] In recent decades, during five public hearings about Title IX, hundreds of members of the public provided direct testimony about the effect of equity on their lives and the lives of their families (Messner and Solomon 2007; Sharrow 2020).[2] In short, the history of engagement and advocacy regarding gender equity issues in college sports provides a strong record of public interest.

With this in mind, it is important to note that, ideally, government officials craft policies that cohere with their constituents' preferences (e.g., Dahl 1971).[3] But this relatively simplistic portrayal often belies substantial normative aspirations (e.g., Disch 2011) and empirical realities. Shapiro (2011, 1003) summarizes the challenges, noting, "there are a great many studies of representation and responsiveness that provide evidence for strong effects of public opinion on government policies at different levels. That said, the causal processes that appear to operate in these and other studies also reveal limits to democracy: Other influences and obstructions are at work, and government actions and policies fall short of what the public wants, even as they move in desired directions" (e.g., Erikson, MacKuen, and Stimson 2002; Page and Shapiro 1992; Soroka and Wlezien 2010). These "other influences and obstructions" include interest groups (Finger 2019), issue publics (Druckman and Jacobs 2015), and the unequal responsiveness to constituent groups by both elected officials and advocacy communities (e.g., Gilens 2012; Strolovitch 2007). Further, responsiveness varies based on the issue, with salient issues often receiving higher levels of response (e.g., Druckman and Jacobs 2015; Lax and Phillips 2009; Shapiro 2011).

Gender equity policies in college sports have seen limited deliberate action from legislators over the past several decades, whether resulting from low salience or robust cross-partisan support for the basics of Title IX. To the extent that legislators have recently debated policy implementation it has been narrowly focused through increased Republican party preoccupation with transgender athletes in high school athletics.

---

[1] Public comments on proposed regulations remain robust to this day. Over 200.000 comments were filed on draft regulations in summer 2022, the increased number presumably driven by increased public awareness of the law, and the regulations process having moved online (Knott 2022).

[2] The hearings occurred in 2002 in Atlanta, Chicago, Colorado Springs, San Diego, and Philadelphia and through an online forum in 2021.

[3] An alternative is the trustee model of representation that does not necessitate direct responsiveness.

Rather than expanding attention to fully implementing gender equity, Republicans have advanced an agenda centered on narrowing participatory eligibility in the girl's/women's category at the exclusion of transgender girls and women, thereby limiting the impacted beneficiary population to cisgender athletes (Sharrow 2021b). Robust discussion of better enforcement for existing policy (i.e., ensuring compliance with current Title IX requirements for athletics) is largely absent. Even so, exploring general public opinion serves two important purposes. First, latent public opinion – that is, nonsalient but underlying sentiment – could be triggered in response to emerging actions of public officials (Key 1961; Zaller 2003). Put another way, in making or enforcing a policy – such as Title IX – policymakers anticipate reactions from the general public, even on low-salience issues. Thus, it is worthwhile to understand the contours of opinions on such policies, even in what might appear to be nascent periods of policymaking.

Second, understanding what drives the general public's attitudes on gender equity policies in college sports provides insight into how different contextual factors may shape beliefs. This includes institutional and sociological experiences that could affect not only an individual's policy support but also the attitudes and behaviors of those in their family and social circles. Given research on the recursive impacts of familial experiences and athletic opportunities generated by Title IX (Sharrow et al. 2018; Sharrow 2020), these contextual factors are particularly central to our theory. We seek to understand the levels of support among the public, and its corollaries, as these could matter for policymakers and society.

Our expectations regarding women as a group among the American public are less straightforward than were our expectations for women student-athletes, coaches, and athletic administrators. The athletic constituency groups directly benefit from gender equity policies and thus we predicted and consistently found large gender gaps in support. Among the general public, gender gaps exist on a host of issues such as the use of military force and social welfare issues (see Burns and Gallagher 2010). However, gender gaps on opinion toward women's issues have been much less consistent – Lizotte (2017, 53) explains, "With respect to equal rights ... gender differences have been very small or nonexistent" (see also Holman and Kalmoe 2021; Huddy, Cassese, and Lizotte 2008). When it comes to gender and sports policy specifically, a 2017 national survey found that women support Title IX at a higher level than do men, albeit by a relatively small amount – 60 percent to 54 percent (YouGov 2017). That said, larger gender gaps emerged along more specific provisions such as the importance of the DOE enforcing Title IX in sports (a gap of 69 percent versus 55 percent, indicating "important" or "very important").[4] A 2022 Pew study found a substantial gender gap on the question of equal funding for men's and women's college sports – 71 percent of women compared to 50 percent of men support equality (Igielnik 2022). Moreover, public opinion on athletic equality issues from previous eras found evidence of a gender gap (Sigelman and Wilcox 2001).

This leaves us some ambiguity for our expectations; however, we expect to find that men and women differ in opinions about our sports equity initiatives for two reasons. First, we suspect that the lack of a robust gender gap in other data about Title IX stems partially from a lack of awareness about the extent of inequalities in college sports. Indeed, the prevalence of celebratory framings that focus on the gains achieved by women under Title IX often overshadows a nuanced conversation about inequalities (e.g., Whiteside and Roessner 2018). Our initiatives call attention to disparities by proposing explicit steps toward equality. We suspect women will be more willing to support overt policies for gender equality (e.g., equal opportunities and equal spending).

Second, we expect that recent high-profile events may have reshaped opinions. From increased attention to sexual misconduct cases discussed in Chapter 3 to the pay equity complaint and subsequent lawsuit by the US women's national soccer team (see English 2021; ESPN 2020), inequalities in sports have become more salient. We anticipate that this knowledge has a more profound effect on women because they likely feel more linked to those experiencing inequalities and therefore are more likely to express support. While we do not test this exact mechanism, we nonetheless arrive at the following hypothesis:

Women will express more support for gender equity initiatives than men, all else constant. (Hypothesis 5–1)

One of the more intriguing findings of the aforementioned 2017 national survey is that adults with daughters who participated in high school or college sports expressed higher support for directing new or existing funds toward equal athletic opportunities for girls and women. They also viewed this as more important than the DOE's federal enforcement of Title IX in sports. These findings align with a burgeoning literature that reveals how family structure can influence political

---

[4] However, the study also reports no subgroup differences on a question about whether colleges are doing enough to ensure equal sports opportunities for female students.

socialization. For example, several studies find that men with daughters tend to hold more liberal attitudes on gender-related public policies (c.f., Lee and Conley 2016; Shafer and Malhotra 2011; Sharrow et al. 2018; Washington 2008). Furthermore, research on the history of Title IX advocacy finds that fathers of daughters who play sports have frequently emerged as allies of female athletes (Sharrow 2020). Given the specificity of our items – concerning precise equity initiatives – we anticipate that having a daughter who plays sports will have a positive impact on both of our main measures. This could emerge via self-interest or via contact as explicated in Chapter 3 – that is, on opinion toward gender equity policies in sports, the interactions that matter are those confined to sports (e.g., parenting a daughter who plays sports rather than a daughter who does not play sports).[5]

Individuals who have (had) a daughter who plays(ed) sports will express more support for gender equity initiatives than those who do (did) not, all else constant. (Hypothesis 5–2)

We also offer expectations about the downstream socialization consequences of participating in competitive sports defined by a sex-segregated system (McDonagh and Pappano 2007). Sex-based segregation is deeply naturalized in athletics (Sharrow 2021a). We expect that participation in a system that normalizes sex separation, while also prioritizing sports for boys and men, depresses support for structure-altering policies among males who participate in and benefit from the system. This most likely develops during high school as youth sports prior to high school tend to be less competitive and, relatively, include more sex integration. Indeed, Title IX becomes the governing mandate for interscholastic athletic programs that often emerge in American communities in high schools (but not necessarily primary schools where school-sponsored teams are uncommon). Segregation becomes more universally normative in interscholastic practices in large measure because Title IX technically governs high school as well.

Further, those who participate in high school sports during their adolescence likely experienced substantial gender inequalities. Enforcement of Title IX at the high school level can be particularly lax – even just a decade ago, one estimate suggested that nearly 30 percent of high schools had "large gender inequality in sports," meaning the percentage of spots on teams allocated to girls was 10 percent or lower than those allocated

---

[5] It is plausible that the extent of the daughter's or daughters' interest/participation in sports might matter (beyond whether they play(ed) or not), but we do not explore that here.

to boys (Wong 2015). A more recent report states that "boys receive more than 1.13 million more high school sports opportunities than girls ... and the gap between high school boys' and girls' participation has not significantly narrowed in the past 20 years" (Staurowsky et al. 2020, 8; see also Staurowsky et al. 2022; Veliz, Snyder, and Sabo 2019). Americans also perceive the resource gap that substantially favors support for boys' sports (YouGov 2017).[6] Men who participated in such a system may have come to see these imbalances as the expectation, as well as the status quo. Consequently, they may be less supportive of equity initiatives. We do not expect the same effect among women since participation means experiencing inequalities that, if anything, will enhance their support for improved equity initiatives.

In developing our expectations for how these conditions may impact opinion, we draw on a study from a parallel context – the military. Scholarship shows that early conscription into sex-segregated military forces leads to diminished levels of tolerance and more politically conservative attitudes (Navajas et al. 2022). For instance, Vogt et al. (2007, 894–95) find members of the US Marine Corps express fewer positive attitudes toward women than members of the other armed forces, a dynamic they suggest may occur because:

the Marine Corps is the only component of service that currently has gender-segregated training. It may be that gender integrated training leads to more positive interactions between the genders during later military service, while gender-segregated training leads to greater adherence to traditional gender-role attitudes ... spending time in a male-dominated work setting such as the military contributes to the development of negative attitudes toward women. (895)

This coheres with our basic idea that socialization in an institutionalized setting, in our case sex-segregated sports in high school, can have long-term downstream consequences. Political science research demonstrates the durable power into adulthood of other experiences in adolescence, such as being raised in a home where partisan politics are salient or where the family benefits from other means-tested policy provisions (e.g., Barnes and Hope 2017; Beck and Jennings 1991; Jennings and Niemi 1974). Thus, we expect that:

---

[6] Gender distinctions start early too; in a survey of girls aged 7–13 who participate in sport, about one-third report being made fun of by boys and indicate that they intend to drop sports prior to high school (Zarrett, Veliz, and Sabo 2020). Interestingly, though, parents now spend more on daughters who play sports than sons (Aspen Institute 2020). As stated, despite these early experiences, we expect high school to be the crucial point in shaping equity views given it is then when sex segregation begins to predominate.

Men who participated in high school sports will express less support for gender equity initiatives than those who did not, all else constant. (Hypothesis 5–3)[7]

This prediction has relevance given our findings in Chapter 3 that sex segregation among college athletes acts as a barrier to bottom-up change. Here, we suggest that the same system presents a hurdle to change from the outside in since it durably reduces support for gender equity policy among some members of the public.

5.2 PRIVATE POLITICS AND GENDER EQUITY INITIATIVES

Also relevant to possibilities for change from the outside in are issue publics – those groups that pay close attention to a given issue. Such individuals can have an outsized impact on policies since they tend to take relevant actions on policy change. This can occur via elected representatives or other governmental channels, but of equal if not contextually greater importance are the marketplace activities undertaken by key constituencies. Specifically, "private politics" refers to individuals and activists mobilizing in the private realm to induce companies or organizations to alter their behaviors and/or to reward them for supporting a favored position. Work on private politics reveals the extent to which consumers can alter the practices of businesses and government (e.g., Abito, Besanko, and Diermeier 2019; Baron and Diermeier 2007; Druckman and Valdes 2019; Endres and Panagopoulos 2017). For example, market behaviors (e.g., boycotts and buycotts) have led companies to change their environmental practices, such as Nestle's efforts to end deforestation, Staples' increased usage of recycled paper, or Zara clothing store's elimination of fur products (Roser-Renouf et al. 2016; also see Hiatt, Grandy, and Lee 2015; Malhotra, Monin, and Tomz 2019; Reid and Toffel 2009). After sustained pressure, consumer forces and the retraction of corporate sponsorship ultimately convinced the reticent leadership of the National Football League's Washington team to drop the franchise's racist name (Sharrow, Tarsi, and Nteta 2021). In some circumstances, policy change comes not via governance structure but due to market demand.[8]

---

[7] We do not expect an independent effect among men who played college sports, since virtually all of them will have played high school sports and thus already been socialized as such.

[8] There are critiques of such approaches to policymaking (e.g., LeBaron and Dauvergne 2014; Strach 2016), but the normative evaluation of these potential pathways is beyond our scope.

This possibility lurks within the realm of college athletics where fans act as a critical consumer constituency. The industry depends on fan support (Nixon 2014), and thus, fan reactions and product preferences matter. If college sports fans demand more gender-equitable policies, the NCAA and colleges/universities would be increasingly incentivized to implement them – if they failed to do so, they will potentially lose fan revenue.[9] At the same time, market pressures are imperfect and imprecise movers of policy (Strach 2016). Grassroots' calls to address gender inequalities in college sports often arise from episodic incidents like fan reactions to the 2021 basketball tournament revelations. Thus, it is worth exploring how college sports fans evaluate gender equity policies. To what extent do the demands of fans differ from those in the general population? Does inequity partially stem from the deprioritization of equity efforts among fans?

Fans make psychic and financial investments in college sports. As such, they have a stake in the status quo (i.e., they have expressed tacit support for current practice) and will likely oppose major changes. Along these lines, Druckman, Howat, and Rodheim (2016) find that fans (relative to nonfans) express less support for pay-for-play reforms that might increase college athlete compensation or unionization efforts among college athletes. This reticence could be even more pronounced on gender equity initiatives, given gender norms in sports. Flores et al. (2020, 383) explain that "Sport is often a hyper-masculine world where aggression is valued, great attention is given to being a 'real man' ... Even sports fandom is a highly gendered environment where female fans of sport need to suppress their femininity to be viewed as authentic fans" (Borer 2009; Crawford and Gosling 2004).[10] Research shows that many sports fans oppose, or are even hostile to, significant shifts to the gendered order, exemplified by the resistance to transgender athletes' participation in the status quo (Bahrampour, Clement, and Guskin 2022). While the gendered initiatives on which we focus may not be seen as completely upending current practice, they nevertheless challenge the extant regime and the gender hierarchy normalized within it. We link this to our concept of

---

[9] In principle, noncompliance with Title IX could also impact the ability of colleges and universities to recruit students, faculty, and/or employees. These market pressures are conceivable, but less central to the theory we posit.

[10] Thorson and Serazio (2018) also speculate that sports culture prioritizes men as exemplified by overwhelming media focus on male sports. They do not find that fan intensity leads to the endorsement of traditional gender roles (despite their hypothesis). However, they note that their measure, which asked about discrimination, sexism, and work/family labor division, may not have fully captured gendered attitudes (397). Their basic argument may better apply to our outcomes focused on policies that explicitly enhance women in sport.

fandom in terms of market investment in college sports, about which we will say more shortly, since that is the mechanism by which change can come via private politics.

As one invests more in college sports (i.e., greater market behavior), they become less supportive of gender equity initiatives, all else constant. (Hypothesis 5–4)

This prediction has substantial implications for gender equity initiatives. Economic considerations drive much of the contemporary calculus of college sports (Clotfelter 2019; Zimbalist 1999). Consequently, if the primary financial stimulus – fans – do not support gender equity initiatives, it will serve as a counterforce to those who look to implement initiatives aimed at achieving greater gender equality. This would represent a substantial challenge to policy change from the outside in.

5.3 SURVEY

We assess these hypotheses with a survey of the public, including fans. As detailed in Chapter 2, we obtained a representative national sample from Bovitz Inc.'s Forthright panel. We conducted our survey from April 30, 2019, to May 9, 2019, with 1,508 individuals.[11] The survey included a host of demographic items (see Table 5.1) as well as some variables we have not used in prior chapters that are crucial for our hypotheses here. To test Hypothesis 5–2, regarding the impact of having a daughter who plays sport, we asked respondents whether they have children (of any age), the gender of each child, and whether they had a daughter or son who plays/played sports.[12]

We asked respondents whether they participated in high school sports, varsity college sports, and/or adult sports leagues. Hypothesis 5–3 suggests a depressive effect on support for gender equity policy among adult men who participated in high school sports. We do not expect an impact from varsity collegiate sports (as noted, given it is duplicative of high school sports). Nor do we anticipate an adult sports league effect since those often are coed. However, both the college and adult measures allow us to assess the impacts of alternative experiences in the statistical models from which we derive our key results (see the appendix). We additionally asked people whether they coach(ed) youth teams (of any sex), many of which

[11] We preregistered our data collection at: https://aspredicted.org/6em45.pdf.
[12] We explored the impact of having a son who plays(ed) sports and find it has no effect on equity opinions; see the appendix.

TABLE 5.1 *Public sample description*

Variable	Mean/percentage
Sex (as self-identified by respondent)	Male: 49%; female: 51%; other: 1%[1]
Race (that best describes the respondent, as self-identified)	White: 70%%; Black: 12%; Hispanic/Latino: 10%; Asian/Pacific Islander: 5%; other: 3%[2]
Religion	Protestant: 22%; Catholic: 21%; Jewish: 3%; other religion: 23%[2]; not religious: 31%[3]
Highest level of education	Less than high school: 3%; high school: 23%; some college: 37%; 4-year college degree: 27%; advanced degree: 11%[4]
Income	< $30,000: 30%; $30,000–$69,999: 35%; $70,000–$99,999: 18%; $100,000–$200,000: 16%: >$200,000: 2%[5]
Age	18–24: 12%; 25–34: 20%; 35–50: 32%; 51–65: 23%; over 65: 14%[6]
Children	Have daughter(s): 42% Have son(s): 42%
Children who play/played sport	Daughter(s) who plays/played sport: 18% Son(s) who plays/played sport: 23%
Playing sports	Played high school: 43% Played varsity college: 10% Play as adult: 20%
Coach(ed) youth team	17%
Political ideology, mean (1–7 scale, with higher scores indicating more conservative)	3.57 (std. dev.: 1.52)
Racial conservativism, mean (1–7 scale, with higher scores indicating more racial conservatism)	3.32 (std. dev.: 1.28)
Hostile sexism, mean (1–7 scale, with higher scores indicating more sexism)	3.50 (std. dev.: 1.70)

[1] The total does not sum to 100 percent due to rounding error.
[2] Less than 1 percent classified themselves as Middle Eastern/North African; less than 1 percent classified themselves as Native American; 1.99 percent classified themselves as "other."
[3] 1.46 percent classified themselves as Muslim; 1.06 percent classified themselves as Hindu; 20.78 percent classified themselves as "other."
[4] The total does not sum to 100 percent due to rounding error.
[5] The total does not sum to 100 percent due to rounding error.
[6] The total does not sum to 100 percent due to rounding error.

are not coed (see also Messner and Bozada-Deas 2009). We describe our measurement strategy for Hypothesis 5–4 in the next section.

In Table 5.1, we present a description of our sample. It matches US Census benchmarks well – as we detail in this chapter's appendix. Relevant to our hypotheses, we find 18.08 percent have a daughter who plays/played a sport. A total of 42.45 percent played high school sports, and while not displayed in the table, 54.18 percent of men played high school sports.

The survey included our key outcome variables as analyzed in prior chapters. This includes our six-item scale of support for gender equity policy (i.e., Title IX support, support for equal opportunities for men and women, greater enforcement of sexual harassment laws, ensuring equal spending for men's and women's teams, and instituting a requirement that women be interviewed for athletic directorships and women's coaching jobs). We again employ the budget allocation exercise where respondents decide the percentage to devote to gender equity initiatives (i.e., equal opportunities, enforcement of sexual harassment laws, support for women pursuing coaching careers) as opposed to student-athlete benefit initiatives (i.e., paying student-athletes, guaranteeing scholarships, guaranteeing medical coverage). Figures 5.1 and 5.2 display the density plots

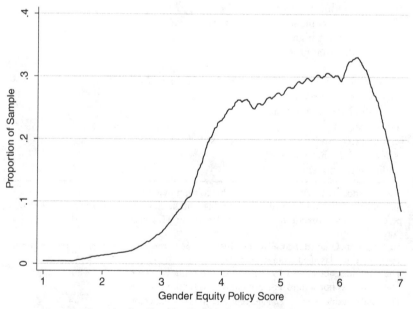

FIGURE 5.1 Sample distribution for gender equity policy (scaled), public

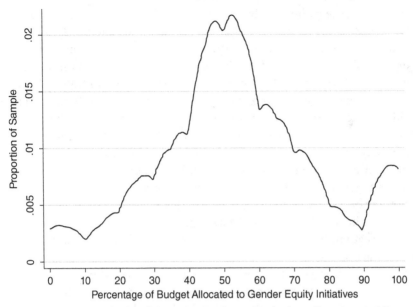

FIGURE 5.2 Sample distribution for gender equity budget allocation, public

of each – as in the prior chapter, the x-axis provides the scores and the
y-axis the proportions of the samples that registered the given scores. The
gender equity distribution measure shows a fair amount of spread with a
mean score of 5.15 (1.12) (on a 1–7 scale).[13] The budget distribution peaks
more with a mean of 54.70 (24.82). Thus, the means of both are above the
respective midpoints. All of our question wordings (including those items
discussed in the next section) appear in this chapter's appendix. Before
turning to the main tests of our hypotheses, we first discuss how we measured sports market fan behavior employed in our tests of Hypothesis 5–4.

5.4 MEASURING COLLEGE MARKET FAN BEHAVIOR

Scholars have studied mass interest in sports or sports fandom from a
variety of angles including exploring the extent of fandom (Wann and
James. 2018), consequences (e.g., violence and alcohol consumption) of
being a fan (e.g., Ostrowsky 2018), its effects on communications and

---

[13] As was noted in Chapters 3 and 4, the y-axis for the gender equity policy figure
(Figure 5.1) differs from the y-axis for the gender equity budget allocation figure
(Figure 5.2) since the former is a 7-point scale while the latter is a 101-point scale.

relationships (e.g., Billings, Butterworth, and Turman. 2017; Earnheardt, Haridakis, and Hugenberg 2013), and gender and fandom (Markovits and Albertson 2012; Tarver 2017; Toffoletti 2017). Our interest is in distinguishing those who drive the market for college sports through the major sources of revenue: television broadcasts, tickets, and apparel sales (see Murphy 2019; NCAA 2021b; Tarver 2017). To identify these individuals, we asked respondents to report (to the best of their memory) how many college sports games/competitions they attended in person during the past year as well as how many they watched (on television or the Internet) during the same time period.[14] Respondents answered on a 0 to 100 game scale. We further queried respondents for the number of clothing or other apparel items they own that feature a college team, on a 0 to 100 item scale. We took the average across these items to construct a "market fan behavior" scale.[15] The survey also included other behavioral measures – less central to major sources of direct revenue to the NCAA and schools but important to understanding the intensity of fan engagement – such as betting on college sports and donating to a sports program (i.e., "other fan behavior" in Table 5.2).[16]

The survey includes a host of other measures to validate the market fan behavior items. We provide an overview of these measures in Table 5.2 that also delineates our aforementioned market-based and other fan behavior items. One measure gauges psychological attachment to college sports via the college sports fandom questionnaire (Absten 2011; Wann 2002). It asks respondents the extent to which they disagree or agree with five statements (on 7-point scales, with higher scores indicating agreement).[17] Examples of the statements include: "I consider myself to be a college sports fan," "My friends see me as a college sports fan," and "Being a college sports fan is very important to me."[18] Another

---

[14] We reminded respondents to consider all seasons and sports and defined "watching" as including cases where they watched the majority or all of the game. As a reminder, the survey occurred prior to the COVID-19 pandemic and thus the pandemic did not affect opportunities to watch and/or attend games/competitions.

[15] The three measures highly correlated with one another; the alpha score for internal consistency is .81.

[16] Donations clearly can play a key role in athletic programs; however, donations among the general population are not particularly large and we do not have data on the attitudes of "big" donors.

[17] The original scale includes eight response options, but we modified it to cohere with other response scales on our survey.

[18] The measures highly correlated with one another; the alpha score for internal consistency is .96.

TABLE 5.2 *Fan measures*

Variable	Items
Market fan behavior	• Number of games/competitions attended in the previous year (0–100) • Number of games/competitions watched on the television/ Internet or listened to in the previous year (0–100) • Number of clothing or other apparel items owned that explicitly features college sport's team (0–100)
Other fan behavior	• Frequency of following college sports (1–5) • Average days a week read about college sports (0–7) • Ever bet on college sports (no/yes) • Amount donated to college sports programs ($0 to $1000)
College sports fandom questionnaire	• Consider yourself a college sports fan (1–7, with higher scores on this and all measures that follow indicating agreement) • Friends see you as a college sports fan (1–7) • Following college sports is the most enjoyable form of entertainment (1–7) • Life would be less enjoyable if not able to follow college sports (1–7) • Being a college sports fan is very important (1–7)
College sport team identity	• Importance of being a fan of favorite college team(s) (1–5) • "College sports fan" describes well when comes to favorite college team(s) (1–5) • How often use "we" or "they" in talking about favorite college team(s) (1–5) • Extent think of self as being a fan of favorite college sports team(s) (1–5)
Fan of sports	• Consider yourself a sports fan (1–6)
Fan of college sports	• Consider yourself a college sports fan (1–6)
Fan of men's college sports	• Consider yourself a fan of men's college sports (1–6)
Fan of women's college sports	• Consider yourself a fan of women's college sports (1–6)
Fan of college football	• Consider yourself a fan of college football (1–6)
Fan of men's college basketball	• Consider yourself a fan of men's college basketball (1–6)

scale focuses instead on identification with a given team (Boyle and Magnusson 2007; Mahony, Madrigal, and Howard 2000; Wann and Branscombe 1993; Wann and Pierce 2003).[19] This uses a social identity scale to measure the extent to which an individual closely identifies with their favorite college team(s). Specifically, it includes four items on 5-point scales, with higher values indicating a stronger identity – such as the importance of being a fan of the team and whether one thinks of the team in terms of "we" rather than "they" (i.e., "college sport team identity" in Table 5.2).[20] While the strength of team fan identity is not our focus, since we are more interested in fandom writ large, it provides a useful point of comparison.

Finally, to gauge how our market fan behavior measures compare across fan contexts, we also included six items all on 6-point scales (ranging from "not a fan at all" to "a very big fan") asking about fandom of sports in general, college sports in general (which is redundant with our college sports fandom questionnaire but on the same scale as these other measures), men's college sports, women's college sports, college football, and men's college basketball.[21]

5.4.1 Validating Market Fan Behavior Measure

To assess the validity of our measure, we explore its relationship with the other fan measures. Recall our main measure includes three items: attendance, watching, and owning team-branded clothes, all on 0 to 100 scales. In Figure 5.3, we display density plots of the variables (again, the x-axis contains the scale(s) and the y-axis the proportion of the sample with the given scores on the relevant variable). All three variables exhibit extreme skews toward 0, although this is particularly true for the measures of attendance and clothing ownership. The mean values for attendance, watching, and clothing items are, respectively, 8.35 (19.08; 1,487), 20.47 (26.43; 1,489), and 9.02 (17.69; 1,427). This illustrates that the college sports market is not dominated by a large number of superfans. Thus, we focus on our (average) scaled measure of market fan behaviors. To get a substantive sense of the scale, consider that those below the median on the scale, on average, report attending .34 (std. dev.: 1.04; $N = 745$)

---

[19] Such scales correlate highly with general fandom (Wann and Pierce 2003).
[20] The measures highly correlated with one another; the alpha score for internal consistency is .96.
[21] We asked additional items about the importance of being a men's and women's college sports fan; they highly correlate with the items on which we focus (at .80 and .78).

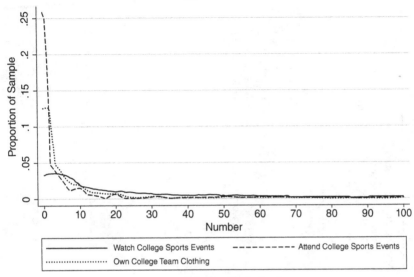

FIGURE 5.3 Market fan behaviors

games in the past year, watching 2.11 (3.16; 744) games in the past year, and owning .81 (1.86; 715) pieces of college sports clothing/apparel. In contrast, the respective means for those above the median on the scale are 16.39 (24.49; 742), 38.80 (26.71; 745), and 17.26 (22.10; 712).

In Table 5.3, we present the mean scores for each of the other variables listed in Table 5.2 (in order) for the below- and above-median respondents on the market fan behavior measure. If our measure is valid, we should see higher scores for the other measures (from Table 5.2) when the market fan behavior is above the median (compared to when it is below the median). This is exactly what we find, with sizeable differences across every measure. Notably, among those above the median for market fan behaviors, fandom for women college sports falls well below fandom for men's college sports generally, as well as below fandom for college football or men's basketball specifically. We also see that our overall college sports fan measure resembles the averages for our men's college sport fan measure, suggesting that when asked about "college sports," respondents often focus entirely on men's college sports.

We further confirm the outlier nature of women's sports fandom by correlating the measures with one another. This explores the extent to which the measures are related to one another. We find that the average correlation between all the measures with one another, sans women's college

TABLE 5.3 *Relationship between market fan behaviors and other fan measures*

Variable (scale)	Market fan behavior below median average (std. dev., N)	Market fan behavior above median average (std. dev., N)	Overall average (std. dev., N)
Frequency of following college sports (1–5)	1.76 (.85; 750)	3.61 (.97; 745)	2.68 (1.30; 1,495)
Average days a week read about college sports (0–7)	.51 (1.14; 751)	3.30 (2.20; 745)	1.90 (2.24; 1,496)
Ever bet on college sports (no/yes)	2.80%	28.73%	15.71%
Amount donated to college sport program ($0 to $1,000)	$3.04 (16.50%; 751)	$139.92 (45.28%; 745)	$68.78 (36.40%; 1,496)
College sports fandom questionnaire (1–7)	$20.55; 711)	$243.07; 657)	$182.35; 1,368)
College sport team identity (1–5)	2.07 (1.37; 751)	5.18 (1.44; 744)	3.62 (2.10; 1,495)
Fan of sports (1–6)	1.63 (.84; 750)	3.47 (.99; 743)	2.55 (1.30; 1,493)
Fan of college sports (single item) (1–6)	2.91 (1.44; 751)	4.84 (1.16; 745)	3.87 (1.62; 1,496)
Fan of men's college sports (single item) (1–6)	2.12 (1.15; 751)	4.53 (1.24; 745)	3.31 (1.70; 1,496)
Fan of women's college sports (single item) (1–6)	2.15 (1.36; 751)	4.60 (1.27; 745)	3.37 (1.80; 1,496)
Fan of college football (1–6)	1.94 (1.12; 750)	3.40 (1.30; 745)	2.66 (1.42; 1,495)
Fan of men's college basketball (1–6)	2.00 (1.23; 750)	4.55 (1.31; 745)	3.27 (1.80; 1,495)
	1.90 (1.21; 750)	4.20 (1.45; 745)	3.04 (1.76; 1,495)

sports, is .79; in contrast, the average correlation between being a fan of women's college sports and the other items is .63. For example, the correlation between general college sports fan and men's college sports fan is .85, while the correlation of general college sports fan and women's college sports fan is .57. This is perhaps unsurprising given the market differences in sports – among them that television and media coverage wildly over-represents men's sports (Cooky et al. 2021) – but the data make clear that men's college sports are more chronically accessible in general discourse about college sports fandom. Most importantly, while we did not differentiate our market fan behavior items by gender of sport, we have little doubt that the bulk of those behaviors reflect a disproportionate interest in men's and not women's college sports, driven in part by the dramatically greater television broadcast coverage of men's college sports.[22]

5.5 SUPPORTING GENDER EQUITY POLICIES

We next directly explore support for gender equity policies among the public and market-driven college sports fans. In Table 5.4, we provide the mean scores on our two main outcome measures for the student-athlete, coach, and athletic administrator data used in the prior chapters, as well as for the public, distinguishing again those above (market fans) and below (nonfans) the median on our market fan behavior measure. The table shows that fans' scores resemble those of athletic administrators, and coaches for both gender equity policies and the gender budget allocation; it also is similar to the student-athletes' gender equity policy score, although not their budget allocation (which is lower for student-athletes). More importantly, we find that those who are nonfans exhibit *significantly higher* support for gender equity on both items (i.e., relative to fans, for gender equity policies, $t1494 = 4.30$, $p < .01$ for a two-tailed test; for the budget allocation, $t1494 = 4.38$; $p < .01$).

These results have three implications for policy change. First, all stakeholder groups express general support for gender equity policies, with

---

[22] We also included a question about why people support their favorite team (allowing for multiple responses). Of the 43 percent who reported having a favorite team, the main reasons included living near the school (31 percent), the team being successful (31 percent), family member having attended the school (27 percent), and the respondent having attended the school (26 percent). The team having a notable television presence also registered a nontrivial 20 percent. This all suggests that school location, size, success, and exposure likely lead to larger fan bases. The latter two reasons also explain, at least in part, why many schools invest as they do in college sports. Finally, we explored the correlates of our market fan behavior measure and the college sports fandom measure; these results can be found in the appendix.

TABLE 5.4 *Average gender equity policy and gender budget allocation scores across samples*

	Student-athletes	Administrators	Coaches	Fans	Nonfans
Gender equity policies	5.09 (std. dev.: 1.29; N: 2531)	5.02 (1.11; 862)	5.07 (1.22; 528)	5.03 (1.15; 745)	5.28 (1.08; 751)
Gender budget allocation	46.23 (21.59; 2531)	51.64 (22.82; 862)	52.85 (23.05; 528)	52.02 (24.30; 745)	57.61 (25.02; 751)

support scores well above the midpoints on the scales and budget attitudes near the midpoints (varying slightly across groups). Yet the context and reality of women's significant marginalization across multiple dimensions of college sports (detailed in Chapter 1) suggest that the scores do not reach the levels needed to stimulate substantial change. Indeed, the equal split of the budget allocation item scores between gender equity and student-athlete benefits spending suggests that gender equity is not prioritized in a context of finite budgets, across stakeholder groups. Second, that market-driven fans show no greater support than those within the college athletics system suggests that change via private politics seems unlikely – that is, the marketplace for college sports does not appear inclined to apply pressure for change relative to what those within the system themselves support. Fans are not overwhelmingly hostile to spending on gender equity spending, but neither do they prioritize it. Third, the significantly higher scores among nonfans mean the general public (e.g., taking the average between fans and nonfans) is mildly more supportive than dedicated fans but probably nowhere near the levels needed to pressure policymakers to implement change from outside the system. More importantly, their high scores reveal the power of the extant institutions – the issue public (i.e., fans) that drive it are *less* supportive of change. They have likely been socialized to enjoy the system in its current form – including the extant marginalization of women's interests. Attitudinally, these activated fans look similar to those stakeholders within the system. The dynamics echo those found in prior chapters: *The institutions that contribute to women's marginalization seem to shape attitudes that accept it.*

We next investigate the correlates of support for equity policies and the gender equity budget allocation among the public. As in the prior chapters, we use statistical models that appear in the chapter's appendix to produce predicted values (with uncertainty and setting other variables at their means) for key groups to test our hypotheses. These models include various control variables that are not central to our hypotheses – demographic control variables as well as others such as whether the respondent played varsity college sports, has a son who plays sports, and/or coaches a youth team. Readers are referred to the appendix for results regarding these variables.[23]

The key groups to test our hypotheses include identifying as female (Hypothesis 5–1), having a daughter who plays/played sports (Hypothesis 5–2), being a male who played high school sports (Hypothesis 5–3), and market fan behavior (Hypothesis 5–4). With respect to market fan behavior, we compare individuals with the minimum and the maximum fan behavior scores for presentational clarity; the results we show are robust to other operationalizations.

In Figures 5.4 and 5.5, we display the results for gender equity policies and budget allocation to gender equity initiatives, respectively. As with the other populations, we find – consistent with Hypothesis 5–1 – women are much more supportive of the gender equity policies ($p < .01$) and budget allocation to gender equity initiatives ($p < .01$). While these are not extremely large movements – for example, the predicted equity policy score for women is 5.29 versus 5.02 for men, which is a 4.5 percent shift – they are nonetheless meaningful.[24] As mentioned, past work on gender gaps in equity policies has produced ambiguous results; our result suggests that women may recognize the potential (if not the reality) for gendered inequalities in a domain persistently defined by androcentric norms.

We also see clear support for Hypothesis 5–2, that having a daughter(s) who plays(/ed) sports leads to more support on both equity policies ($p < .05$) and budget allocation ($p < .01$).[25] As mentioned, this aligns with our student-athlete contact results since learning of the first-hand

---

[23] In the chapter's appendix, we also present statistical results for three other outcome variables: being a fan of men's college sports, being a fan of women's college sports, and support for student-athlete benefit policies – as explained there, these have some relevance to a broader contextual understanding of equality in college sports but do not have a direct bearing on our hypotheses.

[24] This registers as a .15 Cohen's D, which is a small effect size. The effect size for the budget allocation item is .13.

[25] The effect has the same influence among both men and women respondents.

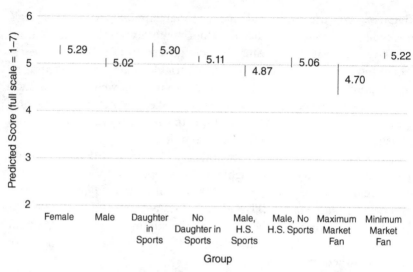

FIGURE 5.4 Predicted gender equity policy scores for the public

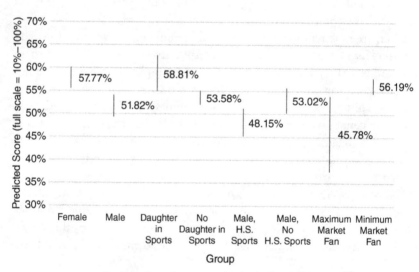

FIGURE 5.5 Predicted gender equity budget allocation for the public

experiences with gendered marginalization, via their daughters (in this case), shapes attitudes.[26] As with the effect of gender identity, the impact is not large (e.g., 3.2 percent on equity policies and 5.2 percentage points

---

[26] The results in the appendix show no evidence of any unique effect of having a daughter that speaks to the issue specificity of what we study.

on budget allocation) but nonetheless is intriguing given it is a typically underappreciated dynamic of policy support.[27]

Perhaps our most intriguing result concerns support for Hypothesis 5–3: *Men* who played high school sports show significantly less support for both outcomes. For equity policies, the drop is from 5.06 to 4.87, or 3.2 percent ($p < .05$); for the budget allocation, men who did not play high school sports allocate 4.9 percentage points more of the budget to equity initiatives ($p < .05$) – thus a history of high school sports participation among men moves them away from distributing a majority of the budget to equity initiatives.[28] We view this as a crucial finding – it suggests that participation in the sex-segregated system, one that defines high school athletics in the same way as it does college, plays a role in socializing men to oppose gender equity policies. Put another way, there is a downstream consequence of segregation that undermines gender equity policy support years later.[29] While not displayed in the figure (see the chapter's appendix), we do not see the same findings for women; in fact, if anything, women who participated in high school sports move toward greater support for equity policies and equity budget allocation (but not significantly so). This might reflect downstream effects of experiencing inequalities as a member of the subordinated group.[30]

Finally, we find support for Hypothesis 5–4 (consistent with Table 5.4). Those who spend more time consuming and supporting college sports (what we call "market fan behaviors") are significantly less supportive of both gender equity policies and the gender budget allocation – respectively by 8.7 percent (5.22 to 4.70) ($p <. 01$) and 10.41 percentage points ($p < .05$).[31] Those who invest in the extant

---

[27] The Cohen's D effect sizes are small – .08 for equity policies and .09 for budget allocation.

[28] The Cohen's D effect size for both outcomes is .09 (i.e., small).

[29] Candace Parker, one of the most accomplished American women's basketball players in history, captures the unequal socialization processes from a girl's/woman's perspective, stating, "This mentality is built over time, from a fourth grader who receives a hand-me-down uniform while the boys receive brand-new ones. That's a mindset being developed through society that you're less than. It's important for people across the board to understand it's not just about college. This is high school. This is elementary..." (Kane 2022, 2).

[30] Also, the results in the appendix show no effects for those who played varsity sports in college, a much smaller and distinctive group. Likewise, we do not find a consistent impact of adult sports participation, perhaps because they are frequently coed.

[31] The respective Cohen D's effect sizes are .12 and .09. Also, the appendix results show that the fan identity variable is, in contrast, positive (and marginally significant for equity policies), illustrating the importance of differentiating self-reported identity from actual

product remain committed to the status quo more so than change that supports the marginalized group.

We thus find clear support for each of our hypotheses. While the substantive sizes of the effects may seem small, they are meaningful when one considers the nature of the barriers. The gender effect can preclude cross-sex coalitions for change among the mass public. More remarkable is that the impact of high school sports on men's attitudes endures into adulthood, even though high school sports participation concluded decades earlier for many in the sample. (We do not find differential effects by age.) And the market fan impact suggests that institutionally college sports face scant private pressures for change from fans.

On the flip side, the positive effect of having a daughter who played/plays sports is promising and it confirms the importance of familial gendered socialization experiences that, in this case, stimulate support. Yet only 18.08 percent of the sample report having a daughter who participates/participated in sports, so this socialization pathway remains an unlikely vehicle for mass change. The main takeaway is that the very factors that perpetuate the marginalization of women reconstitute themselves across early socialization experiences (in high school sports) and a marketplace that prioritizes men's sports. This undermines support that could otherwise potentially emerge through mass legislative pressure or private politics.

5.6 CONCLUSION

In this chapter, we explored attitudes among the public toward equity policies. We differentiated market fans from non-market fans based on a validated measure of behavior. Such behavior is important because fans can put pressure on the NCAA or federal governmental leaders to shift college athletic policy from the outside in. More broadly, this chapter looks at the gender equity opinions of the public who figure as key constituents of any federal law. We find that fans who invest in the college sports market exhibit less support for equity policies than the public writ large. This reflects (and fuels) the privileged status given to men in college athletics, as the advantaged group. That respondents seem to think

---

market behaviors, as behavioral outcomes are more apt to indicate decisions. Finally, note that the predicted values for market behavior differ from those presented in Table 5.4 since there we did not control for other variables and also compared respondents below and above the median score whereas here we look at minimum and maximum values.

dominantly, if not exclusively, of men's college sports when asked about college sports in general accentuates that privileged status. Fans in essence constitute a crucial "issue public" to which leadership in college sports respond. On balance, the conservatizing leanings of fans likely exert more influence (compared to non-fans) on outcomes and on an intractable status quo. Although more progressive views may be expressed at public hearings, exemplified by the perspectives with which we began the chapter, they are fewer in number.[32]

We do, though, discover that socialization processes matter among those who have daughters who play or played sports. We find that parents of sporting daughters offer greater support for equity initiatives. Yet the impact of parenting daughters is constrained by the fact that most American adults do not have athletic daughters who play or played sports. Further, we find that marginalizing institutions once again play a powerful role. Men who participated in athletic institutions that engage in sex segregation – even if that participation transpired decades earlier – are significantly less supportive of gender equity policies and budget allocation. Consequently, the enduring experiences in androcentric institutions also vitiate the otherwise positive effects of high school sports participation evident among women. We thus observe a troubling process of gendering attitudes, among men, that moves them away from supporting gender equity in college sports. More generally, these findings highlight the massive challenge facing marginalized groups: Institutions established to manage stakeholders contribute to marginalization and have far-reaching consequences. This undermines mass policy support in durable ways. Marginalizing institutions that practice sex segregation not only create barriers for change from within but they also affect policy support among the public. Institutions that govern policies socialize those impacted, thereby shaping opinions about the policies (e.g., Michener 2018; Soss 2000). In the long run, these results make clear that many factors undercut the possibilities for mass movements – or even fan movements – for change toward equity from the outside in.

---

[32] This is not to say that all the testimony at the US Department of Education hearings advocated for increased equality; the transcripts reveal wide heterogeneity in opinions.

6

Gender Equality in College Sports and Beyond

College sports is a peculiar institution, embedded in higher education in ways that both pursue and defy the broader academic mission. The purported mission of college sports remains an educational one – the core purpose of the National Collegiate Athletic Association (NCAA) is "to govern competition in a fair, safe, equitable and sportsmanlike manner, and to integrate intercollegiate athletics into higher education so that the educational experience of the student-athlete is paramount" (COIA 2017). Sports formalize play where student-athletes participate for reasons beyond intrinsic enjoyment and receive the many positive benefits of athletic participation, including access to higher educational opportunities as they enter early adulthood (see Gallup 2016; Staurowsky et al. 2020). Yet institutionalized, competitive athletics also blatantly pursue revenue streams and financial profits that benefit almost everyone except the athletes, as university administrators seek heightened school status and potential income on the backs of success-ful sports programs.[1] The race to pursue these ends frequently renders outcomes that run counter to broader educational aims (Bowen and Levin 2003; Clotfelter 2019). According to one football coach who makes more than $10 million a year: "In college, we revenue produce ... the sports that create revenue make it possible for all of those [other] sports to exist" (Blinder 2021). With market forces according unequal opportunities for television contracts and ticket sales to some sports and not others, the American sports culture and current intercollegiate

---

[1] Most NCAA colleges and universities retain non-profit status, though there are a small number of for-profit schools in the NCAA.

athletics system allocates monetary value unevenly across teams which then requires institutions to balance competing values, often in lopsided ways (Shulman and Bowen 2000).

College sports also are an overtly gendered realm. Sex-segregated spaces and male-dominated leadership that have been thoroughly critiqued elsewhere persist in college sports, highlighting additional tensions within the educational mission. Sex-based segregation endures in sports as a legal policy practice, separating (and thereby reifying problematic ideas about) social groups in ways that are illegal in other domains. On issues of race, the US Supreme Court justices concluded in *Brown v. Board of Education*, that "in the field of public education the doctrine of 'separate but equal' has no place. Separate educational facilities are inherently unequal" (*Brown, 397 U.S. at 495*). Although eradicating de facto racial segregation has proven to be excruciatingly difficult (see Anderson 2010), such critique of "separate but equal" logics are now widely applied, at least in principle.[2] De jure integration based on race, sex, disability status, religion, and other categories of difference permeates nearly all spheres of public education. School-sponsored sports, with their sex-segregated teams, remain a glaring exception.[3]

Similarly, many bemoan persistently male-dominated leadership in other sectors of education. A 2018 article asked, "where are all the female college presidents?", noting that only 30 percent of them are women (Moody 2018). This is similar in number to the only 31 percent of full-time female faculty members in US higher education despite five decades of Title IX's implementation in graduate education, a percentage one scholarly expert described as leaving her in a "somber mood" (Kelly 2019).[4] Even so, such comparative statistics dwarf the proportions of women head coaches (21 percent) and head athletic directors (20 percent) (HigherEd Direct 2018; also see Chapter 4), revealing athletics as a laggard even compared to troubling benchmarks.

The impacts of sex segregation and androcentrism on inequality in college sports remain clear. The events of the 2021 NCAA basketball

---

[2] In practice, the road to racial integration is undeniably unfulfilled. Our point is that ideas about segregation in education have been more thoroughly critiqued than have sex-segregated athletics.

[3] Legal jurisprudence and de facto practice have largely worked to eradicate sex exclusionary and segregated structures in nearly every other venue of American life (see, e.g., English 2016; Strum 2004; Turk 2016; Williams 2016).

[4] Among other impacts, the lack of women and gender-diverse faculty undermines research quality given evidence that gender-diverse teams produce more novel and higher-impact scientific ideas (Yang et al. 2022).

tournaments that we weave throughout this book underscore the argument advanced by McDonagh and Pappano (2007) fifteen years ago, that separate is *not* equal in contemporary college sports. Recent evidence abounds of inferior facilities, scheduling, and support for women's athletics. In short, college sports operate as a segregated, economic industry overseen by and largely to the benefit of men. Though such problems are not absent elsewhere in American higher education, they are acute in college sports.

From this perspective, it may be surprising how much celebration accompanies each legislative anniversary of Title IX. Yet even current inequalities look good compared to the circumstances of women's exclusion from sports in 1972. Fifty years hence, such exclusion remains the implicit counterfactual embedded in logics that celebrate the "success" of Title IX. While battles over Title IX's implementation accomplished a tremendous amount, the limits of the policy remain substantial. We offer the analyses in this book to decenter outdated comparisons as the contemporary yardstick for success. As much as Title IX stimulated institutional evolution, it also reinscribed organizational and participatory logics that, in other areas of education, are now eschewed. This book draws to the fore the consequences of sex segregation, male-dominated leadership, and the capitulation toward economic incentives in college sports for gender equity attitudes – showing that they vitiate support for gendered equality, making it difficult to provoke change. A summary of our argument is as follows.

- Despite the passage of Title IX fifty years ago – a law that forbids discrimination in education based on sex – vast inequalities remain between women's and men's college sports programs. These are evident in participation opportunities, expenditures, and the composition of athletic leadership.
- Gender equity initiatives, such as requiring equal opportunities, equal expenditures, and affirmative interviewing of female candidates for leadership positions, could be implemented to address the inequalities in the status quo.
- Policy change towards these equity initiatives could be pursued by student-athletes, coaches and athletic administrators, or the American public, including college sports fans.
- Student-athletes could best pursue such initiatives by creating advocacy coalitions between men and women. This is viable when there are cross-sex interactions that educate men to the plight of women and when male student-athletes (as the empowered majority group)

trust their schools and the NCAA. However, sex segregation in college sports minimizes such interactions, creating a hurdle for change from "below."

- Coaches and athletic administrators could best pursue the initiatives with representation and guidance from leaders, women in particular, pushing for change on behalf of women's interests. Although men *or* women could lead on such change, female leaders exhibit substantially greater support for equity initiatives than male leaders. However, the organizational culture in college sports – where men remain a vast numeric majority – socializes and/or selects women leaders to be less supportive of equity initiatives than those whose interests they represent, that is, female student-athletes. Women who advance up the administrative hierarchy to become heads of athletic departments or head coaches are especially apt to be less supportive of equity. Those best positioned to lead from the top are the least likely to support change. Thus, the organizational culture in the institutions that govern college sports creates a hurdle for change from "above."
- The public could best pursue the gender equity initiatives via exhibiting strong public support, particularly among those who financially invest in college sports by attending and watching games (i.e., fans). But fans exhibit substantially lower support for equity initiatives than nonfans. Further, support is lower among men who played high school sports. Thus, the socializing effects of sex segregation and the market-driven nature of college sports create hurdles for change from the "outside-in."
- These entrenched barriers reveal how structuring institutions prevent change for a marginalized group. They also show that equality will remain unfulfilled if pursued under the established regime. Equality requires institutional change.

Although we see clear lessons from this research for the realm of collegiate athletics, it also illustrates more general insights. Later in this chapter, we offer a detailed discussion of our proposed institutional transformations, but first we consider the implications of our findings for a broader context, in domains beyond college sports.

6.1 LESSONS FOR SEGREGATION, ORGANIZATIONAL CULTURE, AND POLICY FEEDBACK

The book used college sports, with its clearly defined, exogenous organizational parameters, as a case study of how institutions affect opportunities for marginalized groups, more generally. For example, the sex-based division of teams and athletic competition naturalizes sex segregation in institutional practices and thus establishes social homophily within student-athlete life (Sharrow 2017, 2021a). Likewise, men's leadership – particularly in athletic administration where men hold roughly 80 percent of the athletic director positions – remains a defining feature of college athletics. Finally, the explosion of television deals for (predominately men's) college sports broadcasts, starting in the 1980s, paved the way for an economic model of market-driven support for athletics where men's football and basketball enjoy privileged status. The exogeneity of these factors aids in understanding how segregation, organizational culture, and policy feedback (specifically via market demands) shape attitudes about policies targeting marginalized groups. In the subsections that follow, we highlight general lessons derived from our findings.

6.1.1 Segregation and Interpersonal Contact

Sports are premised on competition and thus invoke and rely on eligibility rules to pursue fairness and a purportedly equal playing field. Chief among athletic logics of "fair play" is the ubiquitous (albeit contested) notion that women require competitive venues of their own (Serrano-Durá, Molina, and Martínez-Baena 2021; Sullivan 2011). The enduring practice of dividing sports competition into sex-based venues (which occurs at all levels of competition) can make such organization seem inevitable. However, there exist various alternative models for competitive athletics that group athletes on assorted metrics. The Paralympics, for example, emphasizes "like-with-like athletes, so people of roughly equivalent levels of impairment – or roughly equal functional ability – can compete together fairly" (McGarry 2021). This leads to mixed-sex paralympic categories for rowing, archery, wheelchair rugby, shooting, and more. The 2020 Summer Olympics also included eighteen mixed-gender competitions (e.g., in badminton, equestrian, tennis, swimming relays).[5] Similarly, youth sports are often sex integrated, organized instead on the basis of age cohorts. Other sports, like wrestling and rowing, routinely arrange competition based on weight class and group like-sized competitors often without respect to sex or gender identity.

Increasingly, scholars of policy, law, and sports studies argue that strictly sex-segregated athletics can cause as much harm as good for issues

---

[5] These Olympics were convened in 2021 due to the COVID-19 pandemic.

of gender justice (Buzuvis 2019; Leong 2018; McDonagh and Pappano 2007; Milner and Braddock 2016; Sharrow 2021a), public health (Leong and Bartlett 2019), and transgender inclusion (Buzuvis 2021; Sharrow 2021b).[6] Despite increasing dialogue among some scholars, sex segregation receives scant attention in public discourse. We recognize that for many participants and sports observers, the renegotiation and reclassification of collegiate competitive categories may seem farfetched. Yet the evidence we have presented should invite readers to take pause, particularly insofar as the findings disrupt the assumption that segregated sports currently function without negative consequences. We have shown that current modes of classification operate to the detriment of women's equal opportunity, raising important questions about alternatives.

Surely, sports reclassification would require engaging the careful critiques of gendered binaries, sexist practices, and outright misogyny that generations of feminist scholars have brought to many other aspects of social organization (see Dietz 2003). We hope that our analyses demonstrate the underappreciated negative impacts of status quo practices that make such engagement pressing. We show that in the limited circumstances in college sports where cross-sex interactions are routine, support for equity policies is higher. Thus, any increase in intermingling – formal or informal – among otherwise segregated communities has promising possibilities for those in the marginalized group. It is worth dwelling on this point, as we believe it has implications beyond our focus on sex segregation.[7]

Indeed, social scientists and historians have long studied the impacts of many kinds of segregation that continue to plague American society. These findings, while contingent and distinct to their specific historic and social contexts, hold important points of comparison to college sports. Historic de jure racial segregation in American schools, public institutions, and under Jim Crow laws has infamous legacies that continue to fuel dramatic inequalities by and for the maintenance of White supremacy (e.g., Bischoff and Reardon 2014; Sampson 2012).

---

[6] Conversations in elite athletics remain similarly (though distinctly) complicated by the shifting rules about who "counts" as a woman eligible for competition in the women's categories (Karkazis and Jordan-Young 2018; Pieper 2016).

[7] We acknowledge the basic feminist critiques about "intimate inequalities" and gendered roles – that is, gender integration in many (but not all) families makes all of the lessons prima facia different from other types of segregation. That said, the specific context we explore – hypersegregated environments found in sports – are socially constituted and therefore more similar to elements of race-based segregation and partisan segregation (i.e., what we discuss in this chapter) than are often acknowledged or discussed.

Government-authorized federal mortgage lending practices through-out the middle of the twentieth century that both relied on and natu-ralized race-based neighborhood segregation still haunt American life (Rothstein 2017). Trounstine (2018) shows how such racial segregation in American cities continues to engender vast inequalities in municipal services such as schools, clean water, garbage collection, and parks. This perverse outcome is sustained, in part, from land-use policies that restrict development and that garner support among the White popula-tion (Trounstine 2020). The downstream impacts of racial segregation in housing policy and education persistently benefit White people (e.g., Erickson 2017). Other work shows that early life experiences in racially integrated neighborhoods shape partisan identities over seventy years later (Brown et al. 2021). We perceive lessons from these distinct realms that parallel the circumstances in collegiate athletics. Much as race-based segregation maintains the illusions and empowered status of White supremacist ideologies, sex-based segregation promotes gendered domination that subordinates the status of women through false ideolo-gies of male supremacy. Structures that enact segregation on the bases of race or sex durably produce unequal, downstream outcomes that benefit privileged groups.

Yet gendered and racialized structures are not the only vehicles for enduring, politicized segregation. Scholars also document the troubling emergence of partisan segregation across the United States. Regardless of whether partisanship drives choices about where to live (c.f., Cho, Gimpel, and Hui 2013; Mummolo and Nall 2017), the evidence makes clear that partisans live in areas where they have virtually no exposure to those affiliated with the other party (Brown and Enos 2021). Lee and Bearman (2020) show that, over time, personal networks have become smaller and more homogeneous in terms of partisanship (also see Mason 2018 on partisan demographic sorting). While partisan segregation does not stem from institutionally mandated separation or from ascriptive identities, it still contributes to sectarian partisanship that fuels partisan discrimination and antidemocratic behaviors (Finkel et al. 2020). Social scientists increasingly agree that segregation in many forms remains del-eterious to democratic outcomes even as the ongoing consequences of sex-based segregation have gone largely underexamined. We hope to help change this.

A sharp focus on sex-segregated institutions reveals both the stakes and the possibilities for alternative outcomes, aimed at gender equality as well as other types of effects. In light of the evidence that group-based segregation generates negative impacts, interpersonal contact has long been seen as a route to increased tolerance and understanding between groups (Allport 1954). It is among the most-studied approaches for reducing racial prejudice (e.g., Paluck and Clark 2020) and is widely considered a robust method to reduce partisan animus (e.g., Levendusky and Stecula 2021). The effectiveness of contact on policy processes, though, remains unclear. Paluck, Green, and Green (2019, 5) state, "the jury is still out regarding the contact hypothesis and its efficacy as a policy tool." This stems from insufficient attention to how segregation impacts policy preferences and how contact could be an antidote to such segregation effects.

Our findings on efficacious contact provide insight into the effects of interpersonal relations in general. First, our operationalization of contact identified its prevalence, in terms of both cross-sex contact among student-athletes and policy beneficiary-leader contact between student-athletes and athletic administrators. We found that increased frequency of interactions renders greater impacts on policy support – that is, it is not just the presence of contact that matters but also the amount. This finding aligns with MacInnis and Page-Gould's (2015, 311) argument that the frequency of contact is key to positive outcomes (also see Amsalem and Nir 2021). This suggests the need for continued and consistent intergroup relationships (see also Dahl, Kotsadam, and Rooth 2021).

Second, our results expand scholarly understandings of contact. Our unique case study and research design differs from the bulk of prior work by focusing on policy attitudes rather than evaluations of other groups. In some sense, our focus on policy stances reveals the impact of contact on more crucial outcomes. For instance, the future politics of Title IX are more likely to depend on support for equity policies than on attitudes toward female student-athletes. Policies such as Title IX serve as the accountability mechanism for ending sex discrimination; they also act as the primary bulwark against market-driven models for college sports that accrue value to a narrow subset of men's sports that draw financial support. Analogously, contact that can reduce prejudice among White Americans toward Black Americans certainly matters, but understanding how such attitudinal shifts inform support for policies that address and institutionalize policy responses to enduring inequities likely have a larger impact.

Likewise, partisan animus can be problematic, but not as much as support for antidemocratic policies such as partisan gerrymandering or voter suppression. Voelkel et al. (2023) in fact show there is scant relationship between partisan prejudice and antidemocratic policy views. Similarly, there is no reason to expect that altering group assessments will necessarily generate policy support – particularly when such policies may upend the status of dominant groups. We demonstrate that trust in the policymaking entity constitutes a necessary ingredient for contact to stimulate a change in policy attitudes. This suggests that those who hope to employ contact interventions to pursue policy goals need to consider institutional trust despite the potential endogeneity between removing barriers to contact (e.g., desegregation and bringing people together) and maintaining trust. Indeed, our own data from the student-athlete survey in Chapter 3 reveal a perplexing scenario. In our data, we identified respondents affiliated with institutions that experienced a Title IX Office for Civil Rights (OCR) federal investigation (or lawsuit) concerning practices in athletics or policies addressing sexual misconduct or assault.[8] We find those at such institutions display significantly less trust in their schools than those at schools that did not have investigations.[9] This reveals a tension: Schools that may be most in need of reform (i.e., those under investigation by the federal government) clearly weaken trust among constituent populations that may be a crucial component in such groups pursuing equity initiatives. This reflects a perverse aspect of policy feedback: Policy or practice fails, undermines trust, and the lack of trust makes the push for reform increasingly difficult. This proves notably problematic in nondemocratic organizations, such as schools or the NCAA, since the existing leaders can be durably employed and difficult to replace. Complexities such as this demand more attention in work on contact that seeks to understand the conditions under which policies that benefit marginalized groups garner support (and cultivate coalitions) under challenging circumstances.

Third, work on interpersonal contact typically focuses on microlevel changes with little attention to the institutional setting that structures interactions. Since people typically choose their social environments, self-selection and the likelihood of resulting homophily shape many social

[8] We did this by identifying schools with a recent OCR investigation or lawsuit (on practices of athletics or on policies addressing sexual misconduct) a priori and then using unique survey links depending on whether a respondent was competing for or employed by a given type of school (e.g., a school with no recent investigation, a school with an athletic investigation).

[9] See Reynolds (2019) on the relative growth, but overall dearth, of Title IX investigations over the past three decades.

interactions (Sinclair 2012). However, the exogenous nature of sex seg-regation in college sports teams creates an underappreciated and unde-rutilized research setting for a study of controlled contact. Exogenously sex-segregated institutions are few in contemporary American society, but this setting creates an opportunity to isolate its impact. Furthermore, although few such de jure segregated institutions remain, many de facto male-dominated or male-exclusive settings persist. Consider that lead-ership in college sports exhibits notable administrative malapportion-ment where women tend to work in roles that have less power (e.g., academic advisors instead of athletic directors). Such gendered power imbalance – particularly at the top of the leadership – leads to dimin-ished contact across gendered identity groups (including among athletic administrators who are overwhelmingly men) that, in turn, undercuts policy coalitions and policy reform. Lacking such reform, men's lead-ership over college athletics also remains uncontested. These findings surely apply to many areas of the American workforce where women's leadership and fulsome incorporation remain limited or symbolic (e.g., Edelman 2016).

Institutions, even when not strictly segregated, shape communication and possible coalition formation. This has implications.[10] For example, our findings supplement Trounstine's (2018) finding that racial segrega-tion in American cities generates unequal services for marginalized groups by showing how segregation undermines interpersonal contact between different groups. This can subvert the formation of policy coalitions that could otherwise push for equality. Geographic segregation based on partisanship similarly limits interpartisan interactions, which creates space for misperceptions of political partisan rivals that can undermine policy compromise. Levendusky (2023) shows that when partisans think of friends affiliated with the other party, or engage in discussions with those from the other party, they come to perceive more common ground. This, in turn, can lead to the creation of policies that both parties might support. Our results highlight how segregation can preclude such interac-tions, making it harder for partisans to work with one another (includ-ing, presumably, on issues of gender inequality).

In sum, in most domains of life, segregation – particularly de jure, institutionalized segregation – is understood to be anathema. College

---

[10] Along these lines, Nir (2012) shows that electoral institutions shape the amount and nature of interpersonal discussion (e.g., electoral systems that breed greater competitive-ness lead to more discussion).

sports defy this logic. While debates about competitive fairness remain highly gendered in a structure where men and women rarely compete head to head, our findings highlight the importance of recognizing the limitations embedded in the status quo. Namely, how the strict limiting of cross-sex interactions negatively affects opportunities for women. Segregation presents a key difficulty in the pursuit of equity policies in large part because it marginalizes women within sporting structures. This lesson applies to any segregated context – marginalized groups in such situations may confront both material inequalities and an uphill climb to build coalitions in their interests. Contact provides a route to coalition formation but only if that contact is not prevented by societal and institutional constraints. Any understanding of policy preferences requires consideration of the institutional setting in which people form such preferences. This is a point often lost on political behavior and public policy research that rarely considers the structuring capacities of institutions for governance and representational outcomes.

These results also underscore age-old feminist concerns about the role of binaries in undermining women's full autonomy and potential. Decades of feminist critique reveal the damaging logics of "sex difference" for gendered emancipation (e.g., Dietz 2003; Fausto-Sterling 2000; Jordan-Young 2010; Kenney 1992; Richardson 2015). Our findings emphasize the urgent need to keep critical perspectives on sex-segregated institutions that are premised on such rationales, even those once developed in an attempt to serve women's needs. Much like the protective labor laws that once capped women's workforce participation are now unthinkable (see Novkov 2001; Turk 2016), the future of feminist thought must continue to target the structures of sport. That the institutions purportedly designed to "protect" women in athletic competition undermine their abilities to pursue full equality should be a wakeup call for those committed to women's rights.

Finally, segregation fuels exclusion for an increasingly gender-diverse populous. The recent uptick in proposed state-level legislation targeting transgender people reveals that sports are at the center of struggles for gendered emancipation. Between 2020 and 2023, conservative lawmakers proposed hundreds of anti-trans laws in states across the country that would restrict access to medical care, identification documents, and athletic participation for transgender people (Sharrow 2021b). By early April 2023, twenty-one states had passed anti-trans athletic bans into law. Segregated sports figured centrally in the push to exclude transgender athletes from teams for girls and women (Sharrow 2023). That we find evidence of corrosive effects of sex segregation for cisgender women and girls should underscore the point that institutions, not vulnerable and marginalized groups, must remain the target of critique in battles for gendered liberation. Strict segregation harms both cisgender and transgender athletes, a point lost in the absence of mindful critiques of the status quo (but see Schultz et al. 2022; Sharrow 2021a, 2023). Thus, we recommend that alternative structures for athletic competition move to the fore of debates over the future of college sports as doing so opens new space for less rigid competitive categories and more space for including all people in athletics.

6.1.2 Organizational Culture and Representation

At the same time, our findings bear upon the hope that incorporating women into long-standing, male-dominated institutions will necessarily lead to improved gendered outcomes. These findings add troubling but important nuance to our conclusions, illustrating that cultural change must accompany efforts to include marginalized groups. Women's leadership is necessary, if not sufficient, to gendered change. In realms where women remain excluded as leaders, their full incorporation into male-dominated sectors is also a form of change in and of itself.

While women athletic administrators and coaches have no more special obligation to advocate for gender equity than do men, they have self-interested incentives to do so – increased equity practices could lead to expanded opportunities from which they may directly benefit. Furthermore, from a representational perspective, they serve as descriptive representatives for female student-athletes. Descriptive representation, more generally, refers to leaders sharing the demographic backgrounds of the people they represent (e.g., gender, race, religion). Political institutions sometimes facilitate descriptive representation of marginalized groups to diversify legislative bodies – such as the use of electoral quotas that reserve positions for people from particular backgrounds. Research demonstrates that such quotas make gendered concerns more salient, amplifying women's voices, providing women access to leadership roles, and encouraging men in leadership positions to participate in conversations about gender equity policy (Weeks 2022). In college sports, initiatives that would require interviewing women candidates for high-level appointments could increase the descriptive presence of women leaders who might then act in the interests of female student-athletes or potentially change the engagement of historically disengaged men.[11]

Inherent in these approaches are important questions, such as whether descriptive representation will lead to substantive representation for a given group – that is, whether leaders pursue issues and policies in the interest of that group (Mansbridge 1999). Theoretically, leaders who belong to a marginalized group (e.g., women in college sport) will prioritize policies for that community and pursue them more aggressively than those who are not members of the group.[12] Sizeable literatures explore whether women leaders or representatives advocate for policies in the interests of women (see reviews in Lawless 2015; Wängnerud 2009). One of the most notable strains of work comes from a policy experiment in India: A 1993 constitutional reform reserved one-third of local council positions and one-third of all council leadership positions for women (i.e., quotas, as in the prior discussion). The reserved districts and councils rotated randomly. Scholars show that, in this case, women's leadership led to the creation and enforcement of policies that benefit women (e.g., Chattopadhyay and Duflo 2004; Iyer et al. 2012), although there was also some backlash among male constituents (Brulé 2020).[13] In the American context, evidence suggests that, at least to some extent, women legislators offer more support for women's issues (Dittmar, Sanbonmatsu, and Carroll 2018; Swers 2002), display greater responsiveness to constituents on women's issues (Butler 2014), and more frequently contact federal agencies on behalf of women constituents (Lowande, Ritchie, and Lauterbach 2019), relative to men.[14] Their presence can also have a role modeling effect that stimulates involvement among future generations (Campbell and Wolbrecht 2006; Ladam, Harden, and Windett 2018; Wolbrecht and Campbell 2007).

---

[11] Such affirmative practices to diversify other elements of higher education, like through race-conscious admissions, have proven successful, if not also contentious (Bowen and Bok 1998).

[12] There are a host of ways to think about political group representation (e.g., Mansbridge 2003); as mentioned earlier in the book, we focus on relatively basic portrayals of the most relevant types. Such basic depictions align with public narratives of possible routes to change.

[13] Beaman et al. (2012) find that the quota increased girl's career aspirations à la a role-model effect.

[14] In some instances, the results are more mixed due to exogenous agenda setting power and cross-pressures (e.g., from parties and other constituents). Other work in a comparative context shows that women pursue the end to gender-discriminatory policies (Betz, Fortunato, and O'Brien 2021) and keep electoral promises more than men (Homola 2022).

Our results illustrate that women athletic leaders show similar patterns: All else constant, female coaches and administrators exhibit greater support for gender equity initiatives than do men. However, two aspects of our findings stand out. First, we show that female leaders (particularly athletic administrators and head coaches) exhibit lower levels of support for gender equity initiatives than do female student-athletes. We theorize this stems from the male-dominated organizational culture with which women in sports leadership must cope (Darvin, Hancock, and Williams 2021). Many leadership cultures where men maintain large numeric majorities, such as those in lawmaking bodies, produce similar vectors of exclusion (c.f., Dittmar, Sanbonmatsu, and Carroll 2018). Extant research on gender and representation typically compares women policymakers (i.e., legislators) to men. We acknowledge that such comparison constitutes a meaningful baseline in our case as well; however, we also highlight other relevant dimensions of comparison such as comparing leaders' preferences to those of the constituents with whom they share descriptive features. This ideal descriptive-substantive representation process would entail women leaders reflecting the preferences of their women constituents (see, e.g., Ferland 2020; Reher 2018). In our studies, while women leaders support equity initiatives more than do men, they do not ultimately match the preferences of female student-athletes. Future work on representation could consider the more complicated task of identifying and assessing a constituent baseline instead of focusing on comparisons with other leaders. It should also explore the more fundamental perennial question of how to demand leadership on gender equality issues from empowered men.

Second, support for equity policies among women leaders notably decreases as they advance into positions of greater power – that is, heading an athletic administrative department or being a head coach. We argue that this reflects cultural entrenchment, either via women's socialization and adaptation to the organizational environment or through selection effects that enable the advancement only of those women who best adapt or conform to the extant culture. This is an intriguing aspect of descriptive-substantive representation that deserves study in other political domains. While it is understood that women leaders sometimes distance themselves from more disadvantaged women in organizations (see Chapter 4 and Strolovitch 2007), it remains unclear how advancing up an institutional hierarchy generally shapes their policy opinions.

These types of tensions around conformity and assimilation complicate narratives about descriptive representation. As detailed in

Chapter 4, a long line of theory suggests that those who lead organizations differ from nonleaders. Such distinctions though are not universal (e.g., Diefenbach 2019), so understanding the conditions under which these dynamics occur requires future inquiry. A notable aspect of college sports concerns the lack of direct accountability mechanisms between athletes and leadership; women student-athletes do not necessarily have direct input into who is hired to lead, either in coaching or administrative appointments. In other words, there is no direct parallel between the athletics hiring process and the electoral, legislative policymaking context. Their partial to full occlusion from athletic leadership selection makes it more difficult for student-athletes to ensure representation of their preferences, even within their local institutions.

At the same time, athletes have been subjected to the consequences of broader trends that more generally offer a cautionary lesson for organizations. The concomitant decrease in the number of women coaching women's teams ran parallel with the increase of opportunities for women student-athletes after Title IX. As leadership in the organization/entity become more desirable, those who hold greater power – that is, men – usurp emerging leadership opportunities even as, as our results demonstrate, they retain lower levels of support for equality while enjoying a larger share of leadership. These trends that displaced women's leadership over women's sports highlight a challenge for marginalized groups, both in advancing group members up the hierarchy to ensure the representation of their interests, and to secure the quality of their experiences. Research in other realms demonstrate that male-dominated environments tend to breed cultures permissive of sexual harassment and sex discrimination (Edelman and Cabrera 2020; NASEM 2018). This can, in effect, further marginalize women's interests (Campuzano 2019). Our finding that women in empowered positions hold opinions less supportive of equity initiatives relative to those of women lower in the hierarchy suggests clear limits for future change, particularly because their male counterparts are suboptimal allies.

6.1.3 Policy Feedback, Market Demands, and Socialization

Another relevant dynamic that can shape successive policy over time are the reactions of those with a stake in the policy itself (Mettler and Soss 2004). This introduces complicated dynamics in the political milieu. In Chapter 5, we discussed the policy feedback framework that suggests policies shape ensuing political processes, creating path dependencies that limit avenues for change. College sports purportedly aim to enhance the educational experiences of student-athletes, and Title IX requires that these opportunities should not be limited or denied on the basis of sex. The most direct beneficiaries are student-athletes, although the public retains an interest since education policy involves tax expenditures (in the case of publicly funded institutions and through federally-backed student loans available to many enrollees). The public also has a long history of weighing in on civil rights disputes as key stakeholders in federal policy (Clotfelter 2004; Lee 2002).

We explored public attitudes about gender equity initiatives. We found that those who invest in college sports (i.e., fans) are less supportive of equity. The commercialization of college sports, a trend that has accelerated in recent years with the adoption of sponsorship opportunities for student-athletes, makes the preferences of consumers salient. That these preferences might differ from those of the general public creates a normative conundrum. Many policies have commercial elements; the extent to which such market-driven pressures should influence policy implementation is unsettled. Moreover, in the quasi-private market of college athletics, debates endure about whose preferences ought to matter most – the student-athletes', the public's, or the fans'? Student-athletes could claim they experience the most direct effects of policies that determine their access to equal opportunity irrespective of market demands, but fans could argue that their consumption privileges their priorities in the market outputs. Little work explores the commercial considerations at play in the policy feedback process of such public-private realms leaving open empirical and normative questions.

Furthermore, if fans qualify as stakeholders, our findings suggest that their views (and the views of the public generally) depend on contextual, past experiences. Our data suggest that the socializing role of participation in high school sports leads men who played high school sports to be less supportive of equity initiatives than those who did not. This reveals again that institutions established by policy, that is, sex segregation in school sports, socialize individuals in ways that influence their long-term policy (and perhaps consumer) preferences. While the policy feedback framework highlights path dependency, there has been less investigation into how policies normalize perspectives in adolescence with impacts throughout the life course (but see Barnes 2021; Mettler 2005). Yet political socialization is a burgeoning area of research, particularly regarding the impact of family structure on political attitudes (e.g., Shafer and Malhotra 2011; Sharrow et al. 2018; Washington 2008). Our finding that parents with daughters who play sports are more supportive of gender equity initiatives shows that in some cases the impact is domain and context specific. Clearly, policy attitudes depend on prior socialization and the institutions that structure those experiences (see also Michener 2018).

In sum, our results reveal three nuances to the policy feedback process. First, public policies that are simultaneously enacted in a marketplace require deeper analysis of and accounting for economic forces that shape policy implementation. Second, such circumstances muddle the identification of a policy's constituency. Constituents could be those directly affected and/or those who consume or profit from the policy, particularly if intermediary leaders (i.e., athletic administrators) perceive accountability to both populations. Finally, policies can influence socialization processes that, in turn, transform policy support. This type of path dependency can contribute to policy drift – that is, a failure to appropriately update policies to reflect changing social realities (e.g., Hacker 2004). Research on policy drift is slow to focus on the challenges associated with implementing civil rights protections in a persistently unequal world.

6.2 TITLE IX'S FIFTIETH ANNIVERSARY AND BEYOND

What do these findings suggest for gender equality in sports and the possibilities for reform? We first reflect on events surrounding the fiftieth anniversary of Title IX in 2022. The anniversary drew additional scrutiny due to the glaring inequalities revealed between the 2021 NCAA women's and men's basketball tournaments, the circumstances with which we opened this book. After the release of two external reviews (KHF 2021a, 2021b), the NCAA worked to prevent a repeated display of conspicuous disparities exposed in 2021. This meant expanding the number of qualifying women's teams to match the men's tournament (sixty-eight teams), employing the March Madness branding (previously reserved only for men) at the women's games, and offering equivalent food, swag, and tournament weight rooms. As noted in Chapter 1, the 2022 women's tournament was, by most accounts, extremely successful and much more on par with the men's tournament. These changes notably reflect the demands of pressure from "below" – that is, social media activism – and from the "outside-in" – in the form of market pressures (as we next discuss). That said, it is essential to not overinterpret these changes.

Although the media attention to women's basketball remains high, the circumstances of the sport are exceptional compared to other women's sports. The future of this precise topic of equality in basketball hinges on two issues. First, the external gender equity review by Kaplan Hecker & Fink LLP (KHF) emphasizes that the NCAA has undervalued the women's tournament. Although ESPN paid $34 million for broadcast rights to the women's tournament, the NCAA bundled the rights for sale along with all the other NCAA championships except men's basketball and football (Dosh 2022).[15] The review report suggests that the women's tournament on its own could be worth between $81 million to $112 million annually when the extension is negotiated after the 2024 season. This prospective value could increase, given the substantially growing audience for women's basketball – for example, the 2023 championship game registered 12.6 million viewers, a figure on par with viewership of the 2022 National Basketball Association finals games (Adgate 2023). This dwarfed the impressive ratings from 2022, when viewership for regular season games was up 46 percent and the championship game registered 4.85 million viewers, making it the most-watched college basketball game on ESPN (men or women) since 2008 (Dosh 2022). And women college basketball players have marketed themselves more successfully – using the new name-image-likeness (NIL) rules to sign endorsement deals – than all student-athletes other than football players (Streeter 2022a).

Second, and perhaps even more crucial for the long-term equality prospects in basketball, the future hinges on what the NCAA and the conferences do with the (likely) higher financial returns.[16] Currently, the NCAA distributes revenue from the men's basketball tournament to conferences based on how well the teams from each given conference perform, thereby incentivizing conferences and schools to invest in men's basketball. In contrast, conferences are not compensated based on the performance of the women's teams, meaning there is scant investment incentive. The KHF report (2021a, 93–95) recommends a phased-in even split of future revenues based on the performance of the men's *and* women's teams. That would incentivize investments in women's basketball. As 2022 national champion South Carolina coach Dawn Staley said, "It took a lot of work to keep us where we were. I don't get it...Isn't our money green?" (Witz 2022).

---

[15] Broadcast rights for collegiate football are much more complicated and lucrative. The football national championship is not run by the NCAA but by an external firm that manages the College Football Playoff series.

[16] These decisions are likely to rest largely within the college athletic conferences (e.g., the Big Ten, SEC) given that the new NCAA constitution, adopted in January 2022, delegates more control to conferences.

These circumstances and possibilities are important, but particular. As important as changes to the highest-profile women's collegiate sports may be, basketball players account for an average of 7.3 percent of collegiate women athletes in a given year, according to the NCAA (NCAA 2021e). Beyond basketball, whether funds are used to pursue the types of gender equity initiatives we study remains far from clear. When asked about future revenue distribution, the NCAA president at the time of the 2021 tournaments stated, "There's really only just preliminary discussions about it ... Once you start talking about how you're going to divide resources, then those [discussions] are difficult" (Dosh 2022). In short, the NCAA has enacted some changes under heightened scrutiny, but the future of gender equality remains as uncertain as ever.

Thus, the larger, more looming questions about the status of inequality for women in sports require a broader lens and a more general reflection on the fiftieth anniversary of Title IX. As with previous anniversaries, the spring and summer of 2022 brought a wave of media attention to the legacies of the policy. Even in the midst of the ongoing COVID-19 pandemic, movements for racial justice, soaring inflation, and with floods, droughts, and wildfires ravaging corners of the country, a wealth of coverage around Title IX dappled the mediascape. Certainly, there was evidence of the traditional celebratory coverage – the US Postal Service released Title IX stamps, and professional sports leagues and individual college athletic departments across the country acknowledged the law on player t-shirts, jerseys, and during match-time ceremonies. President Biden noted, "This is what America is all about: possibilities" (Biden 2022).

Yet evidence of growing public detection of its incomplete implementation was equally present – a notable and important contrast to prior anniversary celebrations of the law (Whiteside and Roessner 2018). Indeed, evidence of persistent inequalities manifested in moments large and small. Interest group reports on the fiftieth anniversary, including one from the Women's Sports Foundation (Staurowsky et al. 2022), declared of the first fifty years, "we're not done yet." A four-part docuseries by award-winning producers Dawn Porter and Nicole Newnham, entitled "37 Words," aired on ESPN as a capstone on several months of network coverage. It wove athlete and activist interviews from current and former players with archival footage to acknowledge the uneven history of Title IX. Notably, it shone the spotlight on many women for whom the law's promise fell far short. Focused on the overlapping histories of sex-based discrimination through sexist exclusions, harassment, and anti-trans bigotry in sports and education, the series unflinchingly cast light on policy successes *and* failures to a nationwide audience.

Local protests emerged. Alumni of the San Diego State University (SDSU) women's rowing team, a team whose varsity status was abruptly withdrawn during the 2020–21 season, rowed to a second-place finish in the alumni division at the San Diego Crew Classic, a nationally-prominent race in the collegiate season. As they rowed past the spectator beach, their coxswain unfurled a sign that read "too many female athletes," the language employed by their athletic administration to justify cutting their team, bracing the sign into the breeze to reveal "TITLE IX" etched with black ink on her biceps. (The athletes are now suing SDSU in a class action suit seeking monetary damages for their lost opportunities.) Even the *Sports Illustrated* magazine cover commemorating the anniversary with dozens of photos of women athletes in multiple sports across several generations declared Title IX's legacy merely "The *Pursuit* of Equal Play" (emphasis added).

On June 23, fifty years after Title IX became law, the US Department of Education (DOE) released draft policy guidelines proposing changes to Title IX's enforcement regulations, aiming to "restore crucial protections for students who are victims of sexual harassment, assault, and sexbased discrimination – a critical safety net for survivors that was weakened under previous regulations" (OCR 2022). These proposed regulations culminated a sixteen-month process of review on standing equity policies advanced through the rulemaking process by the Trump administration. Executive Order 14021, announced in the early days of the Biden administration, sought new regulations to guarantee "an educational environment free from discrimination on the basis of sex, including sexual orientation or gender identity." The DOE simultaneously declared it would engage in a separate public rulemaking process regarding athletics, with draft regulations for trans inclusion open for public comment as of Spring, 2023. This despite several public opinion polls on the occasion of its fiftieth anniversary that revealed a majority of Americans know "not much" or "nothing at all" about the law (Clarke, Clement, and Guskin 2022; Igielnik 2022). Even so, by the time the public comment period on draft regulations for campus sexual misconduct concluded in September 2022, the DOE received over 235,000 comments suggesting substantial public interest in the law's future (Knott 2022). Both final revised regulations on harassment and athletics, and the future of public engagement remain to be seen.[17]

---

[17] The polarized stances of the American political parties on trans inclusion also play into these fates. The 2022 midterm election cycle coincided with policy debate, forcing DOE to strategically time the release of new sports guidelines for trans athletes and delaying equality conversations (Quilantan 2022). In the early months of 2023, anti-trans lawmaking has become entrenched on the Republican party agenda.

Certainly, we join other scholars who note that "[u]ncritically cele-
brating Title IX disguises persistent gender inequities in sport" (Hextrum
and Sethi 2022, 656; see also Schultz 2022; Sharrow 2022). Taken in
context, the legacy of Title IX at fifty is fraught and some commentators
offered critical portraits. For instance, the day after the anniversary, a
New York Times editorial entitled (in the print version) "Title IX Hasn't
Done Enough for Women's Sports" concluded,

> If Title IX has set ... girls up to believe they could be treated as equal to boys on
> the playing field or off, that delusion dissolves when real money or power is at
> stake. That's when the bulk of the athletic resources go to men, leaving the women
> those girls become to discover where our society's values really lie. As we muddle
> through the great unfinished business of Titles IX, sports are teaching girls the
> truth. We may be allowed to play, but we are still not equal. (Crouse 2022)

The direct indicators of inequality (see Chapter 1) concur with this assessment, as they remain substantively unchanged in 2022 compared to when
we first entered the field to begin collecting our data (Staurowsky et al.
2022). Even the NCAA report on the fiftieth anniversary acknowledged
that their "efforts to commemorate Title IX's 50th" and their intent to
"model gender equity" "fell short" in recent years (Wilson 2022, 2).
Additionally, evidence abounds of institutional failures to meet the needs
of American women. Several high-profile suicides of female student-
athletes in the 2021–22 school year raise concerns that changes to college
sports – resulting from the pandemic and NIL pressures – may be acutely
challenging for women who are navigating the rapid and novel commercialization dynamics of college sports (Gluckman 2022).

Mental health concerns are especially calamitous for transgender, nonbinary, and gender-diverse athletes. The NCAA abruptly withdrew its
long-standing trans athlete inclusionary guidelines in the spring of 2022
and announced, absent any consultation with stakeholders, their intent to
cede inclusion standards to the national governing body of each individual
sport. This announcement came weeks before the NCAA swimming and
diving championships to which Lia Thomas, a trans woman competing for
the University of Pennsylvania women's team, had qualified. Thomas went
on to win a national title in the Division I women's 500 freestyle (and,
just as notably, placed only fifth and eighth in the 200 and 100 freestyle,
respectively) as the first out-trans competitor to do so in college sport.[18]

---

[18] Before medically transitioning, Thomas also had a successful career in the men's events,
placing second in the men's 500-, 1,000-, and 1,650-yard freestyle at the Ivy League
championships as a sophomore in 2019.

Efforts to ban trans girls and women from the "female" categories acceler-ated during the coverage of her success, during which Fox News broadcast hundreds of anti-trans stories (Paterson 2022). In short, increased atten-tion to the women's competitive category has yet to focus on addressing the acute inequalities that define the experience of participants on women's teams. Instead, anti-trans activists have incited political panics that spread transmisogynistic content under auspices of "protecting women," all while exploiting the institutions designed to *increase* opportunities for women towards antiqueer, exclusionary aims. Increased attention to school-sponsored sports has yet to render policy proposals that would address any of the glaring concerns about sex inequality identified in our analyses (a sobering reality that should underscore the concerns our analyses reveal about the roadblocks to change).

In the same season, and the very day after Title IX's fiftieth anniver-sary, the US Supreme Court announced their ruling in the *Dobbs v. Jackson Women's Health Organization* case, effectively ending a federal constitu-tional right to abortion. Abortion rights emerged virtually simultaneous with Title IX, as the *Roe v. Wade* decision came just seven months after Title IX's passage. It is a right of notable importance to women athletes; indeed, more than 500 women athletes signed an amicus brief to the Supreme Court to defend the federal right to abortion in the recent case (Streeter 2021). Reproductive choice shapes women's athletic careers, allowing them to plan whether or when they want to give birth, timing it with consideration of important windows in their competitive careers. As Streeter (2022b) notes, "a through line connects the right to control one's body with the empower-ment and confidence that are currently sparking extraordinary success for women in sports." Simultaneously, as evidenced by the abrupt retraction of reproductive rights and the ascension of anti-trans lawmaking, gendered policing of bodies is a foremost theme in modern American politics. This contemporary environment defined by uncertainty, stasis, and regression across a host of interconnected, embodied gendered rights highlights the continued (and emerging) challenges confronting women who seek equi-table conditions in sports and education. With that in mind, we turn to our discussion of possibilities for institutional reforms.

6.3 COLLEGE SPORTS AND INSTITUTIONAL REFORM

In this concluding section, we return to our critiques of college sports and how they might be reimagined in the pursuit of gender equality. Fifty years into Title IX's implementation, such critical perspectives are necessary to guide the future of policy. Circumstances have evolved considerably since 1972. Congressional intent when crafting Title IX focused on countering sex bias, gendered exclusions, and employment discrimination in educational settings. Lawmakers primarily sought to ensure opportunities for women in the classroom and academic workplace and to safeguard women's access to colleges and graduate schools (Rose 2018). It took nearly a decade for policymakers to fully identify and specify the compliance implications and regulations for sports and about twenty years for its implementation consequences to become fully palpable (Sharrow 2017). The main governing institution of college sports – the NCAA – opposed Title IX in the first decade of its implementation and discontinued its resistance only when women's sports began to flourish. Over time, it also executed a "hostile takeover" of the Association of Intercollegiate Athletics for Women in order to secure financial rights over women's championship sports (Eckstein 2017, 27). The subsequent steady increase in women's educational and collegiate sports participation is largely remembered as evidence of Title IX's progressive impact as among the most successful and important public policies to advance the rights of American women.

As with most civil rights policies, detractors remain – for instance, critics of Title IX often claim that implementation has led to cuts in men's sports even as most schools remain noncompliant. Yet the ballooning of men's football rosters have more credibly threatened the viability of other men's sports than have women's athletics (Eckstein 2017, 28). Recall that the logics of parity in the "three-part test" consider the head count of all women versus all men, so as football rosters expand opportunities on the men's "side" in recent years many institutions have proven more apt to cut other men's teams (thereby holding the "men's numbers" at relative stasis) before they add new teams for women. Still, regressive framings that ignore these facts and pit non-football playing male athletes against women divert attention away from the persistence of considerable gender inequalities (and, as discussed in Chapter 1, have no normative, legal, or policy basis).

Stopgap measures to address inequality are similarly distracting. For instance, recall from our discussion in Chapter 1 that the 2021 NCAA championship women's softball tournament had a torrid schedule that often forced players to participate in two games a day, some that started near midnight. This contrasted with the NCAA championship men's baseball tournament that included rest days and recreational outings for players. In response to public outcry and an external review, the NCAA agreed to expand the women's tournament by two days (Johnson 2022). This suggests, as with the 2022 basketball tournament, the NCAA will make efforts to avoid gross displays of disparities. While these types of changes are welcome – even from the NCAA's perspective as it allows for more economic profit and less public criticism – they will ultimately do little to address the fundamental inequalities in opportunities and resources that cut across women's sports. In essence, the proffered changes represent only slight improvements glossed over an enduringly sexist status quo.

Just as there are path dependencies in institutional development, there is a status quo bias that shapes public perceptions of political possibilities. Many Americans, perhaps unthinkingly, consider current practice a sufficient success compared to a fifty-year-old baseline that existed prior to equity policy. We argue that this likely explains the celebratory framings of media portrayals – such as *Sports Illustrated*'s description that the policy "forever chang[ed] of the role of women in society," published on Title IX's fortieth legislative anniversary. Similar, although, as mentioned, clearly more nuanced portraits of Title IX were present on its fiftieth anniversary (including in *Sports Illustrated*). We do not aim to fully disagree; new opportunities for women athletes were a crucial and highly consequential step toward equality. Instead, we aim to bring gradation to an otherwise stale framework and to regain traction toward meaningful progress. To do so, we must acknowledge the more complicated reality in which Title IX has changed possibilities for women's lives, when it comes to sports, even as its promise remains unfulfilled.

6.3.1 Title IX and Education

Of course, institutional reforms in college sports exist in the context of the effects of Title IX in postsecondary education more broadly. Title IX prohibited schools from treating students differently based on sex, which meant that the policy outlawed exclusions in admission decisions to particular programs. The impacts are palatable: For instance, before Title IX, women earned 7 percent of law degrees and 9 percent of medical degrees; they now earn half (NCES 2014, 2021). By the 1980s, the historic trend that favored men's attainment of undergraduate degrees durably shifted and today women far outpace men in enrollment and degree completion.

The structural barriers on which we focus (i.e., sex segregation, exclusionary cultures, and market pressures) are less apparent when it comes to educational attainment – a fact that we find telling.[19] First, coeducational opportunities became normative throughout the 1960s and 1970s when even historically sex-exclusionary institutions confronted demands to change (Goldin and Katz 2011; Malkiel 2016). Further, even though women continue to be underrepresented in higher education leadership and elected office, shifts in political culture that empowered women to be educated evolved prior to Title IX extend back as early as the National Defense Education Act of 1958 and the Higher Education Act of 1965 (Rose 2018). Finally, broader cultural change has proven more tractable than policy outcomes. While discrimination and stereotypes about women lead to skewed representation in particular fields, public opinion generally now views women as equally competent as men (Eagly et al. 2020). At the same time, challenges and discrimination facing women in many areas of education persist, illustrated by the simultaneous resurgence of sexist discourses and regressive politics, and the intractable gender pay gap confronting college educated women (e.g., Manne 2017; Schaffner 2020, 2022). However we note that the relative state of equality in education more generally versus the inequalities found in athletics makes clear the necessity of ending the barriers that we identify in sports (see also Sharrow 2021a).[20] It also highlights why, when it comes to sports, equality likely requires moving beyond Title IX.

6.3.2 Moving beyond Title IX in College Sports

We have demonstrated how institutions can undermine equity initiatives. This reveals that advancing toward equality will require more than improved enforcement of Title IX. Our perspective stems foremost from the reality that after a half century, the policy in its current form has been unable to close the notable gaps that we documented. Consequently, the

---

[19] Certainly, exclusionary cultures remain deeply problematic for many women in academe, both specifically in many STEM fields (e.g., GAO 2015; Neumann 2020) and across academe more generally, as the #MeToo movement made evident (e.g., Brodsky 2021; Hirsch and Khan 2020). However much research also demonstrates the breadth and extent of cultural change (e.g., Rose 2018; Steward and Valian 2018).

[20] We also do not mean to minimize other inequalities in education; in some ways education policy has failed to adapt over time. Mettler (2016, 375) explains: "forty years ago the nation's higher-education policies helped to mitigate inequality in college-going. Today, these policies still exist but several policy effects have combined to undermine the extent to which they advance opportunity." The details are quite distinct, but they illustrate that initial policies can drift away from the original intent without policy maintenance and in some sense may even abet inverse outcomes.

prevention of discrimination hinges on the choices of (mostly male) leaders who may be insufficiently incentivized to stridently act on the interests of the marginalized group, particularly when federal enforcement has been limited and slow.

The lack of regulation around equitable spending opens the door for market considerations. And, the college sports market, as we documented, prioritizes men's sports. This facilitates vastly unequal spending on men's teams to meet skewed market demand – and such spending is not entirely inconsistent with Title IX requirements. Equity policy without equal spending mandates legally allows women to receive fewer resources.[21] Our analyses suggest that allowing market considerations to guide practice leads colleges and universities to undercut their full compliance with the intent of equality law. For instance, schools routinely violate the proportionality test of compliance as evidenced by the disproportionate allocation of athletic opportunities to men (i.e., 57 percent of student-athletes are male compared to 43 percent of undergraduates). For these reasons, we argue for increased attention to the insufficiencies of Title IX in its current interpretation, particularly on its silences toward spending.

We advance a forward-thinking assessment of policy that moves beyond current dictates and instead concurs with calls for equal spending, enhanced women's leadership opportunities, and strengthened enforcement of sexual harassment protections. Simultaneously, we highlight the structural factors that undermine policy coalitions that might best pursue these possibilities. We find that possible pathways toward these initiatives face serious roadblocks. Here our argument makes an inferential leap from microlevel evidence to macrolevel solutions. This type of shift in scale presents a long-standing intellectual challenge (e.g., Druckman and Leeper 2012; Eulau 1996). We cannot know with certainty that future alterations to institutions and cultures will necessarily lead to support for the initiatives we study, nor whether such attitudinal shifts will propel eventual change. While more work would (we believe) buoy our perspective, our analyses reveal that attention must be paid to the barriers preventing institutional change in the status quo. We are offering a blueprint for needed changes even if we are unprepared to fully detail strategies for how to pursue it. We hope that our analyses will ensure that those best poised to pursue solutions will address the trenchant roadblocks. Absent our findings, scholars or activists might misdirect their energies

---

[21] Congress debated the funding question in the 1970s but ultimately authorized the lack of an equal spending mandate (Suggs 2005).

or critique in organizing for change. We reveal that without dedicated attention to institutionalized structures, change from the bottom up, top down, or outside in remains unlikely.

6.3.3 Institutional Reforms

Thus, we suggest three institutional reforms. Our first suggestion is for college sports to move toward sex desegregation. This need not take the form of full and immediate sex integration in competition, although such an approach should not be off the table as a long-term goal.[22] Integration could take many intermediary forms that might increase cross-sex contact in ways that meaningfully reshape policy futures. It could involve a commitment to share coaching staffs, facilities, training activities, and practice schedules between men's and women's teams in ways that facilitate more contact among athletes.[23] It could involve the end of the "contact sports exemption," and secure women's right to try out for historically men's teams (see Fields 2005).[24] Integration need not be bidirectional; that is, rules that allow women to participate more easily on "men's" teams could both enable added participation for larger numbers of women athletes and facilitate increased cross-sex contact.[25]

---

[22] Indeed, the National Organization for Women argued for this stance nearly fifty years ago (Sharrow 2017). Sex integration also is fairly typical in many adult recreational sports as dictated by institutions that oversee these sports, such as the National Association of Intercollegiate Gymnastics Clubs (https://naigc.org/what-is-naigc/).

[23] Certain sports such as rowing and golf may facilitate shared arrangements (relative to other sports) due to their infrastructure (e.g., space constraints require more people to use specialized facilities at the same time). See similar analyses on possibilities for track and field (Posbergh and Jette 2022). That said, this type of partial integration also faces limitations. For instance, rowing is only infrequently sponsored at the varsity level for men due to the outsized role it often plays for women in balancing out the roster sizes of men's football (particularly at the NCAA Division I level). In these cases, it is possible to integrate women's varsity rowing facilities with men's rowing at the club level (when it exists); indeed, many men's club programs have benefited from being granted practice facilities out of varsity boathouses constructed to support women's teams, and women often cox for men's programs. That said, these circumstances can facilitate integration among athletes with different relationships to sport (i.e., varsity versus club competition) who therefore confront different stakes with respect to policy change.

[24] For example, women can be denied access to men's "contact sports" teams, including boxing, wrestling, rugby, ice hockey, football, or basketball. Likewise, if a school offers a basketball team for both women and men, the contact sports exemption effectively denies girls or women at that school even the opportunity to try out for the men's team (Fields 2005).

[25] In line with Chapter 3, some research suggests that participation on sex-integrated sports teams may be related to positive shifts in men's attitudes toward women athletes (Anderson 2008).

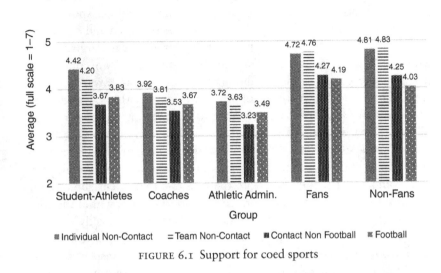

FIGURE 6.1 Support for coed sports

The possibility of coed teams is increasingly discussed among scholars who question the organization of athletics as a strictly sex-segregated system (c.f., Adjepong and Travers 2022; Leong 2018; McDonagh and Pappano 2007; Milner and Braddock 2016; Sharrow 2017, 2021a).

This begs the question of whether college athletic stakeholders support such sex integration. Each of our surveys (with the exception of the student-athlete imagined contact experiment fielded in 2020) included items that asked the extent to which respondents oppose or support allowing women, who are athletically qualified, to participate on men's teams in four different scenarios: individual noncontact sports (e.g., track, tennis, swimming), team noncontact sports (e.g., baseball, rowing, volleyball), contact sports other than football (e.g., basketball, hockey, wrestling), and men's football.[26] All were asked on 7-point scales, with higher scores reflecting more support. We report the average scores in Figure 6.1.[27]

---

[26] Title IX's aforementioned "contact sports exception" denies women the guaranteed opportunity to try out for certain types of men's teams (i.e., boxing, wrestling, rugby, ice hockey, football, basketball, "and other sports in which the purpose or major activity involves bodily contact"), so we crafted questions probing opinion with such distinctions in mind. See 34 C.F.R. § 106.41(b).

[27] The Ns and standard deviations for individual noncontact sports, team noncontact sports, contact sports other than football, and football are as follows. For student-athletes (2,529): 2.03, 2.04, 2.12, 2.15; for coaches (528): 2.16, 2.10, 2.12, 204; for administrators (862): 1.99, 1.93, 1.96, 2.09; for fans (745; 744 for football): 1.86, 1.83, 1.95, 1.99; for nonfans (749; 750 for individual noncontact): 1.88, 1.88, 1.9, 2.04.

Three points stand out. First, all groups of respondents exhibit greater support for integrated participation in noncontact sports than in contact sports (including football). Given the freighted and often sexist understandings of women's physical capacities that undergird segregated structures, we see these differences as predictable. Second, with just two exceptions (athletic administrators' opinions toward contact team sports and football), all of the scores exceed the 3.5 midpoint. There is more support than resistance to the idea of integrative possibilities. Third, student-athletes and the public (both fans and nonfans) show significantly greater support for integration of the noncontact coed teams than do coaches and administrators ($p < .01$ for all relevant comparisons). We infer from these results that latent support for integrating sports, particularly noncontact sports, exists within the constituent groups. This manifests notably among those directly affected (i.e., student-athletes) and those who consume sports; opposition comes more from those entrenched in the extant system. We suspect support would be even higher for other initiatives that promote other forms of cross-sex athletic engagement, such as integrated practice facilities, combined practices, and shared personnel. If these preferences translated into actions, the downstream effects could include increased support for equity policies, and potentially to broader conversations about integrated competition as well.

Such partial integration – whether involving more shared facilities and activities or integrated teams – could productively blur perceptions of "necessary" sex-based boundaries. This too would likely benefit transgender and gender-diverse athletes seeking access to teams that affirm their gender identity as well as the affirming social and educational benefits of sports afforded to their cisgender peers. Enabling marginalized athletes (i.e., transgender and nonbinary athletes as well as cisgender women) to select their preferred team would align with principles of nondiscrimination and increase the diversity of participants in historically male-exclusive spaces. Small cohorts of cisgender women have already begun to pursue participation in sports such as men's football (e.g., Brassil 2020; McKinney 2019); policy should fully support them and others.

Some may argue that this could have a negative effect on the success of teams historically reserved only for men – yet there is neither evidence for this claim nor does it square with the mission of college sports.[28]

[28] Notably, similar arguments were deployed to resist women's full integration into military forces, including combat units (e.g., MacKenzie 2015).

In the aforementioned words of the NCAA's mission statement, "the educational experience of the student-athlete is paramount" (COIA 2017), not their participation on certain sex-exclusive teams. Surely, learning about distinct life experiences of those involved in similar activities (i.e., sports), regardless of sex, coheres with the mission of college education (e.g., broadening horizons, building tolerance, and learning new perspectives). Integration would also invariably increase cross-sex interactions, and our data make clear these could facilitate the formation of coalitions committed to equality. In the long term, sports teams could resemble models used elsewhere in education where historically-women's colleges, for example, have become spaces for cisgender women and gender-diverse people alike, while historically men's colleges (such as the Virginia Military Institute or the Citadel) have come to admit all qualified applicants irrespective of their sex assigned at birth.[29]

Desegregation should be considered not only at the collegiate level. Extant practice makes it most imaginable in youth sports where children often have their first competitive athletic (and play) experiences in sex-integrated environments. Sports, as currently practiced, could then socialize them into gender integration that, as our data show, can have long-term effects. More assertively pursuing integrated environments for children and adolescents might help to denaturalize the seeming inevitability of collegiate segregation. Engaging this conversation (rather than operating on presumptions about "necessary" sex segregation) could enable educators to carefully consider the implications of segregation of any sort at key points in an individual's social development.[30] Part of this dialogue should involve decoupling sex segregation and the relative "seriousness" of sports competition – the former need not be a marker of the latter.[31]

---

[29] Other scholarship explores the possibilities and tensions involved in these approaches in education (Davis 2018; Nanney and Brunsma 2017; Williams 2016).

[30] Another possible initiative could entail creating more integrated experiences based on age/school year cohort. For example, all first-year students, across sports, could partake in shared (integrated) experiences such as orientations and tutoring sessions. This would align individuals in terms of their developmental experiences (and could be pursued at any level of education).

[31] As we briefly noted in Chapter 1, there are potential benefits of segregation on outcomes other than policy beliefs. Some evidence suggests Black people who live in more segregated areas exhibit greater happiness (Herbst and Lucio 2016) and less depression (except in cases of extreme segregation) (Bécares, Nazroo, and Jackson 2014). This aligns with work on how individuals from marginalized groups who find themselves in unfamiliar environments can experience negative consequences from efforts to strive and cope (e.g., Jury et al. 2017) or from experiencing microaggressions (e.g., Hernández and

A second set of reforms are needed to alter the leadership structures of college sport, including affirmative hiring of currently underrepresented candidates (i.e., women or gender-diverse people). Such concerns are creeping into the zeitgeist; for example, a 2019 *New York Times* editorial asked, "Where Are All the Women Coaches: Title IX Got Women Playing College Sports. Now It's Time to Let Them Lead" (Hutchins, Curry, and Flaherty 2019). Unfortunately, the grossly unequal representation of women in coaching and higher-level administration does not garner nearly the attention of other inequities in education. Women's incorporation into university faculty, for example, has been a longtime objective of policymakers and advocates, even as women in athletic leadership have increasingly been culled from the flock. Of course, some of this has been driven by a cruel irony; men showed scant interest in coaching women's team until the teams became more visible and highly salaried, thanks in part to Title IX. Thus, women's collegiate athletics have been captured by androcentric imperialism, a feature that serves to render women's interest more vulnerable to the caprice of men's leadership.

Addressing these trends requires both a process and a willing cohort of advocates. Although some policy change will likely come through deliberative or contentious methods (here, as everywhere), initial steps could be straightforward, as evidenced in the proposed hiring practices that we explored. Such proposals could require a shift toward requiring at least one woman be interviewed for head coaching jobs for women's teams and for athletic director appointments. While the success of such a rule in providing opportunities for racial minority coaches in the National Football League (NFL) has generated some debate (i.e., the Rooney Rule), evidence also exists for its success (e.g., DuBois 2015).[32]

Villodas 2020). This point has been made in the context of college athletics with regard to low-socioeconomic student-athletes (Druckman and Rothschild 2018). This general idea aligns with some of the concerns of why girls and women drop out of sports, more generally – due to social stigma and decreased quality of experiences (Staurowsky et al. 2020, 2022). That said, we make two points in response. First, most work finds harmful impacts of segregation on social and material outcomes (e.g., Do, Locklar, and Florsheim 2019). Second, when it comes strictly to sports sex segregation, the negative outcomes could potentially be counteracted if integration was normalized at an early age and maintained without bias.

[32] Another approach would be to institute explicit quotas requiring a certain number of women hold a set of leadership positions. For instance, the United Kingdom's Labour Party commits to having 50 percent of all winnable parliamentary seats selected from All Women Shortlists (Wäckerle 2022). The NCAA designation of a "Senior Woman Administrator" already implicitly requires the employment of at least one woman in athletic leadership.

As in the NFL, these proposals could also be unilaterally adopted by institutions and/or incentivized by the NCAA. Policy change *could* come from new forms of leadership that directly address inequalities by pursuing the initiatives we have studied. We expect that such change would require credible requests from mobilized constituencies, but it is worth at least noting that leaders retain the capacity, in many contexts, to act without awaiting a potentially high-profile social movement. We hope that some readers might consider the ways in which they can use their power to make direct policy change.

However, the most powerful possibilities for systemic change remain in activating broad-based coalitions. Women's leadership, if supported by cohort demands, can have important downstream effects. Having women in more positions of power can alter the organizational culture that vitiates support for equity policies, including among women. Even though our research design is unable to isolate the precise cultural dynamics that suppressed support for such policies among women in leadership roles (e.g., socialization, selection, or another factor), it seems clear that increasing the number of women in such positions would make a difference by increasing critical mass in the number of potential advocates. While we acknowledge the need to be cautious in asserting a specific critical mass level (Dahlerup 2006), evidence suggests that women face negative stereotyped evaluations particularly in settings where they have been historically underrepresented (Bordalo et al. 2016; Coffman 2014). This is true in sports settings: Extant work shows that one of the most notable hurdles in hiring women in sports leadership roles concerns stereotypical hiring perceptions, such as perceiving women to have more family obligations and less competence (Darvin, Hancock, and Williams 2021; Staurowsky et al. 2020).

Moreover, women accurately perceive that they receive less support from institutions where men hold the majority of positions (Born, Ranehill, and Sandberg 2022). This means that the gender composition of any group matters a great deal (e.g., Karpowitz and Mendelberg 2014). For instance, Stoddard, Karpowitz, and Preece (2021) show that "lone women" are less able to shape a group's decisions than women in majority-women groups. They further show that lone women's decreased authority stems from men's behaviors. They conclude that "the typical 'lean in' strategies cannot overcome these barriers. It is not difficult to imagine what effect this devaluation might have on women's opportunities to advance in their workplaces" (32). When there are fewer women present in an organization, there are negative consequences for women's ability to enact change; increasing the number of women is not a guarantee of change but it also can have considerable effects (especially if or when they can become a majority).

Additionally, initiatives that increase the number of women leaders can have important role-model effects. Under particular conditions, seeing women in leadership sparks the interest of girls and young women (e.g., Campbell and Wolbrecht 2006; Wolbrecht and Campbell 2017). Such proposed revisions to hiring practices could enhance the efficacy of extant NCAA women's leadership initiatives, such as WeCoach, which aims to ensure a steady pipeline of future women athletic leaders (NCAA WeCoach 2021). A robust and diverse pipeline of women is vital to ensure a broad pool of candidates for promotion to head leadership roles: a large group that seek out such jobs and then once obtaining them have enough organizational support (e.g., via a critical mass) to feel enfranchised to act.

A third set of reforms involve ensuring market insulation for college sports. A common public narrative, as noted earlier and discussed in detail in Chapter 1, holds that football and men's basketball serve as necessary revenue generators for other sports. However, this narrative is more mythos than fact; at many schools, particularly outside of the athletic top tier, those sports operate in financial deficit (Fort and Winfree 2013, chap. 1; Matheson, O'Connor, and Herberger 2012).[33] Moreover, claiming special treatment for some sports goes against the spirit of equality and the letter of the law – federal funding of colleges and universities require nondiscrimination across all programing, regardless of additional external or private funding streams. Federal student aid and loan money flow through nearly every American college and university through the students they enroll. Thus federal law holds that all higher education institutions are at least quasi-publicly funded (Sharrow 2013). We propose that funding streams directed at college sports need additional insulations against external interests, by developing policies that place limits on funders seeking to use private means to fund select sports. These limits, at the extreme, could fully prohibit private funding. Alternatively, perhaps more practical solutions could require private funding to be justified as enhancing the educational experiences of student-athletes – given that continues to be the stated goal of college sports. This might require that some portion of any external funding be directed to supporting educational/curricular programming or enhancements that directly serve the pathways to degrees for student-athletes.

---

[33] The rise of conference media subscription programs and streaming services also makes it more difficult to even identify which sports drive revenues.

Overall, the need for financial reform was cast into sharp relief with the COVID-19 pandemic. The economic burdens created by the pandemic led to the selective cutting of sports teams by colleges and universities. We found, in other work, that when these threats arose, male student-athletes were relatively quick to deprioritize equity in favor of maintaining benefits (Druckman and Sharrow 2020). More generally, we reiterate that reforms that enable schools to pay less attention to market demands and more attention to public preferences on equality could better embolden schools to implement policies such as equal spending – a practice that recent Pew polling data reveal is supported by 61 percent of Americans (Igielnik 2022). After all it is the general public, and not merely monied fans, whose interests federal laws such as Title IX should reflect.

Of course, perhaps the most straightforward route for reform entails athletic administrators across higher education, within the NCAA, and at every college and university in the country *unilaterally* acting in accordance with the proposals we put forth and studied. Support for gender equality, though varied among stakeholders, is impressively high, on average. A step back to reflect on the weight of our data affirms that Americans, whether among the general public or within targeted policy constituencies, support gender equality initiatives more than they oppose them. That athletic institutions routinely fall short of achieving equality in the face of public sentiment is telling and reflects the various institutional perversions we have identified. While we suspect that policy change *will* require broad-based coalitional support, we would be remiss not to mention that those in power *could* take action immediately without waiting for a social movement. Should this book land on the desk of college presidents, current athletic directors, or leadership of the NCAA, we hope that its lessons might stir them to do better with the resources and institutional decisions they command. Equality is in grasp for leaders with vision.

Likewise, lawmakers and bureaucrats at the federal level could take more concrete actions. We find evidence across the American public of powerful if latent support for a gender equitable future. The change already enacted through the implementation of Title IX inspires many Americans, so much so that they are often willing to overlook the nuanced policy failures that we document in favor of progressive narratives of policy success. Rather than resting on those laurels, lawmakers and federal bureaucrats could see a rare opportunity to aggressively pursue public policy that might push our society towards unrealized equality. They too could reflect on constituent demands for policy change and create enforcement provisions to bring deeper meaning to Title IX's promise.

The progressive narrative of Title IX's potential likely remains so powerful because it taps into a story about American liberalism that we as a
people desperately want to believe could be true. That we are partially,
but not yet wholly there could inspire Americans – and our political leaders in particular – to strive to do better in pursuit of a fully equal future.
An example would be better funding for the Office for Civil Rights and
increased authorization of its enforcement capacities. Policies could be
revised in accordance with the initiatives we studied. Federal funds to
support women's sports could be earmarked. All of our recommendations *could* flow from responsible lawmaking in the public interest. We
are not so naïve to believe changes come so easily, but it is worth noting
that lawmakers hold substantial power to initiate change.

On balance, as careful students of political history we recognize policy change rarely occurs without a struggle, we emphasize the need for
continued careful and critical assessments of gender equity. Our findings
reveal that the structures of college sports remain problematic. Of course,
the success of institutional reforms that we advocate remains speculative,
given inherent implementation questions and the need for broad-based
leadership to support them. Even if changes increase support for gender equality among key stakeholders, support does not ensure mobilization (given collective action challenges) and mobilization does not ensure
change. Regardless, a critical first step is to alter normative expectations.
In an athlete-centered segment honoring Title IX that was broadcast during the 2022 ESPY awards, Olympic gold medalist, Chloe Kim, suggested
an important paradigm shift: "We [must] refuse to be happy with the
minimum, because more than it has been does not mean it's where it
should be" (Lopez 2022). Our data and analyses have focused on equality in opportunities, resources, and experiences – a focus we believe
appropriate for a fifty-year retrospective on the status of Title IX. While
Title IX's implementation has advanced college athletics closer toward
women's full inclusion, it no longer suffices to attend merely on the shift
from what was to what is.

The future stories we tell about public policy need to temporally contextualize the achievements, and shortcomings of Title IX in expanding athletic opportunities for women. It is worth noting its large and
crucial impact on developing opportunities for women in the late 1970s
and the early 1980s. But success today – even by standards of participation proportionality, much less equality across other domains – has not
been met. Reflecting on Title IX at fifty, former college and professional
women's basketball coach and current broadcast announcer, Caroline

Peck noted: "We celebrate the legislation. But let's be clear, the fact that it had to exist, that it still has to exist, is a damning indictment on our culture" (Lopez 2022). Indeed, the pursuit of equal treatment has long been and will continue to be a struggle. Policy discussions must be measured against full equality, invoking more than mere participation opportunities in realizing the promise of Title IX. The quality of experience for all athletes matters as does creating a culture of upward mobility in the profession. With sports at the center of our projections about social change, how we evolve in the next fifty years of Title IX will surely hold a mirror to American society writ large. Although Title IX will always be a landmark civil rights policy worthy of celebration, staid celebrations alone are unlikely to render broader goals. Forward thinking involves acknowledging the ways in which equality remains unfulfilled.

References

Abito, Jose Muguel, David Besanko, and Daniel Diermeier. 2019. *Corporate Reputation and Social Activism: Strategic Interaction, Firm Behavior, and Social Welfare*. New York: Oxford University Press.

Absten, Sarah. 2011. "Factors That Influence Team Identification: Sport Fandom and the Need for Affiliation." MA Thesis: Western Kentucky University.

Acosta, Vivian, and Linda Carpenter. 2014. "Women in Intercollegiate Sport: A Longitudinal, National Study, Thirty Seven Year Update, 1977–2014." www.acostacarpenter.org/.

Adgate, Brad. 2023. "March Madness Finals Ratings Set a Record High For Women, Record Low for Men." *Forbes*. www.forbes.com/sites/bradadgate/2023/04/05/ratings-for-the-march-madness-finals-games-sets-a-record-high-women-and-a-record-low-men/ (April 5, 2023).

Adjepong, Anima, and Travers. 2022. "The Problem with Sex Segregated Sport." *Engaging Sport: The Society Pages*. https://thesocietypages.org/engagingsports/2022/12/09/the-problem-with-sex-segregated-sport/.

Adler, Peter, and Patricia Adler. 1985. "From Idealism to Pragmatic Detachment: The Academic Performance of College Athletes." *Sociology of Education* 58(4): 241–50.

Allport, Gordon. 1954. *The Nature of Prejudice*. Reading, MA: Addison-Wesley.

Amsalem, Eran, and Lilach Nir. 2021. "Does Interpersonal Discussion Increase Political Knowledge? A Meta-Analysis." *Communication Research* 48(5): 619–41.

Anderson, Elizabeth. 2010. *The Imperative of Integration*. Princeton, NJ: Princeton University Press.

Anderson, Eric. 2008. "'I Used to Think Women Were Weak': Orthodox Masculinity, Gender Segregation, and Sport." *Sociological Forum* 23(2): 257–80.

Andersson, Henrik, and Sirus H. Dehdari. 2021. "Workplace Contact and Support for Anti-immigration Parties." *American Political Science Review* 114(4): 1159–74.

Arvate, Paulo Roberto, Gisele Walczak Galilea, and Isabela Todescat. 2018. "The Queen Bee: A Myth? The Effect of Top-Level Female Leadership on Subordinate Females." *The Leadership Quarterly* 29(5): 533–48.

Aspen Institute. 2020. "Survey: Sports Parents Now Spend More Money on Girls than Boys." Project Play: Aspen Institute. www.aspenprojectplay.org/news/sports-parents-now-spend-more-money-on-girls-than-boys (November 9, 2020).

Associated Press (AP). 2021. "Trademark 'March Madness' Missing in Women's NCAA Tournament." Associated Press. https://apnews.com/article/womens-basketball-womens-college-basketball-basketball-trademarks-march-madness-a28035676a5d0c6d42394407b4b1fede (August 11, 2021).

Aswell, Sarah. 2018. "Female Athletes Who Are Demanding Equality in the Sports World." SheKnows.com. www.sheknows.com/entertainment/slideshow/8147/female-athletes-demanding-equality/ (December 21, 2020).

Baccellieri, Emma. 2021. "The Many Shining Disparities between Men's and Women's College Basketball." *Sports Illustrated*. www.si.com/college/2021/04/19/daily-cover-womens-tournament-equality-initiative-daily-cover (November 29, 2021).

Bahrampour, Tara, Scott Clement, and Emily Guskin. 2022. "Most Americans Oppose Trans Athletes in Female Sports, Poll Finds." *Washington Post*. www.washingtonpost.com/dc-md-va/2022/06/13/washington-post-umd-poll-most-americans-oppose-transgender-athletes-female-sports/ (June 14, 2022).

Barnes, Carolyn. 2021. *State of Empowerment: Low-Income Families and New Welfare State*. Ann Arbor, MI: University of Michigan Press.

Barnes, Carolyn, and Elan Hope. 2017. "Means-Tested Public Assistance Programs and Adolescent Political Socialization." *Journal of Youth and Adolescence* 46(7): 1611–21.

Barnett, Barbara, and Marie Hardin. 2011. "Advocacy from the Liberal Feminist Playbook: The Framing of Title IX and Women's Sports in News Releases from the Women's Sports Foundation." *International Journal of Sport Communication* 4(2): 178–97.

Baron, David P., and Daniel Diermeier. 2007. "Strategic Activism and Nonmarket Strategy." *Journal of Economics and Management Strategy* 16(3): 599–634.

Barra, Allen. 2012. "Female Athletes, Thank Nixon." *New York Times*. www.nytimes.com/2012/06/17/opinion/sunday/female-athletes-thank-nixon.html (May 20, 2020).

Bass, Amy. 2002. *Not the Triumph but the Struggle: The 1968 Olympics and the Making of the Black Athlete*. Minneapolis, MN: University of Minnesota Press.

Beaman, Lori, Esther Duflo, Rohini Pande, and Petia Topalova. 2012. "Female Leadership Raises Aspirations and Educational Attainment for Girls: A Policy Experiment in India." *Science* 335(6068): 582–86.

Bécares, Laia, James Nazroo, and James Jackson. 2014. "Ethnic Density and Depressive Symptoms among African Americans: Threshold and Differential Effects across Social and Demographic Subgroups." *American Journal of Public Health* 104(12): 2334–41.

Beck, Paul, and M. Kent Jennings. 1991. "Family Traditions, Political Periods, and the Development of Partisan Orientations." *The Journal of Politics* 53(3): 742–63.

Beckwith, Karen, and Kimberly Cowell-Meyers. 2007. "Sheer Numbers: Critical Representation Thresholds and Women's Political Representation." *Perspectives on Politics* 5(3): 553–65.

Bedolla, Lisa García. 2007. "Intersections of Inequality: Understanding Marginalization and Privilege in the Post-Civil Rights Era." *Politics & Gender* 3(2): 232–48.

Béland, Daniel, Andrea Campbell, and R. Kent Weaver. 2022. *Policy Feedback: How Policies Shape Politics*. New York: Cambridge University Press.

Belanger, Kelly. 2017 *Invisible Seasons: Title IX and the Fight for Equity in College Sports*. Syracuse, NY: Syracuse University Press.

Bell, Derrick. 2004. *Silent Covenants: Brown V. Board of Education and the Unfulfilled Hopes for Racial Reform*. New York: Oxford University Press.

Bell, Richard C. 2007. "History of Women in Sport Prior to Title IX." *The Sport Journal* 10(2). https://thesportjournal.org/article/a-history-of-women-in-sport-prior-to-title-ix/ (January 11, 2021).

Betz, Timm, David Fortunato, and Diana Z. O'Brien. 2021. "Women's Descriptive Representation and Gendered Import Tax Discrimination." *American Political Science Review* 115(1): 307–15.

Biden, Joseph. 2022. "Statement by President Joe Biden on the 50th Anniversary of Title IX." The White House Office of the Press Secretary. www.whitehouse.gov/briefing-room/statements-releases/2022/06/23/statement-by-president-joe-biden-on-the-50th-anniversary-of-title-ix/ (October 1, 2022).

Bigler, Rebecca S., and Julie Milligan Hughes. 2010. "Reasons for Skepticism about the Efficacy of Simulated Social Contact Interventions." *American Psychologist* 65(2): 132–33.

Billings, Andrew C., and Jason Edward Black. 2018. *Mascot Nation: The Controversy over Native American Representations in Sports*. Urbana-Champaign, IL: University of Illinois Press.

Billings, Andrew C., Michael L. Butterworth, and Paul D. Turman. 2017. *Communication and Sport: Surveying the Field*, 3rd ed. New York: SAGE Publications.

Bischoff, Kendra, and Sean F. Reardon. 2014. "Residential Segregation by Income, 1970–2009." In *Diversity and Disparities: America Enters a New Century*, ed. John Logan. New York: The Russell Sage Foundation, 208–33.

Blinder, Alan. 2021. "Q and A: Nick Saban, 7 Titles in, on Offenses, Defenses and Changes in College Sports." *New York Times*. www.nytimes.com/2021/08/30/sports/ncaafootball/nick-saban-alabama.html (December 6, 2021).

Blount, Rachel. 2020. "400 March to Protest Gophers' Proposed Cut of Three Men's Teams." *Star Tribune*. www.startribune.com/400-march-to-protest-gophers-proposed-cut-of-three-men-s-teams/572436372/ (September 27, 2020).

Bordalo, Pedro, Katherine Coffman, Nicola Gennaioli, and Andrei Shleifer. 2016. "Stereotypes." *Quarterly Journal of Economics* 131(4): 1753–94.

Borer, Michael Ian. 2009. "Negotiating the Symbols of Gendered Sports Fandom." *Social Psychology Quarterly* 72(1): 1–4.

Born, Andreas, Eva Ranehill, and Anna Sandberg. 2022. "Gender and Willingness to Lead: Does the Gender Composition of Teams Matter?" *The Review of Economics and Statistics* 104(2): 259–75.

Borzi, Pat. 2014. "Citing Budget, Minnesota-Duluth Cuts Ties with Women's Hockey Coach." *New York Times*: www.nytimes.com/2014/12/18/sports/citing-budget-minnesota-duluth-cuts-ties-with-womens-hockey-coach.html (July 22, 2016).

Bos, Angela, Jill Greenlee, Mirya Holman et al. 2022. "This One's for the Boys: How Gendered Political Socialization Limits Girls' Political Ambition and Interest." *American Political Science Review* 116(2): 484–501.

Boschert, Sherry. 2022. *37 Words: Title IX and Fifty Years of Fighting Sex Discrimination*. New York: The New Press.

Bowen, William, and Derek Bok. 1998. *The Shape of the River: Long-Term Consequences of Considering Race in College and University Admissions*. Princeton, NJ: Princeton University Press.

Bowen, William G., and Sarah A. Levin. 2003. *Reclaiming the Game: College Sports and Educational Values*. Princeton, NJ: Princeton University Press.

Boyle, Brett A., and Peter Magnusson. 2007. "Social Identity and Brand Equity Formation: A Comparative Study of Collegiate Sports Fans." *Journal of Sport Management* 21(4): 497–520.

Brake, Deborah. 2010. *Getting in the Game: Title IX and the Women's Sports Revolution*. New York: New York University Press.

Branch, Taylor. 2011. "The Shame of College Sports." *The Atlantic*. www.theatlantic.com/magazine/archive/2011/10/the-shame-of-college-sports/308643/ (November 1, 2020).

Brassil, Gillian. 2020. "Sarah Fuller, with a Kickoff, Is the First Woman to Play Football in a Power 5 Game." *New York Times*. www.nytimes.com/2020/11/28/sports/sarah-fuller-woman-kicker-vanderbilt.html (December 21, 2020).

Brodsky, Alexandra. 2021. *Sexual Justice: Supporting Victims, Ensuring Due Process, and Resisting the Conservative Backlash*. New York: Macmillan Publishing.

Brown, Jacob R., and Ryan D. Enos. 2021. "The Measurement of Partisan Sorting for 180 Million Voters." *Nature Human Behaviour* 5(8): 998–1008.

Brown, Jacob R., Ryan D. Enos, James Feigenbaum, and Soumyajit Mazumder. 2021. "Childhood Cross-Ethnic Exposure Predicts Political Behavior Seven Decades Later: Evidence from Linked Administrative Data." *Science Advances* 7(24): eabe8432.

Brown, Robert, and James Frank. 2006. "Race and Officer Decision Making: Examining Differences in Arrest Outcomes between Black and White Officers." *Justice Quarterly* 23(1): 96–126.

Brown, Wendy. 1988. *Manhood and Politics: A Feminist Reading in Political Theory*. Lanham, MD: Rowman & Littlefield.

    1995. *States of Injury: Power and Freedom in Late Modernity*. Princeton, NJ: Princeton University Press.

Bruch, Sarah K., Myra Marx Ferree, and Joe Soss. 2010. "From Policy to Polity: Democracy, Paternalism, and the Incorporation of Disadvantaged Citizens." *American Sociological Review* 75(2): 205–26.

Brulé, Rachel E. 2020. "Reform, Representation, and Resistance: The Politics of Property Rights' Enforcement." *Journal of Politics* 82(4): 1390–405.

Burns, Nancy, and Donald Kinder. 2012. "Categorical Politics: Gender, Race and Public Opinion." In *New Directions in Public Opinion*, ed. Adam J. Berinsky. New York: Routledge, 151–79.

Burns, Nancy, and Katherine Gallagher. 2010. "Public Opinion on Gender Issues: The Politics of Equity and Roles." *Annual Review of Political Science* 13: 425–43.

Burton, Laura J., and Sarah Leberman. 2017. *Women in Sport Leadership: Research and Practice for Change*. New York: Routledge.

Butler, Daniel. 2014. *Representing the Advantaged: How Politicians Reinforce Inequality*. New York: Cambridge University Press.

Butler, Daniel M., and Charles Crabtree. 2021. "Audit Studies in Political Science." In *Advances in Experimental Political Science*, eds. James N. Druckman, and Donald P. Green. Cambridge: Cambridge University Press, 42–55.

Buzuvis, Erin. 2006. "Survey Says ... A Critical Analysis of the New Title IX Policy and a Proposal for Reform." *Iowa Law Review* 91: 821–83.

2017. "Coaches in Court: Legal Challenges to Sex Discrimination in College Athletics." *Tennessee Journal of Race, Gender, & Social Justice* 6(1): 41–66.

2019. "Attorney General v. MIAA at Forty Years: A Critical Examination of Gender Segregation in High School Athletics in Massachusetts." *Texas Journal on Civil Liberties & Civil Rights* 25(1): 1–37.

2021. "Law, Policy, and the Participation of Transgender Athletes in the United States." *Sport Management Review* 24(3): 439–51.

Buzuvis, Erin, and Kristine Newhall. 2012. "Equality beyond the Three-Part Test: Exploring and Explaining the Invisibility of Title IX's Equal Treatment Requirement." *Marquette Sports Law Review* 22(2): 427–59.

Cahn, Susan. 1995. *Coming on Strong: Gender and Sexuality in Twentieth-Century Women's Sport*. Cambridge, MA: Harvard University Press.

Callegaro, Mario, Ana Villar, David S. Yeager, and Jon A. Krosnick. 2014. "A Critical Review of Studies Investigating the Quality of Data Obtained with Online Panels Based on Probability and Nonprobability Samples." In *Online Panel Research: A Data Quality Perspective*, eds. Mario Callegaro, Reg Baker, Jelke Bethlehem, Anja S. Göritz, Jon A. Krosnick, and Paul J. Lavrakas. Hoboken, NJ: Wiley, 23–53.

Callison, Kevin, and Aaron Lowen. 2022. "The Long-Run Effects of Adolescent Athletic Participation on Women's Health." *Economics and Human Biology* 44: 101087.

Campbell, Andrea. 2003. *How Policies Make Citizens: Senior Political Activism and the American Welfare State*. Princeton, NJ: Princeton University Press.

2012. "Policy Makes Mass Politics." *Annual Review of Political Science* 15: 333–51.

Campbell, David, and Christina Wolbrecht. 2006. "See Jane Run: Women Politicians as Role Models for Adolescents." *Journal of Politics* 68(2): 233–47.

Campuzano, Mariela V. 2019. "Force and Inertia: A Systematic Review of Women's Leadership in Male-Dominated Organizational Cultures in the United States." *Human Resource Development Review* 18(4): 437–69.

Canaday, Margot. 2009. *The Straight State: Sexuality and Citizenship in Twentieth-Century America*. Princeton, NJ: Princeton University Press.

Carroll, Susan. 2002. "Representing Women: Congresswomen's Perceptions of Their Representational Roles." In *Women Transforming Congress*, ed. Cindy Simon Rosenthal. Norman, OK: University of Oklahoma Press, 50–68.

Center for American Women in Politics (CAWP). 2021. "Women in Elective Office 2021." Center for American Women and Politics, Eagleton Institute of Politics, Rutgers University-New Brunswick. https://cawp.rutgers.edu/women-elective-office-2021 (May 20, 2021).

Chalabaev, Aïna, Philippe Sarrazin, Paul Fontayne et al. 2013. "The Influence of Sex Stereotypes and Gender Roles on Participation and Performance in Sport and Exercise: Review and Future Directions." *Psychology of Sport and Exercise* 14(2): 136–44.

Chattopadhyay, Prithviraj, Malgorzata Tluchowska, and Elizabeth George. 2004. "Identifying the Ingroup: A Closer Look at the Influence of Demographic Dissimilarity on Employee Social Identity." *The Academy of Management Review* 29(2): 180–202.

Chattopadhyay, Raghabendra, and Esther Duflo. 2004. "Women as Policy Makers: Evidence from a Randomized Policy Experiment in India." *Econometrica* 72(5): 1409–43.

Cho, Wendy K. Tam, James G. Gimpel, and Iris S. Hui. 2013. "Voter Migration and the Geographic Sorting of the American Electorate." *Annals of the Association of American Geographers* 103(4): 856–70.

Chudacoff, Howard. 2015. *Changing the Playbook: How Power, Profit, and Politics Transformed College Sports*. Urbana-Champaign, IL: University of Illinois Press.

Clarke, Liz, Scott Clement, and Emily Guskin. 2022. "Most Americans Support Gender Equity in Sports Scholarships, Poll Finds." *Washington Post*. www.washingtonpost.com/sports/2022/06/22/title-ix-poll-americans-support-gender-equity/ (August 20, 2022).

Clayton, Amanda, and Pär Zetterberg. 2018. "Quota Shocks: Electoral Gender Quotas and Government Spending Priorities Worldwide." *Journal of Politics* 80(3): 916–32.

Clotfelter, Charles T. 2004. *After Brown: The Rise and Retreat of School Desegregation*. Princeton, NJ: Princeton University Press.

2019. *Big-Time Sports in American Universities*, 2nd ed. New York: Cambridge University Press.

Coalition on Intercollegiate Athletics (COIA). 2017. "NCAA Mission Statement." www.thecoia.org/wp-content/uploads/2017/10/NCAA-Mission-Statement-COIA-version-with-NCAA-Current-Statements.pdf (December 6, 2020).

Coffman, Katherine Baldiga. 2014. "Evidence on Self-Stereotyping and the Contribution of Ideas." *The Quarterly Journal of Economics* 129(4): 1625–60.

Cohen, Cathy J. 1999. *The Boundaries of Blackness: AIDS and the Breakdown of Black Politics*. Chicago, IL: University of Chicago Press.

Commission on College Basketball (CCB). 2018. *Commission on College Basketball: Report and Recommendations to Address the Issues Facing Collegiate Basketball*. https://ncaaorg.s3.amazonaws.com/compliance/cbreform/2018CCB_ReportFinal.pdf (February 20, 2023).

Cooky, Cheryl. 2017. "'We Cannot Stand Idly By': A Necessary Call for a Public Sociology of Sport." *Sociology of Sport Journal* 34(1): 1–11.

Cooky, Cheryl, and Mary G. McDonald. 2005. "'If You Let Me Play': Young Girls' Insider-Other Narratives of Sport." *Sociology of Sport Journal* 22(2): 158–77.

Cooky, Cheryl, and Michael Messner. 2018. *No Slam Dunk: Gender, Sport and the Unevenness of Social Change*. New Brunswick, NJ: Rutgers University Press.

Cooky, Cheryl, LaToya D. Council, Maria A. Mears, and Michael A. Messner. 2021. "One and Done: The Long Eclipse of Women's Televised Sports, 1989–2019." *Communication and Sport* 9(3): 347–71.

Cowell-Meyers, Kimberly, and Laura Langbein. 2009. "Linking Women's Descriptive and Substantive Representation in the United States." *Politics & Gender* 5(4): 491–518.

Crawford, Garry, and Victoria K. Gosling. 2004. "The Myth of the 'Puck Bunny': Female Fans and Men's Ice Hockey." *Sociology* 38(3): 477–93.

Crenshaw, Kimberle. 1989. "Demarginalizing the Intersection of Race and Sex: A Black Feminist Critique of Antidiscrimination Doctrine, Feminist Theory and Antiracist Politics." *The University of Chicago Legal Forum* 39: 139–68.

——— 1991. "Mapping the Margins: Intersectionality, Identity Politics, and Violence against Women of Color." *Stanford Law Review* 43(6): 1241–99.

Crisp, Richard J., Sofia Stathi, Rhiannon N. Turner, and Senel Husnu. 2009. "Imagined Intergroup Contact: Theory, Paradigm, and Practice." *Social and Personality Psychology Compass* 3(1): 1–18.

Crouse, Lindsay. 2022. "We Can Do Better than Title IX." *New York Times.* www.nytimes.com/2022/06/22/opinion/title-ix.html (June 26, 2022).

Cunningham, George. 2015. *Diversity and Inclusion in Sport Organizations*, 3rd ed. London: Taylor & Francis.

Cunningham, George, Pamela Wicker, and Nefertiti A. Walker. 2021. "Editorial: Gender and Racial Bias in Sport Organizations." *Frontiers in Sociology* 6: 684066. https://doi.org/10.3389/fsoc.2021.684066.

Dahl, Gordon, Andreas Kotsadam, and Dan-Olof Rooth. 2021. "Does Integration Change Gender Attitudes? The Effect of Randomly Assigning Women to Traditionally Male Teams." *The Quarterly Journal of Economics* 136(2): 987–1030.

Dahl, Robert. 1971. *Polyarchy: Participation and Opposition.* New Haven, CT: Yale University Press.

Dahlerup, Drude. 2006. "The Story of the Theory of Critical Mass." *Politics & Gender* 2(4): 511–22.

Darling-Hammond, Sean, Randy T. Lee, and Rodolfo Mendoza-Denton. 2021. "Interracial Contact at Work: Does Workplace Diversity Reduce Bias?" *Group Processes and Intergroup Relations* 24(7): 1114–31.

Dartmouth College. 2020. "Dartmouth Athletics Announcement FAQ." https://dartmouthsports.com/sports/2020/7/9/athletics-announcement-faq-200709.aspx (November 19, 2020).

Darvin, Lindsey. 2020. "Voluntary Occupational Turnover and the Experiences of Former Intercollegiate Women Assistant Coaches." *Journal of Vocational Behavior* 116(A): 103349. https://doi.org/10.1016/j.jvb.2019.103349.

Darvin, Lindsey, Meg Hancock, and Sarah Williams. 2021. "Perceptions of the Sport Leadership Labyrinth through the Career Pathways of Intercollegiate Women Administrators." *SN Social Sciences.* https://doi.org/10.1007/s43545-021-00289-1.

Dauber, Michele Landis, and Meghan O. Warner. 2019. "Legal and Political Responses to Campus Sexual Assault." *Annual Review of Law and Social Science* 15: 311–33.

Davis, Alexander K. 2018. "Toward Exclusion through Inclusion: Engendering Reputation with Gender-Inclusive Facilities at Colleges and Universities in the United States, 2001–2013." *Gender & Society* 32(3): 321–47.

Davis, Heath Fogg. 2017. *Beyond Trans: Does Gender Matter?* New York: New York University Press.

Deaner, Robert, Shea Balish, and Michael Lombardo. 2016. "Sex Differences in Sports Interest and Motivation: An Evolutionary Perspective." *Evolutionary Behavioral Sciences* 10(2): 73–97.

DeBell, Matthew. 2018. "Best Practices for Creating Survey Weights." In *The Palgrave Handbook of Survey Research*, eds. David Vannette and Jon Krosnick. London: Palgrave Macmillan, 159–62.

Derks, Belle, Colette Van Laar, and Naomi Ellemers. 2006. "Striving for Success in Outgroup Settings: Effects of Contextually Emphasizing Ingroup Dimensions on Stigmatized Group Members' Social Identity and Performance Styles." *Personality and Social Psychology Bulletin* 32(5): 576–88.

2016. "The Queen Bee Phenomenon: Why Women Leaders Distance Themselves from Junior Women." *Leadership Quarterly* 27(3): 456–69.

Dhar, Diva, Tarun Jain, and Seema Jayachandran. 2022. "Reshaping Adolescents' Gender Attitudes: Evidence from a School-Based Experiment in India." *American Economic Review* 112(3): 899–927.

Diefenbach, Thomas. 2019. "Why Michels' 'Iron Law of Oligarchy' Is Not an Iron Law – and How Democratic Organisations Can Stay 'Oligarchy-Free.'" *Organization Studies* 40(4): 545–62.

Dietz, Mary G. 2003. "Current Controversies in Feminist Theory." *Annual Review of Political Science* 6: 399–431.

Dinich, Heather. 2021. "NCAA President Mark Emmert Admits Inequality but Wants Women's Basketball Leaders to Push Progress." ESPN. www.espn .com/womens-college-basketball/story/_/id/31172132/ncaa-president-mark-emmert-admits-inequality-wants-women-basketball-leaders-push-progress (August 11, 2021).

Disch, Lisa. 2011. "Toward a Mobilization Conception of Democratic Representation." *American Political Science Review* 105(1): 100–114.

Dittmar, Kelly. 2015. "Encouragement Is Not Enough: Addressing Social and Structural Barriers to Female Recruitment." *Politics & Gender* 11(4): 759–65.

Dittmar, Kelly, Kira Sanbonmatsu, and Susan Carroll. 2018. *A Seat at the Table: Congresswomen's Perspectives on Why Their Presence Matters.* New York: Oxford University Press.

Dittmar, Kelly, Kira Sanbonmatsu, Susan J. Carroll, Debbie Walsh, and Catherine Wineinger. 2017. *Representation Matters: Women in the U.S. Congress.* New Brunswick, NJ: Center for American Women and Politics, Eagleton Institute of Politics, Rutgers University.

Dixon, John, Kevin Durrheim, Colin G. Tredoux et al. 2010. "Challenging the Stubborn Core of Opposition to Equality: Racial Contact and Policy Attitudes." *Political Psychology* 31(6): 831–55.

Do, D. Phuong, Lindsay R. B. Locklar, and Paul Florsheim. 2019. "Triple Jeopardy: The Joint Impact of Racial Segregation and Neighborhood Poverty on the Mental Health of Black Americans." *Social Psychiatry and Psychiatric Epidemiology* 54(5): 533–41.

Dobbin, Frank. 2009. *Inventing Equal Opportunity*. Princeton, NJ: Princeton University Press.

Dodson, Debra L. 2006. *The Impact of Women in Congress*. New York: Oxford University Press.

Dosh, Kristi. 2022. "NCAA Bullish on Change for Women's Basketball Tournament Revenue and Distribution." *Forbes*. www.forbes.com/sites/kristidosh/2022/03/31/ncaa-bullish-on-change-for-womens-basketball-tournament-revenue-and-distribution/?sh=70efe45b2303 (May 11, 2022).

Druckman, James N. 2022. "A Framework for the Study of Persuasion." *Annual Review of Political Science* 25: 65–88.

Druckman, James N., and Donald P. Green. 2013. "Mobilizing Group Membership: The Impact of Personalization and Social Pressure E-Mails." *Sage Open* 3(2): 2158244013492781.

Druckman, James N., and Elizabeth A. Sharrow. 2020. "Public Opinion, Crisis, and Vulnerable Populations: The Case of Title IX and COVID-19." *Politics & Gender* 16(4): 1084–92.

Druckman, James N., and Jacob E. Rothschild. 2018. "Playing with Pain: Social Class and Pain Reporting among College Student-Athletes." *Sport Journal*: 1–15.

Druckman, James N., and Julia Valdes. 2019. "How Private Politics Alters Legislative Responsiveness." *Quarterly Journal of Political Science* 14(1): 115–30.

Druckman, James N., and Kjersten R. Nelson. 2003. "Framing and Deliberation: How Citizens' Conversations Limit Elite Influence." *American Journal of Political Science* 47(4): 729–45.

Druckman, James N., and Lawrence R. Jacobs. 2015. *Who Governs? Presidents, Public Opinion, and Manipulation*. Chicago, IL: University of Chicago Press.

Druckman, James N., and Matthew S. Levendusky. 2019. "What Do We Measure When We Measure Affective Polarization?" *Public Opinion Quarterly* 83(1): 114–22.

Druckman, James N., and Richard Shafranek. 2020. "The Intersection of Racial and Partisan Discrimination: Evidence from a Correspondence Study of Four-Year Colleges." *The Journal of Politics* 82(4): 1602–06.

Druckman, James N., and Thomas J. Leeper. 2012. "Learning More from Political Communication Experiments: Pretreatment and Its Effects." *American Journal of Political Science* 56(4): 875–96.

Druckman, James N., Adam J. Howat, and Andrew Rodheim. 2016. "The Influence of Race on Attitudes about College Athletics." *Sport in Society* 19(7): 1020–39.

Druckman, James N., Adam J. Howat, and Jacob E. Rothschild. 2019. "Political Protesting, Race, and College Athletics: Why Diversity among Coaches Matters." *Social Science Quarterly* 100(4): 1009–22.

Druckman, James N., Jacob Rothschild, and Elizabeth Sharrow. 2018. "Gender Policy Feedback: Perceptions of Sex Equity, Title IX, and Political Mobilization among College Athletes." *Political Research Quarterly* 71(3): 642–53.

Druckman, James N., Matthew Levendusky, and Audrey McLain. 2018. "No Need to Watch: How the Effects of Partisan Media Can Spread via Interpersonal Discussions." *American Journal of Political Science* 62(1): 99–112.

Druckman, James N., Mauro Gilli, Samara Klar, and Joshua Robison. 2014a. "Athlete Support for Title IX." *The Sport Journal*. http://thesportjournal .org/article/athlete-support-for-title-ix/.

2014b. "The Role of Social Context in Shaping Student-Athlete Opinions." *PloS ONE* 9(12): e115159.

Druckman, James N., Sophie Trawalter, Ivonne Montes, Alexandria Frenden- dall, Noah Kanter, and Allison Paige Rubenstein. 2018. "Racial Bias in Sport Medical Staff's Perceptions of Others' Pain." *Journal of Social Psychology* 158(6): 721–29.

DuBois, Cynthia. 2015. "The Impact of 'Soft' Affirmative Action Policies on Minority Hiring in Executive Leadership: The Case of the NFL's Rooney Rule." *American Law and Economics Review* 18(1): 208–33.

Eagly, Alice, and Linda Carli. 2007. "Women and the Labyrinth of Leadership." *Harvard Business Review* 85(9): 62–71.

Eagly, Alice, and Steven Karau. 2002. "Role Congruity Theory of Prejudice toward Female Leaders." *Psychological Review* 109(3): 573–98.

Eagly, Alice, Christa Nater, David Miller, Michèle Kaufmann, and Sabine Sczesny. 2020. "Gender Stereotypes Have Changed: A Cross-Temporal Meta-Analysis of U.S. Public Opinion Polls from 1946 to 2018." *American Psychologist* 75(3): 301–15.

Earnheardt, Adam, Paul Haridakis, and Barbara Hugenberg, eds. 2013. *Sports Fans, Identity, and Socialization: Exploring the Fandemonium.* Lanham, MD: Lexington Books.

Eckstein, Rick. 2017. *How College Athletics Are Hurting Girls' Sports: The Pay-to-Play Pipeline.* New York: Rowman & Littlefield.

Edelman, Lauren. 2016. *Working Law: Courts, Corporations, and Symbolic Civil Rights.* Chicago, IL: University of Chicago Press.

Edelman, Lauren, and Jessica Cabrera. 2020. "Sex-Based Harassment and Sym- bolic Compliance." *Annual Review of Law and Social Science* 16: 361–83.

Edwards, Amanda Ross. 2010. "Why Sport? The Development of Sport as a Policy Issue in Title IX of the Education Amendments of 1972." *Journal of Policy History* 22(3): 300–36.

Elchlepp, Kimberly. 2021. "Women's Championships Cap Impressive Season of Growth across ESPN Networks with Women's College World Series." ESPN. https://espnpressroom.com/us/press-releases/2021/06/womens-champion ships-cap-impressive-season-of-growth-across-espn-networks-with-wom ens-college-world-series/ (December 14, 2021).

Endres, Kyle, and Costas Panagopoulos. 2017. "Boycotts, Buycotts, and Political Consumerism in America." *Research and Politics* 4(4): 1–9.

Enemark, Daniel, Clark C. Gibson, Mathew D. McCubbins, and Brigitte Seim. 2016. "Effect of Holding Office on the Behavior of Politicians." *Proceed- ings of the National Academy of Sciences of the United States of America* 113(48): 13690–95.

English, Ashley. 2016. "Rewriting Title IX: The Department of Education's Response to Feminists' Comments in the Rulemaking Process." *Politics & Gender* 12(3): 491–517.

2021. "Is It a Four-Star Movement? Policy Transformation and the US Women's National Soccer Team's Campaign for Equal Pay." *Social Science Quarterly* 102(4): 1966–81.

Epstein, Adam, and Kathryn Kisska-Schulze. 2016. "Northwestern University, the University of Missouri, and the 'Student-Athlete': Mobilization Efforts and the Future." *Journal of Legal Aspects of Sport* 26: 71–105.

Erickson, Ansley. 2017. *Making the Unequal Metropolis: School Desegregation and Its Limits.* Chicago, IL: University of Chicago Press.

Erikson, Robert, Michael MacKuen, and James Stimson. 2002. *The Macro Polity.* New York: Cambridge University Press.

ESPN. 2020. "USWNT Lawsuit versus U.S. Soccer Explained: Defining the Pay Gaps, What's at Stake for Both Sides." ESPN Online. www.espn.com/soccer/united-states-usaw/story/4071258/uswnt-lawsuit-versus-us-soccer-explained-defining-the-pay-gapswhats-at-stake-for-both-sides (December 21, 2020).

Eulau, Heinze. 1996. *Micro-Macro Dilemmas in Political Science: Personal Pathways through Complexity.* Norman, OK: University of Oklahoma Press.

Ewing, Eve. 2020. "I'm a Black Scholar Who Studies Race, Here's Why I Capitalize 'White.'" *Medium.* https://zora.medium.com/im-a-black-scholar-who-studies-race-here-s-why-i-capitalize-white-f94883aa2dd3 (October 20, 2022).

Faludi, Susan. 1991. *Backlash: The Undeclared War against American Women.* New York: Anchor Books.

Fausto-Sterling, Anne. 2000. *Sexing the Body: Gender Politics and the Construction of Sexuality.* New York: Basic Books.

Ferland, Benjamin. 2020. "A Gender Gap in Party Congruence and Responsiveness?" *Politics & Gender* 16(1): 174–98.

Festle, Mary Jo. 1996. *Playing Nice: Politics and Apologies in Women's Sports.* New York: Columbia University Press.

Fields, Sarah. 2005. *Female Gladiators: Gender, Law, and Contact Sport in America.* Urbana-Champaign, IL: University of Illinois Press.

Fine, Cordelia. 2010. *Delusions of Gender: How Our Minds, Society, and Neurosexism Create Difference.* New York: W.W. Norton.

Finger, Leslie K. 2019. "Interest Group Influence and the Two Faces of Power." *American Politics Research* 47(4): 852–86.

Fink, Janet S., Nicole M. LaVoi, and Kristine E. Newhall. 2016. "Challenging the Gender Binary? Male Basketball Practice Players' Views of Female Athletes and Women's Sports." *Sport in Society* 19 (8–9): 1316–31.

Finkel, Eli J., Christopher A. Bail, Mina Cikara et al. 2020. "Political Sectarianism in America." *Science* 370(6516): 533–36.

Fishbein, Martin, and Icek Ajzen. 2010. *Predicting and Changing Behavior: The Reasoned Action Approach.* New York: Taylor & Francis.

Fishel, Andrew. 1976. "Organizational Positions on Title IX: Conflicting Perspectives on Sex Discrimination in Education." *The Journal of Higher Education* 47(1): 93–103.

Fishel, Andrew, and Janice Pottker. 1977. *National Politics and Sex Discrimination in Education*. Lexington, MA: Lexington Books.

Flamholtz, Eric G., and Yvonne Randle. 2014. "Implications of Organizational Life Cycles for Corporate Culture and Climate." In *The Oxford Handbook of Organizational Climate and Culture*, eds. Benjamin Schneider and Karen Barbera. New York: Oxford University Press, 235–56.

Flores, Andrew R., Donald P. Haider-Markel, Daniel C. Lewis, Patrick R. Miller, Barry L. Tadlock, and Jami K. Taylor. 2020. "Public Attitudes about Transgender Participation in Sports: The Roles of Gender, Gender Identity Conformity, and Sports Fandom." *Sex Roles* 83(5–6): 382–98.

Fording, Richard, Joe Soss, and Sanford Schram. 2011. "Race and the Local Politics of Punishment in the New World of Welfare." *American Journal of Sociology* 116(5): 1610–57.

Fort, Rodney, and Jason Winfree. 2013. *15 Sports Myths and Why They're Wrong*. Palo Alto, CA: Stanford University Press.

Fraser, Nancy. 2009. *Scales of Justice: Reimagining Political Space in a Globalizing World*. New York: Columbia University Press.

Gallup. 2016. *Understanding Life Outcomes of Former NCAA Student-Athletes*. Washington, DC: Gallup World Headquarters. www.gallup.com/services/189056/understanding-life-outcomes-former-ncaa-student-athletes.aspx (February 15, 2019).

——— 2020. "A Study of NCAA Student-Athletes: Undergraduate Experiences and Post-college Outcomes." www.gallup.com/education/312941/ncaa-student-athlete-outcomes-2020.aspx (June 1, 2020).

Galvin, Daniel J. 2012. "The Transformation of Political Institutions: Investments in Institutional Resources and Gradual Change in the National Party Committees." *Studies in American Political Development* 26(1): 50–70.

Galvin, Daniel J., and Jacob S. Hacker. 2020. "The Political Effects of Policy Drift: Policy Stalemate and American Political Development." *Studies in American Political Development* 34(2): 216–38.

Gavora, Jessica. 2002. *Tilting the Playing Field: Schools, Sports, Sex, and Title IX*. New York: Encounter Books.

Gerber, Ellen W. 1974. *The American Woman in Sport*. Boston, MA: Addison-Wesley Publishing Company.

Gilens, Martin. 2012. *Affluence and Influence*. Princeton, NJ: Princeton University Press.

Gluckman, Nell. 2022. "'It's Definitely a Crisis': Why Women in College Sports Are Struggling with Mental Health." *Chronicle of Higher Education*. www.chronicle.com/article/its-definitely-a-crisis-why-women-in-college-sports-are-struggling-with-mental-health (May 10, 2022).

Goldin, Claudia, and Lawrence F. Katz. 2011. "Putting the 'Co' in Education: Timing, Reasons, and Consequences of College Coeducation from 1835 to the Present." *Journal of Human Capital* 5(4): 377–417.

Goldman, Tom. 2012. "40 Years on, Title IX Still Shapes Female Athletes." National Public Radio. www.npr.org/2012/06/22/155529815/40-years-on-title-ix-still-shapes-female-athletes (December 21, 2022).

Goss, Kristin. 2012. *The Paradox of Gender Equality: How American Women's Groups Gained and Lost Their Public Voice*. Ann Arbor, MI: University of Michigan Press.

Grasgreen, Allie. 2012. "Equal Opportunity, Unequal Interest?" *Inside Higher Ed.* www.insidehighered.com/news/2012/11/15/lower-female-interest-sports-calls-title-ix-application-question-study-says (April 30, 2020).

Gravely, Alexis. 2021. "Thoughts from the Public on Title IX." *Inside Higher Ed.* www.insidehighered.com/news/2021/06/08/department-education-begins-title-ix-public-hearings (June 10, 2021).

Griffin, Pat. 2012. "'Ain't I a Woman?' Transgender and Intersex Student Athletes in Women's Collegiate Sports." In *Transfeminist Perspectives: In and Beyond Transgender and Gender Studies*, ed. Anne Enke. Philadelphia, PA: Temple University Press, 98–111.

Griffin, Pat, and Helen Carroll. 2010. *On the Team: Equal Opportunity for Transgender Student Athletes*. Washington, DC: National Center for Lesbian Rights. www.nclrights.org/get-help/resource/on-the-team-equal-opportunities-for-transgender-student-athletes/ (May 5, 2012).

Grossman, Joanna. 2016. *Nine to Five: How Gender, Sex, and Sexuality Continue to Define the American Workplace*. New York: Cambridge University Press.

Guiliano, Jennifer. 2015. *Indian Spectacle: College Mascots and the Anxiety of Modern America*. New Brunswick, NJ: Rutgers University Press.

Hacker, Jacob. 2004. "Privatizing Risk without Privatizing the Welfare State: The Hidden Politics of Social Policy Retrenchmen in the United States." *American Political Science Review* 98(2): 243–60.

Han, Hahrie, Elizabeth McKenna, and Michelle Oyakawa. 2021. *Prisms of the People: Power & Organizing in Twenty-First-Century America*. Chicago, IL: University of Chicago Press.

Hanlon, Philip. 2021. "Important Announcement about Athletics." Dartmouth Office of the President. https://president.dartmouth.edu/news/2021/01/important-announcement-about-athletics (November 19, 2021).

Hanson, Katherine, Vivian Guilfoy, and Sarita Pillai. 2009. *More Than Title IX: How Equity in Education Has Shaped the Nation*. Lanham, MD: Rowman & Littlefield.

Hardin, Marie, and Erin Whiteside. 2009. "Sports Reporters Divided Over Concerns about Title IX." *Newspaper Research Journal* 30(1): 58–71.

Hardin, Marie, Scott Simpson, Erin Whiteside, and Kim Garris. 2007. "The Gender War in U.S. Sport: Winners and Losers in News Coverage of Title IX." *Mass Communication & Society* 10(2): 211–33.

Harnois, Catherine E. 2017. "Intersectional Masculinities and Gendered Political Consciousness: How Do Race, Ethnicity and Sexuality Shape Men's Awareness of Gender Inequality and Support for Gender Activism?" *Sex Roles* 77(3–4): 141–54.

Hartmann, Douglas. 2003. *Race, Culture, and the Revolt of the Black Athlete: The 1968 Olympic Protests and Their Aftermath*. Chicago, IL: University of Chicago Press.

Hässler, Tabea, Johannes Ullrich, Michelle Bernardino et al. 2020. "A Large-Scale Test of the Link between Intergroup Contact and Support for Social Change." *Nature Human Behaviour* 4(4): 380–86.

Hawkesworth, Mary. 2003. "Congressional Enactments of Race–Gender: Toward a Theory of Raced–Gendered Institutions." *American Political Science Review* 97(4): 529–50.

Hawkins, Billy. 2010. *The New Plantation: Black Athletes, College Sports, and Predominantly White NCAA Institutions.* New York: Springer.

Hensley-Clancy, Molly. 2021a. "Colleges Cut Sports to Save Money amid the Pandemic, Then Came the Title IX Lawsuits." *Washington Post.* www.washingtonpost.com/sports/2021/03/25/college-sports-cuts-title-ix/ (November 24, 2021).

———. 2021b. "NCAA Vows to Improve Conditions at Women's Basketball Tournament, as Outcry Continues." *Washington Post.* www.washingtonpost.com/sports/2021/03/19/ncaa-women-basketball-weight-room/ (August 11, 2021).

———. 2021c. "Pressure Mounts on NCAA as House Democrats Demand Answers over Tournament Disparities." *Washington Post.* www.washingtonpost.com/sports/2021/03/24/ncaa-tournament-house-democrats-megan-rapinoe/ (March 25, 2021).

Herbst, Chris M., and Joanna Lucio. 2016. "Happy in the Hood? The Impact of Residential Segregation on Self-Reported Happiness." *Journal of Regional Science* 56(3): 494–521.

Hernández, Rafael J., and Miguel T. Villodas. 2020. "Overcoming Racial Battle Fatigue: The Associations between Racial Microaggressions, Coping, and Mental Health Among Chicana/o and Latina/o College Students." *Cultural Diversity and Ethnic Minority Psychology* 26(3): 399–411.

Hetherington, Marc. 2005. *Why Trust Matters: Declining Political Trust and the Demise of American Liberalism.* Princeton, NJ: Princeton University Press.

Hetherington, Marc, and Thomas J. Rudolph. 2015. *Why Washington Won't Work: Polarization, Political Trust, and the Governing Crisis.* Chicago, IL: University of Chicago Press.

Hextrum, Kirsten. 2021. *Special Admission: How College Sports Recruitment Favors White Suburban Athletes.* New Brunswick, NJ: Rutgers University Press.

Hextrum, Kirsten, and Simran Sethi. 2022. "Title IX at 50: Legitimating State Domination of Women's Sport." *International Review for the Sociology of Sport* 57(5): 655–72.

Hiatt, Shon R., Jake B. Grandy, and Brandon H. Lee. 2015. "Organizational Responses to Public and Private Politics: An Analysis of Climate Change Activists and U.S. Oil and Gas Firms." *Organization Science* 26(6): 1769–86.

HigherEdDirect. 2018. "Female Athletic Directors Almost Double Since 1990, Still Lag at D-I Programs." Higher Education Publications, Inc. https://hepinc.com/newsroom/female-athletic-directors-show-growth-since-1990-still-lag-at-d-i-programs/ (December 6, 2020).

Hill, Glynn, Des Bieler, and Cindy Boren. 2021. "As Complaints of Gender Inequity Mount, NCAA President Mark Emmert Agrees to a Review." *Washington Post.* www.washingtonpost.com/sports/2021/03/23/mark-emmert-ncaa-womens-basketball-inequity/ (November 5, 2021).

Hindman, Lauren C., and Nefertiti A. Walker. 2020. "Sexism in Professional Sports: How Women Managers Experience and Survive Sport Organizational Culture." *Journal of Sport Management* 34(1): 64–76.

Hirsch, Jennifer S., and Shamus Khan. 2020. *Sexual Citizens: A Landmark Study of Sex, Power, and Assault on Campus*. New York: W.W. Norton.

Holman, Mirya R., and Nathan P. Kalmoe. 2021. "The Polls–Trends: Sexual Harassment." *Public Opinion Quarterly* 85(2): 706–718.

Holman, Mirya R., Anna Mahoney, and Emma Hurler. 2021. "Let's Work Together: Bill Success via Women's Cosponsorship in U.S. State Legislatures." *Political Research Quarterly* 75(3): 676–90.

Homola, Jonathan. 2022. "The Effects of Women's Descriptive Representation on Government Behavior." *Legislative Studies Quarterly* 47(2): 295–308.

Honig, Bonnie. 2021. *Shell-Shocked: Feminist Criticism after Trump*. New York: Fordham University Press.

Hoover, John. 2021. "Patty Gasso: Softball Amenities Are 'Kind of Shameful; I'm Committed to Help This Change.'" *Sports Illustrated*. www.si.com/college/oklahoma/softball/patty-gasso-softball-amenities-are-kind-of-shameful-im-committed-to-help-this-change (August 11, 2021).

Hopkins, Casey S., Chris Hopkins, Samantha Kanny, and Amanda Watson. 2022. "A Systematic Review of Factors Associated with Sport Participation among Adolescent Females." *International Journal of Environmental Research and Public Health* 19(6): 3353.

Howat, Adam J. 2021. "The Role of Value Perceptions in Intergroup Conflict and Cooperation." *Politics, Groups, and Identities* 9(4): 657–80.

Htun, Mala, and S. Laurel Weldon. 2012. "The Civic Origins of Progressive Policy Change: Combating Violence against Women in Global Perspective, 1975–2005." *American Political Science Review* 106(3): 548–69.

2018. *The Logics of Gender Justice: State Action on Women's Rights around the World*. New York: Cambridge University Press.

Huckfeldt, Robert, Jeanette Mendez, and Tracy Osborn. 2004. "Disagreement, Ambivalence, and Engagement: The Political Consequences of Heterogeneous Networks." *Political Psychology* 25(1): 65–95.

Huddy, Leonie, Erin Cassese, and Mary-Kate Lizotte. 2008. "Gender, Public Opinion, and Political Reasoning." In *Political Women and American Democracy*, eds. Christina Wolbrecht, Karen Beckwith, and Lisa Baldez. New York: Cambridge University Press, 31–49.

Humberstone, Barbara. 2009. "Sport Management, Gender and the 'Bigger Picture'. Challenging Changes in Higher Education – A Partial Auto/Ethnographical Account." *Sport Management Review* 12(4): 255–62.

Husnu, Senel, and Richard John Crisp. 2011. "Enhancing the Imagined Contact Effect." *The Journal of Social Psychology* 151(1): 113–16.

Hutchins, Carol, Edniesha Curry, and Meredith Flaherty. 2019. "Where Are All the Women Coaches." *New York Times*. www.nytimes.com/2019/12/31/opinion/Women-coaching-sports-title-ix.html (December 6, 2020).

IBA Worldtour. 2021. "How Many Profitable College Football Programs?" https://ibaworldtour.com/how-many-profitable-college-football-programs/ (April 30, 2021).

Igielnik, Ruth. 2022. "Most Americans Who Are Familiar with Title IX Say It's Had a Positive Impact on Gender Equality." Pew Research Center. www.pewresearch.org/fact-tank/2022/04/21/most-americans-who-are-familiar-with-title-ix-say-its-had-a-positive-impact-on-gender-equality/ (April 29, 2022).

Iyer, Lakshmi, Anandi Mani, Prachi Mishra, and Petia Topalova. 2012. "The Power of Political Voice: Women's Political Representation and Crime in India." *American Economic Journal: Applied Economics* 4(4): 165–93.

Jacobs, Lawrence, and Suzanne Mettler. 2018. "When and How New Policy Creates New Politics: Examining the Feedback Effects of the Affordable Care Act on Public Opinion." *Perspectives on Politics* 16(2): 345–63.

Janusz, Bernadetta, and Maciej Walkiewicz. 2018. "The Rites of Passage Framework as a Matrix of Transgression Processes in the Life Course." *Journal of Adult Development* 25(3): 151–59.

Jennings, M. Kent, and Richard Niemi. 1974. *The Political Character of Adolescence: The Influence of Families and Schools.* Princeton, NJ: Princeton University Press.

Johnson, Greg. 2022. "Women's College World Series Adds Two Days." NCAA. com. www.ncaa.com/news/softball/article/2021-09-08/womens-college-world-series-adds-two-days (September 15, 2022).

Jones, Philip Edward. 2014. "Does the Descriptive Representation of Gender Influence Accountability for Substantive Representation?" *Politics & Gender* 10(2): 175–99.

Jordan-Young, Rebecca. 2010. *Brain Storm: The Flaws in the Science of Sex Differences.* Cambridge, MA: Harvard University Press.

Jury, Mickaël, Annique Smeding, Nicole M. Stephens, Jessica E. Nelson, Cristina Aelenei, and Céline Darnon. 2017. "The Experience of Low-SES Students in Higher Education: Psychological Barriers to Success and Interventions to Reduce Social-Class Inequality." *Journal of Social Issues* 73(1): 23–41.

Kaestner, Robert, and Xin Xu. 2010. "Title IX, Girls' Sports Participation, and Adult Female Physical Activity and Weight." *Evaluation Review* 34(1): 52–78.

Kalla, Joshua, and David Broockman. 2020. "Reducing Exclusionary Attitudes through Interpersonal Conversation: Evidence from Three Field Experiments." *American Political Science Review* 114(2): 410–25.

——— 2022. "Voter Outreach Campaigns Can Reduce Affective Polarization among Implementing Political Activists: Evidence from Inside Three Campaigns." *American Political Science Review* 116(4): 1516–22.

Kane, Colleen. 2022. "Q&A with Candace Parker on Her Title IX Documentary, Media Future, and Being an Icon." *Chicago Tribune.* www.chicagotribune.com/sports/sky/ct-chicago-sky-candace-parker-title-ix-documentary-20220721-mcvej6m2kzfgdnhpyjualu64zq-story.html (October 25, 2022).

Kane, Mary Jo. 2016. "A Socio-cultural Examination of a Lack of Women Coaches in Sport Leadership Positions." In *Women in Sports Coaching,* ed. Nicole M. LaVoi. New York: Routledge, 35–48.

Kane, Mary Jo, and Nicole LaVoi. 2018. "An Examination of Intercollegiate Athletic Directors' Attributions Regarding the Underrepresentation of Female Coaches in Women's Sports." *Women in Sport and Physical Activity Journal* 26(1): 3–11.

Kaplan Hecker & Fink LLP (KHF). 2021a. "NCAA External Gender Equity Review: Phase 1." https://ncaagenderequityreview.com/ (October 27, 2021). 2021b. "NCAA External Gender Equity Review: Phase II." https://ncaagendere quityreview.com/.

Karkazis, Katrina, and Rebecca Jordan-Young. 2018. "The Powers of Testosterone: Obscuring Race and Regional Bias in the Regulation of Women Athletes." *Feminist Formations* 30(2): 1–39.

Karkazis, Katrina, Rebecca Jordan-Young, Georgiann Davis, and Silvia Camporesi. 2012. "Out of Bounds? A Critique of the New Policies on Hyperandrogenism in Elite Female Athletes." *The American Journal of Bioethics* 12(7): 3–16.

Karpowitz, Christopher, and Tali Mendelberg. 2014. *The Silent Sex: Gender, Deliberation, and Institutions*. Princeton, NJ: Princeton University Press.

Katz, Matthew, Nefertiti A. Walker, and Lauren C. Hindman. 2018. "Gendered Leadership Networks in the NCAA: Analyzing Affiliation Networks of Senior Woman Administrators and Athletic Directors." *Journal of Sport Management* 32(2): 135–49.

Katzenstein, Mary Fainsod. 1998. *Faithful and Fearless: Moving Feminist Protest inside the Church and Military*. Princeton, NJ: Princeton University Press.

Keeter, Scott, Nick Hatley, Courtney Kennedy, and Arnold Lau. 2017. "What Low Response Rates Mean for Telephone Surveys." Pew Research. www .pewresearch.org/methods/2017/05/15/what-low-response-rates-mean-for-telephone-surveys/ (November 24, 2020).

Kelly, Bridget Turner. 2019. "Though More Women Are on College Campuses, Climbing the Professor Ladder Remains a Challenge." Brookings Institute. www.brookings.edu/blog/brown-center-chalkboard/2019/03/29/though-more-women-are-on-college-campuses-climbing-the-professor-ladder-remains-a-challenge/ (December 23, 2020).

Kenney, Sally Jane. 1992. *For Whose Protection?: Reproductive Hazards and Exclusionary Policies in the United States and Britain*. Ann Arbor, MI: University of Michigan Press.

Key, Vladimir Orlando. 1961. *Public Opinion and American Democracy*. New York: Knopf.

Kihl, Lisa, and Matt Soroka. 2012. "The Legitimacy of a Federal Commission as a Deliberative Democratic Process: The Case of the Secretary's Commission on Opportunity in Athletics." *Administration & Society* 45(1): 38–71.

Kihl, Lisa, Vicki Schull, and Sally Shaw. 2016. *Gender Politics in US College Athletic Departments: The Case of the University of Minnesota Merger*. New York: Springer.

Kim, Nuri, James S. Fishkin, and Robert C. Luskin. 2018. "Intergroup Contact in Deliberative Contexts: Evidence from Deliberative Polls." *Journal of Communication* 68(6): 1029–51.

Kliegman, Julie. 2021. "Current and Former Transgender College Athletes Pressure NCAA on Stance." *Sports Illustrated*. www.si.com/college/2021/05/26/current-former-transgender-college-athletes-pressure-ncaa-stance (May 26, 2021).

Klinkner, Philip, and Rogers M. Smith. 1999. *The Unsteady March: The Rise and Decline of Racial Equality in America*. Chicago, IL: University of Chicago Press.

Knott, Katherine. 2022. "Thousands Weigh in on New Title IX Rules." *Inside Higher Ed.* www.insidehighered.com/news/2022/09/14/thousands-weigh-new-title-ix-rules (September 16, 2022).

Krosnick, Jon A., and Matthew K. Berent. 1993. "Comparisons of Party Identification and Policy Preferences: The Impact of Survey Question Format." *American Journal of Political Science* 37(3): 941–64.

Kuchenbrandt, Dieta, Friederike Eyssel, and Sarah Katharina Seidel. 2013. "Cooperation Makes It Happen: Imagined Intergroup Cooperation Enhances the Positive Effects of Imagined Contact." *Group Processes and Intergroup Relations* 16(5): 635–47.

Kumar, Aishwarya. 2020. "The Heartbreaking Reality – and Staggering Numbers – of NCAA Teams Cut during the Pandemic." ESPN. www.espn.com/olympics/story/_/id/30116720/the-heartbreaking-reality-staggering-numbers-ncaa-teams-cut-pandemic (November 19, 2020).

Ladam, Christina, Jeffrey J. Harden, and Jason H. Windett. 2018. "Prominent Role Models: High-Profile Female Politicians and the Emergence of Women as Candidates for Public Office." *American Journal of Political Science* 62(2): 369–81.

Lapchick, Richard. 2020. "The 2020 Racial and Gender Report Card." The Institute for Diversity and Ethics in Sport, University of Central Florida. www.tidesport.org/racial-gender-report-card (April 20, 2021).

LaVoi, Nicole, and Anna Baeth. 2018. "Women and Sports Coaching." In *The Palgrave Handbook of Feminism and Sport, Leisure and Physical Education*, eds. Louise Mansfield, Jayne Caudwell, Belinda Wheaton, and Beccy Watson. London: Palgrave Macmillan, 149–62.

LaVoi, Nicole M., and Julia K. Dutove. 2012. "Barriers and Supports for Female Coaches: An Ecological Model." *Sports Coaching Review* 1(1): 17–37.

LaVoi, Nicole, Courtney Boucher, and Sarah Silbert. 2019. *Head Coaches of Women's Collegiate Teams: A Comprehensive Report on NCAA Division I institutions, 2018–19.* Minneapolis, MN: The Tucker Center for Research on Women and Girls in Sport.

Lawless, Jennifer. 2015. "Female Candidates and Legislators." *Annual Review of Political Science* 18: 349–66.

Lawless, Jennifer, and Richard Fox. 2005. *It Takes a Candidate: Why Women Don't Run for Office.* New York: Cambridge University Press.

2010. *It Still Takes a Candidate: Why Women Don't Run for Office.* New York: Cambridge University Press.

Lax, Jeffrey R., and Justin H. Phillips. 2009. "Gay Rights in the States: Public Opinion and Policy Responsiveness." *American Political Science Review* 103(3): 367–86.

LeBaron, Genevieve, and Peter Dauvergne. 2014. *Protest Inc.: The Corporatization of Activism.* New York: John Wiley & Sons.

LeBlanc, Diane, and Allys Swanson. 2016. *Playing for Equality: Oral Histories of Women Leaders in the Early Years of Title IX.* Jefferson, NC: McFarland & Company, Inc.

Lee, Byungkyu, and Dalton Conley. 2016. "Does the Gender of Offspring Affect Parental Political Orientation?" *Social Forces* 94(3): 1103–27.

Lee, Byungkyu, and Peter Bearman. 2020. "Political Isolation in America." *Network Science* 8(3): 333–55.

Lee, Taeku. 2002. *Mobilizing Public Opinion: Black Insurgency and Racial Attitudes in the Civil Rights Era.* Chicago, IL: University of Chicago Press.

Leong, Nancy. 2018. "Against Women's Sports." *Washington University Law Review* 95(5): 1249–90.

Leong, Nancy, and Emily Bartlett. 2019. "Sex Segregation in Sports as a Public Health Issue." *Cardozo Law Review* 40(4): 1813–56.

Leonhardt, David. 2021. "Massages for Men, Doubleheaders for Women." *New York Times.* www.nytimes.com/2021/06/04/briefing/college-sports-gender-inequality.html (June 4, 2021).

Lerman, Amy, and Katherine McCabe. 2017. "Personal Experience and Public Opinion: A Theory and Test of Conditional Policy Feedback." *The Journal of Politics* 79(2): 624–41.

Levendusky, Matthew S. 2023. *Our Common Bonds: Using What Americans Share to Help Bridge the Partisan Divide.* Chicago, IL: University of Chicago Press.

Levendusky, Matthew S., and Dominik A. Stecula. 2021. *We Need to Talk: How Cross-Party Dialogue Reduces Affective Polarization.* New York: Cambridge University Press.

Lizotte, Mary-Kate. 2017. "The Gender Gap in Public Opinion: Exploring Social Role Theory as an Explanation." In *The Political Psychology of Women in U.S. Politics,* eds. Angela Bos and Monica Schneider. New York: Routledge, 51–70.

Lopez, Isabelle. 2022. "The 2022 ESPYS, hosted by Stephen Curry, Celebrated the Biggest Achievements, Performance, and Moments of the Year in Sports." *ESPN Press Room.* https://espnpressroom.com/us/press-releases/2022/07/the-2022-espys-hosted-by-stephen-curry-celebrated-the-biggest-achieve ments-performances-and-moments-of-the-year-in-sports/ (March 1, 2023).

Lowande, Kenneth, Melinda Ritchie, and Erinn Lauterbach. 2019. "Descriptive and Substantive Representation in Congress: Evidence from 80,000 Congressional Inquiries." *American Journal of Political Science* 63(3): 644–59.

Lucivero, Gabrielle. 2021. "UConn Women's Rowers Protest School's Decision to Cut Program." NBC Connecticut. www.nbcconnecticut.com/news/sports/dog-house/uconn-womens-rowers-protest-schools-decision-to-cut-pro gram/2470123/ (September 27, 2021).

Lupia, Arthur, and Mathew McCubbins. 1998. *The Democratic Dilemma: Can Citizens Learn What They Need to Know?* New York: Cambridge University Press.

Luther, Jessica. 2016. *Unsportsmanlike Conduct: College Football and the Politics of Rape.* New York: Akashic Books.

MacInnis, Cara C., and Elizabeth Page-Gould. 2015. "How Can Intergroup Interaction Be Bad If Intergroup Contact Is Good? Exploring and Reconciling an Apparent Paradox in the Science of Intergroup Relations." *Perspectives on Psychological Science* 10(3): 307–27.

MacKenzie, Megan. 2015. *Beyond the Band of Brothers: The U.S. Military and the Myth That Women Can't Fight.* New York: Cambridge University Press.

Mahony, Daniel F., Robert Madrigal, and Dennis Howard. 2000. "Using the Psychological Commitment to Team (PCT) Scale to Segment Sport Consumers Based on Loyalty." *Sport Marketing Quarterly* 9(1): 15–25.

Malhotra, Neil, Benoit Monin, and Michael Tomz. 2019. "Does Private Regulation Preempt Public Regulation?" *American Political Science Review* 113(1): 19–37.

Malkiel, Nancy Weiss. 2016. *"Keep the Damned Women Out": The Struggle for Coeducation*. Princeton, NJ: Princeton University Press.

Manne, Kate. 2017. *Down Girl: The Logic of Misogyny*. New York: Oxford University Press.

Mansbridge, Jane. 1999. "Should Blacks Represent Blacks and Women Represent Women? A Contingent 'Yes.'" *The Journal of Politics* 61(3): 628–57.

2003. "Rethinking Representation." *American Political Science Review* 97(4): 515–28.

Markovits, Andrei S., and Emily K. Albertson. 2012. *Sportista: Female Fandom in the United States*. Philadelphia, PA: Temple University Press.

Mason, Lilliana. 2018. *Uncivil Agreement: How Politics Became Our Identity*. Chicago, IL: University of Chicago Press.

Matheson, Victor A., Debra J. O'Connor, and Joseph H. Herberger. 2012. "The Bottom Line: Accounting for Revenues and Expenditures in Intercollegiate Athletics." *International Journal of Sport Finance* 7(1): 30–45.

McCants, Rashad. 2018. *Plantation Education: The Exploitation of the Modern-Day Athlete-Student*. New York: Simon & Schuster.

McCoy, Jenny. 2020. "13 Times Women in Sports Fought for Equality." *Glamour Magazine*. www.glamour.com/story/13-times-women-in-sports-fought-for-equality (December 21, 2020).

McDonagh, Eileen. 2010. "It Takes a State: A Policy Feedback Model of Women's Political Representation." *Perspectives on Politics* 8(1): 69–91.

McDonagh, Eileen, and Laura Pappano. 2007. *Playing with the Boys: Why Separate Is Not Equal in Sports*. New York: Oxford University Press.

McGarry, Andrew. 2021. "What Are the Classifications for the Tokyo Paralympics? How Do They Work?" Australian Broadcasting Corporation. www.abc.net.au/news/2021-08-24/what-are-the-classifications-for-the-tokyo-paralympics-/100378012?utm_campaign=abc_news_web&utm_content=link&utm_medium=content_shared&utm_source=abc_news_web (December 6, 2021).

McGraw, Muffet. 2021. @Muffet McGraw (March 20, 2021). Twitter Page. https://twitter.com/MuffetMcGraw/status/1373321930485473287 (August 8, 2021).

McKinney, Kelsey. 2019. "More High School Girls Are Playing Tackle Football Than Ever." *Deadspin*. https://deadspin.com/more-high-school-girls-are-playing-tackle-football-than-1837378141 (May 8, 2020).

Meredith, Luke. 2017. "NCAA Title IX Report: Spending up, Gender Gaps Remain." Associated Press. https://apnews.com/article/7b4e53eb40094a3b8337f322b715e57a (August 15, 2020).

Mervosh, Sarah, and Christina Caron. 2019. "8 Times Women in Sports Fought for Equality." *New York Times*. www.nytimes.com/2019/03/08/sports/women-sports-equality.html?smid=url-share (December 21, 2020).

Messner, Michael. 2002. *Taking the Field: Women, Men, and Sports*. Minneapolis, MN: University of Minnesota Press.

Messner, Michael, and Nancy Solomon. 2007. "Social Justice and Men's Interests: The Case of Title IX." *Journal of Sport & Social Issues* 31(2): 162–78.

Messner, Michael, and Suzel Bozada-Deas. 2009. "Separating the Men from the Moms: The Making of Adult Gender Segregation in Youth Sports." *Gender & Society* 23(1): 49–71.

Mettler, Suzanne. 1998. *Dividing Citizens: Gender and Federalism in New Deal Public Policy.* Ithaca, NY: Cornell University Press.

2005. *Soldiers to Citizens: The G.I. Bill and the Making of the Greatest Generation.* New York: Oxford University Press.

2016. "The Policyscape and the Challenges of Contemporary Politics to Policy Maintenance." *Perspectives on Politics* 14(2): 369–90.

Mettler, Suzanne, and Joe Soss. 2004. "The Consequences of Public Policy for Democratic Citizenship: Bridging Policy Studies and Mass Politics." *Perspectives on Politics* 2(1): 55–73.

Meuleman, Bart, Koen Abts, Peter Schmidt, Thomas F. Pettigrew, and Eldad Davidov. 2020. "Economic Conditions, Group Relative Deprivation and Ethnic Threat Perceptions: A Cross-National Perspective." *Journal of Ethnic and Migration Studies* 46(3): 593–611.

Michels, Robert. 1911. *Political Parties: A Sociological Study of the Oligarchical Tendencies of Modern Democracies.* London: Jarrold and Sons.

Michener, Jamila. 2018. *Fragmented Democracy: Medicaid, Federalism, and Unequal Politics.* New York: Cambridge University Press.

Michener, Jamila, and Margaret Teresa Brower. 2020. "What's Policy Got to Do with It? Race, Gender & Economic Inequality in the United States." *Daedalus* 149(1): 100–18.

Miles, Eleanor, and Richard J. Crisp. 2014. "A Meta-Analytic Test of the Imagined Contact Hypothesis." *Group Processes & Intergroup Relations* 17(1): 3–26.

Milner, Adrienne N., and Jomills Henry Braddock. 2016. *Sex Segregation in Sports: Why Separate Is Not Equal.* New York: Praeger.

Minta, Michael D., and Nadia E. Brown. 2014. "Intersecting Interests: Gender, Race, and Congressional Attention to Women's Issues." *Du Bois Review* 11(2): 253–72.

Miscenko, Darja, and David V. Day. 2016. "Identity and Identification at Work." *Organizational Psychology Review* 6(3): 215–47.

Miyagi, Miriam, Eartha Mae Guthman, and Simón(e) Dow-Kuang Sun. 2021. "Transgender Rights Rely on Inclusive Language." *Science* 374(6575): 1568–69.

Mo, Cecilia, and Katharine M. Conn. 2018. "When Do the Advantaged See the Disadvantages of Others? A Quasi-experimental Study of National Service." *American Political Science Review* 112(4): 721–41.

Moody, Josh. 2018. "Where Are All the Female College Presidents?" *Forbes.* www.forbes.com/sites/joshmoody/2018/07/05/where-are-all-the-female-college-presidents/?sh=47ff3b334ae2 (December 6, 2020).

Mousa, Salma. 2020. "Building Social Cohesion between Christians and Muslims through Soccer in Post-ISIS Iraq." *Science* 369(6505): 866–70.

Mummolo, Jonathan, and Clayton Nall. 2017. "Why Partisans Do Not Sort: The Constraints on Political Segregation." *Journal of Politics* 79(1): 45–59.

Mummolo, Jonathan, and Erik Peterson. 2019. "Demand Effects in Survey Experiments: An Empirical Assessment." *American Political Science Review* 113(2): 517–29.

Murphy, Chris. 2019. "Madness, Inc.: How Everyone Is Getting Rich off College Sports – Except the Players." www.murphy.senate.gov/download/madness-inc (December 13, 2019).

Murray, Caitlin. 2019. *The National Team: The Inside Story of the Women Who Changed Soccer*. New York: Abrams Books.

Musto, Michela, Cheryl Cooky, and Michael A. Messner. 2017. "'From Fizzle to Sizzle!' Televised Sports News and the Production of Gender-Bland Sexism." *Gender & Society* 31(5): 573–96.

Mutz, Diana C. 2006. *Hearing the Other Side: Deliberative versus Participatory Democracy*. New York: Cambridge University Press.

Mutz, Diana C, Paul M. Sniderman, and Richard A. Brody. 1996. "Political Persuasion: The Birth of a Field of Study." In *Political Persuasion and Attitude Change*, eds. Diana C. Mutz, Paul M. Sniderman, and Richard A. Brody. Ann Arbor, MI: University of Michigan Press, 1–14.

Nair, Chenicheri Sid, Phillip Adams, and Patricie Mertova. 2008. "Student Engagement: The Key to Improving Survey Response Rates." *Quality in Higher Education* 14(3): 225–32.

Nanney, Megan, and David L. Brunsma. 2017. "Moving Beyond Cis-Terhood: Determining Gender through Transgender Admittance Policies at U.S. Women's Colleges." *Gender & Society* 31(2): 145–70.

National Academies of Sciences, Engineering, and Medicine (NASEM). 2018. *Sexual Harassment of Women: Climate, Culture, and Consequences in Academic Sciences, Engineering, and Medicine*. Washington, DC: The National Academies Press. https://nap.nationalacademies.org/catalog/24994/sexual-harassment-of-women-climate-culture-and-consequences-in-academic (May 1, 2019).

National Coalition for Women and Girls in Education (NCWGE). 2017. *Title IX at 45: Advancing Opportunity through Equity in Education*. Washington, DC: NCWGE.

———. 2022. *Title IX at 50: A Report by the National Coalition for Women and Girls in Education*. Washington, DC: NCWGE.

National Collegiate Athletic Association (NCAA). 1993. *Final Report of the NCAA Gender-Equity Task Force*. Indianapolis, IN: National Collegiate Athletic Association.

———. 2016. "Division I Time Demands Survey." www.ncaa.org/about/resources/division-i-research (June 9, 2019).

———. 2017a. *45 Years of Title IX: The Status of Women in Intercollegiate Athletics*. Indianapolis, IN: National Collegiate Athletic Association.

———. 2017b. "NCAA Board of Governors Policy on Campus Sexual Violence." www.ncaa.org/sports/2017/8/17/ncaa-board-of-governors-policy-on-campus-sexual-violence.aspx (August 1, 2022).

———. 2019a. "Estimated Probability of Competing in College Athletics." https://ncaaorg.s3.amazonaws.com/research/pro_beyond/2019RES_ProbabilityBeyondHSFiguresMethod.pdf (April 25, 2020).

———. 2019b. "NCAA GOALS Study." www.ncaa.org/about/resources/research/ncaa-goals-study (September 10, 2020).

———. 2021a. "Gender Equity and Title IX." *NCAA.org*. www.ncaa.org/about/resources/inclusion/gender-equity-and-title-ix (December 28, 2021).

2021b. "NCAA Finances." www.ncaa.org/finances (November 12, 2021).

2021c. "NCAA Gender Equity Planning: Best Practices." NCAA.org. https://ncaaorg.s3.amazonaws.com/inclusion/bestprac/NCAAInc_BestPracticeGenderEquity.pdf (December 29, 2021).

2021d. "NCAA Governance." NCAA.org. www.ncaa.org/governance (December 29, 2021).

2021e. *NCAA Sports Sponsorship and Participation Rates Report, 2021.* Indianapolis, IN: National Collegiate Athletic Association.

National Council for Educational Statistics, US Department of Education (NCES). 2014. "'Degrees and Other Formal Awards Conferred' Surveys, 1965–66 through 1985–86; Integrated Postsecondary Education Data System (IPEDS), 'Completions Survey' (IPEDS-C:87–99); IPEDS Fall 2000 through Fall 2012, Completions Component; and Degrees Conferred Pro." *Earned Degrees Conferred, 1869–70 through 1964–65; Higher Education General Information Survey (HEGIS).* http://nces.ed.gov/programs/digest/d13/tables/dt13_318.10.asp?current=yes (March 25, 2021).

2021. "Undergraduate Enrollment." *The Condition of Education 2021.* https://nces.ed.gov/programs/coe/indicator/cha (December 14, 2021).

National Women's Law Center (NWLC), and Poverty & Race Research Action Council (PRRAC). 2015. *Finishing Last: Girls of Color and School Sports Opportunities.* Washington, DC: National Women's Law Center.

Neumann, John. 2020. *GAO Reports (GAO-20-187) Sexual Harassment in STEM Research: Agencies Have Taken Actions, but Need Complaint Procedures, Overall Plans, and Better Collaboration.* Washington, DC: US Government Accountability Office.

Navajas, Gabriela Ertola, Paula A. López Villalba, Martín A. Rossi, and Antonia Vazquez. 2022. "The Long-Term Effect of Military Conscription on Personality and Beliefs." *The Review of Economics and Statistics* 104(1): 133–41.

Nir, Lilach. 2012. "Cross-National Differences in Political Discussion: Can Political Systems Narrow Deliberation Gaps?" *Journal of Communication* 62(3): 553–70.

Nixon, Howard. 2014. *The Athletic Trap: How College Sports Corrupted the Academy.* Baltimore, MD: Johns Hopkins University Press.

Norton, Anne. 2004. *Ninety-Five Theses on Politics, Culture, and Method.* New Haven, CT: Yale University Press.

Novkov, Julie. 2001. *Constituting Workers, Protecting Women: Gender, Law and Labor in the Progressive Era and New Deal Years.* Ann Arbor, MI: University of Michigan Press.

O'Brien, Ruth. 2001. *Crippled Justice: The History of Modern Disability Policy in the Workplace.* Chicago, IL: University of Chicago Press.

O'Keefe, Daniel J. 2021. "Persuasive Message Pretesting Using Non-behavioral Outcomes: Differences in Attitudinal and Intention Effects as Diagnostic of Differences in Behavioral Effects." *Journal of Communication* 71(4): 623–45.

Obama, Barack. 2012a. "President Obama on Title IX's Impact." ESPN-W Online. http://espn.go.com/espnw/title-ix/article/7737386/espnw-title-ix-president-obama-discusses-importance-title-ix. (May 24, 2013).

2012b. "President Obama Reflects on the Impact of Title IX." *Newsweek.* www.newsweek.com/president-obama-reflects-impact-title-ix-65097 (February 8, 2017).

Office for Civil Rights in the US Department of Education (OCR). 1979. Federal Register, Vol. 44, No. 239. A "Policy Interpretation: Title IX and Intercollegiate Athletics." www2.ed.gov/about/offices/list/ocr/docs/t9interp.html (March 25, 2021).

——— 1996. "Clarification of Intercollegiate Athletics Policy Guidance: The Three-Part Test." www2.ed.gov/about/offices/list/ocr/docs/clarific.html (March 25, 2021).

——— 2020. "Requirements under Title IX of the Education Amendments of 1972." www2.ed.gov/about/offices/list/ocr/docs/interath.html (March 25, 2021).

——— 2022. "The U.S. Department of Education Releases Proposed Changes to Title IX Regulations, Invites Public Comment." www.ed.gov/news/press-releases/us-department-education-releases-proposed-changes-title-ix-regulations-invites-public-comment (September 5, 2022).

Olson, Eric. 2021. "Coaches: Venue, Coverage Diminish NCAA Volleyball Tournament." Associated Press. https://apnews.com/article/basketball-omaha-volleyball-college-sports-8842e4a296a8bb3d509d5d0fa344442d (August 6, 2021).

Ostrowsky, Michael K. 2018. "Sports Fans, Alcohol Use, and Violent Behavior: A Sociological Review." *Trauma, Violence, and Abuse* 19(4): 406–19.

Ottaway, Amanda. 2018. *The Rebounders: A Division I Basketball Journey.* Lincoln, NE: University of Nebraska Press.

Page, Benjamin, and Robert Shapiro. 1992. *The Rational Public: Fifty Years of Trends in Americans' Policy Preferences.* Chicago, IL: University of Chicago Press.

Paluck, Elizabeth, and Chelsey S. Clark. 2020. "Can Playing Together Help Us Live Together?" *Science* 369(6505): 769–70.

Paluck, Elizabeth, Hana Shepherd, and Peter Aronow. 2016. "Changing Climates of Conflict: A Social Network Driven Experiment in 56 Schools." *Proceedings of the National Academy of Sciences* 113(3): 566–71.

Paluck, Elizabeth, Seth Green, and Donald Green. 2019. "The Contact Hypothesis Re-evaluated." *Behavioural Public Policy* 3(2): 129–58.

Paluck, Elizabeth, Roni Porat, Chelsey S. Clark, and Donald P. Green. 2021. "Prejudice Reduction: Progress and Challenges." *Annual Review of Psychology* 72: 533–60.

Paolini, Stefania, Fiona White, Linda Tropp et al. 2021. "Intergroup Contact Research in the 21st Century: Lessons Learned and Forward Progress if We Remain Open." *Journal of Social Issues* 77(1): 11–37.

Pape, Madeleine. 2020. "Gender Segregation and Trajectories of Organizational Change: The Underrepresentation of Women in Sports Leadership." *Gender & Society* 34(1): 81–105.

Paterson, Alex. 2022. "'Doom & Groom': Fox News Has Aired 170 Segments Discussing Trans People in the Past Three Weeks." Media Matters for America. www.mediamatters.org/fox-news/doom-groom-fox-news-has-aired-170-segments-discussing-trans-people-past-three-weeks (April 10, 2022).

Petrocelli, John V., Jacob L. Martin, and Winston Y. Li. 2010. "Shaping Behavior through Malleable Self-Perceptions: A Test of the Forced-Agreement Scale Effect (FASE)." *Journal of Research in Personality* 44(2): 213–21.

Pettigrew, Thomas F., and Linda R. Tropp. 2006. "A Meta-Analytic Test of Intergroup Contact Theory." *Journal of Personality and Social Psychology* 90(5): 751–83.

2011. *When Groups Meet: The Dynamics of Intergroup Contact.* New York: Taylor & Francis.

Pettinicchio, David. 2019. *Politics of Empowerment: Disability Rights and the Cycle of American Policy Reform.* Palo Alto, CA: Stanford University Press.

Phillips, Patti. 2021. "Women Athletic Directors? Not in Most Elite NCAA Conferences, Where Men Still Hold Outsize Advantage." *USA Today.* www .usatoday.com/story/opinion/2021/05/10/ncaa-title-ix-equity-women-ath letic-director-power-schools/4989933001/ (August 1, 2022).

Pickett, Moneque Walker, Marvin P. Dawkins, and Jomills Henry Braddock. 2012. "Race and Gender Equity in Sports: Have White and African American Females Benefited Equally from Title IX?" *American Behavioral Scientist* 56(11): 1581–603.

Pieper, Lindsay Parks. 2016. *Sex Testing: Gender Policing in Women's Sports.* Urbana-Champaign, IL: University of Illinois Press.

Pierson, Paul. 1993. "When Effect Becomes Cause: Policy Feedback and Political Change." *World Politics* 45(4): 595–628.

2004. *Politics in Time: History, Institutions, and Social Analysis.* Princeton, NJ: Princeton University Press.

Pollock, Mica. 2008. *Because of Race: How Americans Debate Harm and Opportunity in Our Schools.* Princeton, NJ: Princeton University Press.

Posbergh, Anna and Shannon Jette. 2022. "'Track's Coed, I Never Thought of It as Separate': Challenging, Reproducing, and Negotiating Gender Stereotypes in Track and Field." *Sociology of Sport Journal* 39(1): 47–55.

Proctor, Andrew. 2022. "Marginalization as a Structural Constraint: How Group Position Shapes Out-Group Hostility." *Political Research Quarterly* 75(4): 1113–30.

Quilantan, Bianca. 2022. "Democrats Aren't Eager to Talk about Transgender Athletes; the GOP Can't Get Enough." *Politico.* www.politico.com/ news/2022/10/10/democrats-arent-eager-to-talk-about-transgender-ath letes-the-gop-cant-get-enough-00060931 (October 20, 2022).

Reher, Stefanie. 2018. "Gender and Opinion–Policy Congruence in Europe." *European Political Science Review* 10(4): 613–35.

Reid, Erin M., and Michael W. Toffel. 2009. "Responding to Public and Private Politics: Corporate Disclosure of Climate Change Strategies." *Strategic Management Journal* 30(11): 1157–78.

Reingold, Beth. 2000. *Representing Women: Sex, Gender, and Legislative Behavior in Arizona and California.* Chapel Hill, NC: University of North Carolina Press.

Repo, Jemima. 2016. *The Biopolitics of Gender.* New York: Oxford University Press.

Reynolds, Celene. 2019. "The Mobilization of Title IX across Colleges and Universities, 1994–2014." *Social Problems* 66(2): 245–73.

Rhoden, William. 2006. *Forty Million Dollar Slaves: The Rise, Fall, and Redemption of the Black Athlete.* New York: Crown Publishers.

Richardson, Sarah. 2015. *Sex Itself: The Search for Male and Female in the Human Genome.* Chicago, IL: University of Chicago Press.

Ritter, Gretchen. 2006. *The Constitution as Social Design: Gender and Civic Membership in the American Constitutional Order.* Palo Alto, CA: Stanford University Press.

Roessner, Amber, and Erin Whiteside. 2016. "Unmasking Title IX on Its 40th Birthday: The Operation of Women's Voices, Women's Spaces, and Sporting Myth Narratives in the Commemorative Coverage of Title IX." *Journalism* 17(5): 583–99.

Romero, Melissa, and Mary Yarrison. 2012. "Pro Female Athletes Celebrate the 40th Anniversary of Title IX at the Newseum." *The Washingtonian.* www .washingtonian.com/blogs/wellbeing/fitness/pro-female-athletes-celebrate-the-40th-anniversary-of-title-ix-at-the-newseum.php (June 23, 2012).

Rose, Deondra. 2018. *Citizens by Degree: Higher Education Policy and the Changing Gender Dynamics of American Citizenship.* New York: Oxford University Press.

Roser-Renouf, Connie, Lucy Atkinson, Edward Maibach, and Anthony Leiserowitz. 2016. "The Consumer as Climate Activist." *International Journal of Communication* 10: 4759–83.

Rothstein, Richard. 2017. *The Color of the Law: A Forgotten History of How Our Government Segregated America.* New York: Liveright Publishing Corporation.

Sabiston, Catherine. 2020. *The Rally Report: Encouraging Action to Improve Sport for Women and Girls.* Toronto: Canadian Women & Sport. https:// womenandsport.ca/resources/research-insights/rally-report/.

Sabo, Don, Philip Veliz, and Ellen Staurowsky. 2016. *Beyond X's and O's: Gender Bias and Coaches of Women's College Sports.* East Meadow, NY: Women's Sports Foundation.

Saguy, Abigail C., and Mallory E. Rees. 2021. "Gender, Power, and Harassment: Sociology in the #MeToo Era." *Annual Review of Sociology* 47: 417–35.

Sampson, Robert J. 2012. *Great American City: Chicago and the Enduring Neighborhood Effect.* Chicago, IL: University of Chicago Press.

Sanbonmatsu, Kira. 2006. *Where Women Run: Gender and Party in the American States.* Ann Arbor, MI: University of Michigan Press.

Schaffner, Brian. 2020. *The Acceptance and Expression of Prejudice during the Trump Era.* New York: Cambridge University Press.

2022. "The Heightened Importance of Racism and Sexism in the 2018 U.S. Midterm Elections." *British Journal of Political Science* 52(1): 492–500.

Schein, Edgar H. 2004. *Organizational Culture and Leadership,* 3rd ed. San Francisco, CA: Jossey-Bass.

Schubert, Arline, George Schubert, and Cheryl Schubert-Madsen. 1991. "Changes Influenced by Litigation in Women's Intercollegiate Athletics." *Seton Hall Journal of Sport Law* 1: 237–68.

Schull, Vicki, Sally Shaw, and Lisa A. Kihl. 2012. "'If A Woman Came In … She Would Have Been Eaten Up Alive': Analyzing Gendered Political Processes in the Search for an Athletic Director." *Gender & Society* 27(1): 56–81.

Schultz, Jaime. 2014. *Qualifying Times: Points of Change in U.S. Women's Sport.* Urbana-Champaign, IL: University of Illinois Press.

———. 2022. "Title IX at 50: A Critical Celebration." *Women in Sport and Physical Activity Journal* 30(2): 97–108.

Schultz, Jamie, Anna Baeth, Anne Lieberman et al. 2022. "The Future of Women's Sport Includes Transgender Women and Girls." In *Justice for Trans Athletes*, eds. Ali Green and Helen Lenskyj, 17–29. Bingley, UK: Emerald Publishing.

Serrano-Durá, José, Pere Molina, and Alejandro Martínez-Baena. 2021. "Systematic Review of Research on Fair Play and Sporting Competition." *Sport, Education and Society* 26(6): 648–62.

Shafer, Emily Fitzgibbons, and Neil Malhotra. 2011. "The Effect of a Child's Sex on Support for Traditional Gender Roles." *Social Forces* 90(1): 209–22.

Shannon, Brian. 2018. "The Revised NCAA Division I Governance Structure after Three Years: A Score Card." *Texas A&M Law Review* 5(1): 65–103.

Shapiro, Robert Y. 2011. "Public Opinion and American Democracy." *Public Opinion Quarterly* 75(5): 982–1017.

Sharrow, Elizabeth A. 2013. "Forty Years 'on the Basis of Sex': Title IX, the 'Female Athlete,' and the Political Construction of Sex and Gender." PhD dissertation, University of Minnesota.

———. 2017. "'Female Athlete' Politic: Title IX and the Naturalization of Sex Difference in Public Policy." *Politics, Groups, and Identities* 5(1): 46–66.

———. 2020. "A 'Bridge to Our Daughters': Title IX Fathers and Policy Development." In *Stating the Family: New Directions in the Study of American Politics*, eds. Julie Novkov and Carol Nackenoff. Lawrence, KS: University Press of Kansas, 127–63.

———. 2021a. "Sex Segregation as Policy Problem: A Gendered Policy Paradox." *Politics, Groups, and Identities* 9(2): 258–79.

———. 2021b. "Sports, Transgender Rights and the Bodily Politics of Cisgender Supremacy." *Laws* 10(3): 63. https://doi.org/10.3390/laws10030063.

———. 2022. "Title IX's Interpretation Has Reshaped Athletics in Good and Bad Ways." *Washington Post.* www.washingtonpost.com/outlook/2022/06/20/title-ixs-interpretation-has-reshaped-athletics-good-bad-ways/ (June 23, 2022).

———. 2023. "Public Policy as Trans Harm: Troubling Administrative Governance through Transfeminst Sports Studies." *Transgender Studies Quarterly* 10(2): 100–15.

Sharrow, Elizabeth A., Jesse Rhodes, Tatishe Nteta, and Jill Greenlee. 2018. "The First Daughter Effect: The Impact of Fathering Daughters on Men's Preferences on Gender Equality Issues." *Public Opinion Quarterly* 82(3): 493–523.

Sharrow, Elizabeth A., Melinda R. Tarsi, and Tatishe M. Nteta. 2021. "What's in a Name? Symbolic Racism, Public Opinion, and the Controversy over the NFL's Washington Football Team Name." *Race and Social Problems* 13(2): 110–21.

Shulman, James L., and William G. Bowen. 2000. *The Game of Life: College Sports and Educational Values.* Princeton, NJ: Princeton University Press.

Sidorsky, Kaitlin N., and Wendy J. Schiller. 2023. *Inequality Across State Lines: How Policymakers Have Failed Domestic Violence Victims in the United States.* New York: Cambridge University Press.

Siegele, Jessica, Robin Hardin, Elizabeth Taylor, and Allison Smith. 2020. "'She Is the Best Female Coach': NCAA Division I Swimming Coaches' Experiences of Sexism." *Journal of Intercollegiate Sport* 13(1): 93–118.

Sigelman, Lee, and Clyde Wilcox. 2001. "Public Support for Gender Equality in Athletics Programs." *Women & Politics* 22(1): 85–96.

Sigelman, Lee, and Paul J. Wahlbeck. 1999. "Gender Proportionality in Intercollegiate Athletics: The Mathematics of Title IX Compliance." *Social Science Quarterly* 80(3): 518–38.

Simien, Evelyn M., Nneka Arinze, and Jennifer McGarry. 2019. "A Portrait of Marginality in Sport and Education: Toward a Theory of Intersectionality and Raced-Gendered Experiences for Black Female College Athletes." *Journal of Women, Politics and Policy* 40(3): 409–27.

Simon, Rita James, ed. 2005. *Sporting Equality: Title IX Thirty Years Later.* Edison, NJ: Transaction Publishers.

Sinclair, Betsy. 2012. *The Social Citizen: Peer Networks and Political Behavior.* Chicago, IL: University of Chicago Press.

Skocpol, Theda. 1992. *Protecting Soldiers and Mothers: The Political Origins of Social Policy in United States.* Cambridge, MA: Harvard University Press.

Smith, Rogers M. 1997. *Civic Ideals: Conflicting Visions of Citizenship in U.S. History.* New Haven, CT: Yale University Press.

———. 2022. "Legal Civic Orders and Equitable Lived Citizenships." *American Political Science Review* 116(1): 101–15.

Smith, Ronald. 1990. *Sports and Freedom: The Rise of Big-Time College Athletics.* New York: Oxford University Press.

Solinger, Rickie. 2019. *Pregnancy and Power: A History of Reproductive Politics in the United States (Revised Edition).* New York: NYU Press.

Soroka, Stuart, and Christopher Wlezien. 2010. *Degrees of Democracy: Politics, Public Opinion, and Policy.* New York: Cambridge University Press.

Soss, Joe. 2000. *Unwanted Claims: The Politics of Participation in the U.S. Welfare System.* Ann Arbor, MI: University of Michigan Press.

Stangl, Jane Marie, and Mary Jo Kane. 1991. "Structural Variables That Offer Explanatory Power for the Underrepresentation of Women Coaches Since Title IX: The Case of Homologous Reproduction." *Sociology of Sport Journal* 8(1): 47–60.

Stathi, Sofia, and Richard J. Crisp. 2008. "Imagining Intergroup Contact Promotes Projection to Outgroups." *Journal of Experimental Social Psychology* 44(4): 943–57.

Staurowsky, Ellen J. 2018. "College Athletes as Employees and the Politics of Title IX." In *Sport and the Neoliberal University: Profit, Politics, and Pedagogy*, ed. Ryan King-White. New Brunswick, NJ: Rutgers University Press, 97–128.

Staurowsky, Ellen, and Ainslie Rhoads. 2020. "Title IX Athletics Coordinators in NCAA Division I Institutions: Roles, Responsibilities, and Potential Conflicts of Interests." *Journal of Issues in Intercollegiate Athletics* 13: 381–404.

Staurowsky, Ellen, and Erianne A Weight. 2013. "Discovering Dysfunction in Title IX Implementation NCAA Administrator Literacy, Responsibility, and Fear." *Journal of Applied Sport Management* 5(1): 1–30.

Staurowsky, Ellen J., Courtney L. Flowers, Erin Buzuvis et al. 2022. *50 Years of Title IX: We're Not Done Yet*. East Longmeadow, NY: Women's Sports Foundation.

Staurowsky, Ellen J., Mary Jane DeSousa, Kathleen Miller et al. 2015. *Her Life Depends on It III: Sport, Physical Activity, and the Health and Well-Being of American Girls and Women*. East Meadow, NY: Women's Sports Foundation.

Staurowsky, Ellen J., Nicholas Watanabe, Joseph Cooper et al. 2020. *Chasing Equity: The Triumphs, Challenges, and Opportunities in Sports for Girls and Women*. New York: Women's Sports Foundation.

Stevenson, Betsey. 2010. "Beyond the Classroom: Using Title IX to Measure the Return to High School Sports." *The Review of Economics and Statistics* 92(2): 284–301.

Steward, Abigail, and Virginia Valian. 2018. *An Inclusive Academy: Achieving Diversity and Excellence*. Cambridge, MA: MIT Press.

Stoddard, Olga, Chris Karpowitz, and Jessica Preece. 2020. "Strength in Numbers: A Field Experiment in Gender, Influence, and Group Dynamics." IZA Discussion Paper 13742.

Strach, Patricia. 2016. *Hiding Politics in Plain Sight: Cause Marketing, Corporate Influence, and Breast Cancer Policymaking*. New York: Oxford University Press.

Streeter, Kurt. 2022a. "The N.C.A.A. Undervalued Women's Basketball. Marketers Didn't." *New York Times*. www.nytimes.com/2022/03/28/sports/ncaa basketball/womens-march-madness-endorsements.html (May 11, 2022).

2022b. "The Day the Supreme Court Crashed the Title IX Party." *New York Times*. www.nytimes.com/2022/06/25/sports/title-ix-anniversary-roe-wade .html (June 25, 2022).

2021. "Why Scores of Female Athletes Are Speaking Out on Abortion Rights." *New York Times*. www.nytimes.com/2021/09/27/sports/women-athletes-abortion-rights-brief.html (September 28, 2021).

Strolovitch, Dara Z. 1998. "Playing Favorites: Public Attitudes toward Race and Gender-Targeted Anti-discrimination Policy." *National Women's Studies Association Journal* 10(3): 27–53.

2007. *Affirmative Advocacy: Race, Class, and Gender in Interest Group Politics*. Chicago, IL: University of Chicago Press.

Strolovitch, Dara Z., Janelle S. Wong, and Andrew Proctor. 2017. "A Possessive Investment in White Heteropatriarchy? The 2016 Election and the Politics of Race, Gender, and Sexuality." *Politics, Groups, and Identities* 5(2): 353–63.

Strum, Philippa. 2004. *Women in the Barracks: The VMI Case and Equal Rights*. Lawrence, KS: University Press of Kansas.

Suggs, Welch. 2005. *A Place on the Team: The Triumph and Tragedy of Title IX*. Princeton, NJ: Princeton University Press.

Sullivan, Claire F. 2011. "Gender Verification and Gender Policies in Elite Sport: Eligibility and 'Fair Play.'" *Journal of Sport & Social Issues* 35(4): 400–19.

Sullivan, John, and John Transue. 1999. "The Psychological Underpinnings of Democracy: A Selective Review of Research on Political Tolerance, Interpersonal Trust, and Social Capital." *Annual Review of Psychology* 50: 625–51.

Sweet, Paige. 2021. *The Politics of Surviving: How Women Navigate Domestic Violence and Its Aftermath*. Berkeley, CA: University of California Press.

Swers, Michele. 2002. *The Difference Women Make: The Policy Impact of Women in Congress*. Chicago, IL: University of Chicago Press.

Tarver, Erin. 2017. *The I in Team: Sports Fandom and the Reproduction of Identity*. Chicago, IL: University of Chicago Press.

Tate, Katherine. 2003. *Black Faces in the Mirror: African Americans and Their Representatives in the U.S. Congress*. Princeton, NJ: Princeton University Press.

Taylor, Elizabeth A., and Robin Hardin. 2016. "Female NCAA Division I Athletic Directors: Experiences and Challenges." *Women in Sport and Physical Activity Journal* 24(1): 14–25.

Thorson, Emily A., and Michael Serazio. 2018. "Sports Fandom and Political Attitudes." *Public Opinion Quarterly* 82(2): 391–403.

Threadcraft, Shatema. 2016. *Intimate Justice: The Black Female Body and the Body Politic*. New York: Oxford University Press.

Toffoletti, Kim. 2017. *Women Sport Fans: Identification, Participation, Representation*. New York: Routledge.

Tormos, Fernando. 2017. "Intersectional Solidarity." *Politics, Groups, and Identities* 5(4): 707–20.

Tropp, Linda, Özden Melis Ulug, and Mete Sefa Uysal. 2021. "How Intergroup Contact and Communication about Group Differences Predict Collective Action Intentions among Advantaged Groups." *International Journal of Intercultural Relations* 80: 7–16.

Trounstine, Jessica. 2018. *Segregation by Design: Local Politics and Inequality in American Cities*. New York: Cambridge University Press.

——— 2020. "The Geography of Inequality: How Land Use Regulation Produces Segregation." *American Political Science Review* 114(2): 443–55.

Troutman, Kelly, and Mikaela Durfur. 2007. "From High School Jocks to College Grads: Assessing the Long-Term Effects of High School Sport Participation on Female's Educational Attainment." *Youth & Society* 38(4): 443–62.

Turk, Katherine. 2016. *Equality on Trial: Gender and Rights in the Modern American Workplace*. Philadelphia, PA: University of Pennsylvania Press.

US Bureau of Labor Statistics (BLS). 2021. *Women in the Labor Force: A Databook*, Report 1097. Washington, DC: US Bureau of Labor Statistics. www.bls.gov/opub/reports/womens-databook/2021/home.htm (February 22, 2023).

US Department of Education (DOE). 2021a. *Equity in Athletics Data Analysis*. Washington, DC: US Department of Education Office of Postsecondary Education. http://ope.ed.gov/athletics/ (May 24, 2021).

US Department of Education (DOE). 2021b. *Transcript of 2021 Virtual Public Hearing on Title IX of the Education Amendments of 1972*. Washington, DC: US Department of Education Office for Civil Rights. www2.ed.gov/about/offices/list/ocr/docs/202106-titleix-publichearing-complete.pdf (December 1, 2021).

US Department of Justice (DOJ). 2021. *Application of Bostock v. Clayton County to Title IX of the Education Amendments of 1972*. Washington, DC: US

Department of Justice Civil Rights Division. www.justice.gov/crt/page/
file/1383026/download (May 8, 2021).

US Government Accountability Office (GAO). 2015. *Women in STEM Research:
Better Data and Information Sharing Could Improve Oversight of Federal
Grant-Making and Title IX Compliance.* Washington, DC: U.S. Government
Accountability Office.

Ugarriza, Juan, and Didier Caluwaerts, eds. 2014. *Democratic Deliberation in
Deeply Divided Societies: From Conflict to Common Ground.* New York:
Springer.

Van Doorn, Marjoka. 2014. "The Nature of Tolerance and the Social Circumstances in Which It Emerges." *Current Sociology* 62(6): 905–27.

Van Dyke, Nella, and Bryan Amos. 2017. "Social Movement Coalitions: Formation, Longevity, and Success." *Sociology Compass* 11(7): e12489.

Van Mol, Christof. 2017. "Improving Web Survey Efficiency: The Impact of an
Extra Reminder and Reminder Content on Web Survey Response." *International Journal of Social Research Methodology* 20(4): 317–27.

Vavreck, Lynn, and Douglas Rivers. 2008. "The 2006 Cooperative Congressional Election Study." *Journal of Elections, Public Opinion and Parties* 18(4):
355–66.

Veliz, Philip, Marjorie Snyder, and Don Sabo. 2019. *The State of High School
Sports in America: An Evaluation of the Nation's Most Popular Extracurricular Activity.* New York: Women's Sports Foundation.

Verbrugge, Martha H. 1988. *Able-Bodied Womanhood: Personal Health and
Social Change in Nineteenth-Century Boston.* New York: Oxford University
Press.

2012. *Active Bodies: A History of Women's Physical Education in Twentieth-
Century America.* New York: Oxford Unive rsity Press.

Voelkel, Jan G., James Chu, Michael N. Stagnaro et al. 2023. "Interventions
Reducing Affective Polarization Do Not Necessarily Improve Anti-democratic
Attitudes." *Nature Human Behaviour* 7(1): 55–64.

Vogt, Dawne, Tamara Bruce, Amy Street, and Jane Stafford. 2007. "Attitudes
toward Women and Tolerance for Sexual Harassment among Reservists."
Violence against Women 13(9): 879–900.

Vogt, W. Paul. 1997. *Tolerance and Education: Learning to Live with Diversity
and Difference.* Thousand Oaks, CA: SAGE Publications.

Wäckerle, Jens. 2022. "Parity or Patriarchy? The Nomination of Female Candidates in British Politics." *Party Politics* 28(1): 10–23.

Wahman, Michael, Nikolaos Frantzeskakis, and Tevfik Murat Yildirim. 2021.
"From Thin to Thick Representation: How a Female President Shapes Female
Parliamentary Behavior." *American Political Science Review* 115(2): 360–78.

Walker, Nefertiti A., and Trevor Bopp. 2011. "The Underrepresentation of
Women in the Male-Dominated Sport Workplace: Perspectives of Female
Coaches." *Journal of Workplace Rights* 15(1): 47–64.

Wallsten, Kevin, Tatishe M. Nteta, Lauren A. McCarthy, and Melinda R. Tarsi.
2017. "Prejudice or Principled Conservatism? Racial Resentment and White
Opinion toward Paying College Athletes." *Political Research Quarterly*
70(1): 209–22.

Walton, Theresa, and Michelle Helstein. 2008. "Triumph of Backlash: Wrestling Community and the 'Problem' of Title IX." *Sociology of Sport Journal* 25(3): 369–86.

Wängnerud, Lena. 2009. "Women in Parliaments: Descriptive and Substantive Representation." *Annual Review of Political Science* 12: 51–69.

Wann, Daniel L. 2002. "Preliminary Validation of a Measure for Assessing Identification as a Sport Fan: The Sport Fandom Questionnaire." *International Journal of Sport Management* 3: 103–15.

Wann, Daniel L., and Jeffrey D. James. 2018. *Sport Fans: The Psychology and Social Impact of Fandom*. New York: Routledge.

Wann, Daniel L., and Nyla Branscombe. 1993. "Sports Fans: Measuring Degree of Identification with Their Team." *International Journal of Sport Psychology* 24(1): 1–17.

Wann, Daniel L., and Stephanie Pierce. 2003. "Measuring Sport Team Identification and Commitment: An Empirical Comparison of the Sport Spectator Identification Scale and the Psychological Commitment to Team Scale." *North American Journal of Psychology* 5(3): 365–72.

Ware, Susan. 2011. *Game, Set, Match: Billie Jean King and the Revolution in Women's Sports*. Chapel Hill, NC: University of North Carolina Press.

Washington, Ebonya. 2008. "Female Socialization: How Daughters Affect Their Legislator Fathers' Voting on Women's Issues." *American Economic Review* 98(1): 311–32.

WeCOACH, Inc. 2021. "NCAA Women Coaches Academy." https://wecoachsports.org/programs-events/wca/ (November 3, 2021).

Weeks, Ana Catalona. 2022. *Making Gender Salient: From Gender Quota Laws to Policy*. New York: Cambridge University Press.

Weldon, S. Laurel. 2002. *Protest, Policy, and the Problem of Violence Against Women: A Cross-National Comparison*. Pittsburgh, PA: University of Pittsburgh Press.

⸻. 2011. *When Protest Makes Policy: How Social Movements Represent Disadvantaged Groups*. Ann Arbor, MI: University of Michigan Press.

Wells, Janelle E., Melanie Sartore-Baldwin, Nefertiti A. Walker, and Cheryl E. Gray. 2021. "Stigma Consciousness and Work Outcomes of Senior Woman Administrators: The Role of Workplace Incivility." *Journal of Sport Management* 35(1): 69–80.

West, Jenna. 2021. "NCAA Committee Asks for Investigation into Unequal Accommodations at Women's Tournament." *Sports Illustrated*. www.si.com/college/2021/03/19/ncaa-committee-asks-investigation-womens-ncaa-tournament-weight-room (August 5, 2021).

Whisenant, Warren A. 2003. "How Women Have Fared as Interscholastic Athletic Administrators since the Passage of Title IX." *Sex Roles* 49(3–4): 179–84.

Whiteside, Erin, and Amber Roessner. 2018. "Forgotten and Left Behind: Political Apathy and Privilege at Title IX's 40th Anniversary." *Communication & Sport* 6(1): 3–24.

Whiteside, Erin, and Marie Hardin. 2008. "The Rhetoric and Ideology behind Title IX: An Analysis of U.S. Newspaper Editorials, 2002–2005." *Women in Sport and Physical Activity Journal* 17(1): 54–67.

Wicherts, Jelte M., Coosje Veldkamp, Hilde Augusteijn, Marjan Bakker, Robbie van Aert, and Marcel van Assen. 2016. "Degrees of Freedom in Planning, Running, Analyzing, and Reporting Psychological Studies: A Checklist to Avoid P-Hacking." *Frontiers in Psychology* 7: 1832.

Wiley, Shaun, Cailey Ann Kirby, Julia Richards, and April E. Stockfisch. 2021. "Positive Contact with Feminist Women as a Predictor of Feminist Solidarity, Gender Privilege Awareness, and Public and Domestic Support for Gender Equality in Straight Men." *Sex Roles* 85(11–12): 688–706.

Will, George. 2002. "A Train Wreck Called Title IX." *Newsweek*. www.news week.com/train-wreck-called-title-ix-145717 (November 30, 2020).

Wille, Bart, and Filip De Fruyt. 2014. "Vocations as a Source of Identity: Reciprocal Relations between Big Five Personality Traits and RIASEC Characteristics Over 15 Years." *Journal of Applied Psychology* 99(2): 262–81.

Williams, Juliet A. 2016. *The Separation Solution: Single-Sex Education and the New Politics of Gender Equality*. Berkeley, CA: University of California Press.

Wilson, Amy. 2022. *The State of Women in College Sports*. Indianapolis, IN: National Collegiate Athletic Association.

Witz, Bill. 2022. "Her Video Spurred Changes in Women's Basketball. Did They Go Far Enough?" *New York Times*. www.nytimes.com/2022/03/15/sports/ncaabasketball/womens-march-madness-sedona-prince.html (March 22, 2022).

Wolbrecht, Christina, and David Campbell. 2007. "Leading by Example: Female Members of Parliament as Political Role Models." *American Journal of Political Science* 51(4): 921–39.

——— 2017. "Role Models Revisited: Youth, Novelty, and the Impact of Female Candidates." *Politics, Groups, and Identities* 5(3): 418–34.

Women's Basketball Coaches Association (WBCA). 2021. "Our Fair Shot." https://ourfairshot.com/ (August 1, 2022).

Women's Sports Foundation (WSF). 2020. "Do You Know the Factors Influencing Girls' Participation in Sports?" www.womenssportsfoundation.org/do-you-know-the-factors-influencing-girls-participation-in-sports/ (August 1, 2022).

Wong, Alia. 2015. "Where Girls Are Missing Out on High-School Sports." *The Atlantic*. www.theatlantic.com/education/archive/2015/06/girls-high-school-sports-inequality/396782/ (November 9, 2020).

Wong, Janelle. 2008. *Democracy's Promise: Immigrants and American Civic Institutions*. Ann Arbor, MI: University of Michigan Press.

Wu, Judy Tzu-Chun, and Gwendolyn Mink. 2022. *Fierce and Fearless: Patsy Takemoto Mink, First Woman of Color in Congress*. New York: NYU Press.

Wulf, Steve. 2012. "Title IX: 37 Words That Changed Everything." *ESPN-W Online*. http://espn.go.com/espnw/title-ix/article/7722632/37-words-changed-everything (September 1, 2016).

Wushanley, Ying. 2004. *Playing Nice and Losing: The Struggle for Control of Women's Intercollegiate Athletics, 1960–2000*. Syracuse, NY: Syracuse University Press.

Yang, Yang, Tanya Tian, Teresa Woodruff, Benjamin Jones, and Brian Uzzi. 2022. "Gender-Diverse Teams Produce More Novel and Higher-Impact Scientific Ideas." *Proceedings of the National Academy of Sciences of the United States of America*, 119(36): e2220084119.

Yanus, Alixandra, and Karen O'Connor. 2016. "To Comply or Not to Comply: Evaluating Compliance with Title IX of the Educational Amendments of 1972." *Journal of Women, Politics & Policy* 37(3): 341–58.

YouGov. 2017. *Title IX and Girls in Sport*. East Meadow, NY: Women's Sports Foundation.

Young, Iris Marion. 2000. *Inclusion and Democracy*. New York: Oxford University Press.

Zaller, John. 2003. "Coming to Grips with V.O. Key's Concept of Latent Opinion." In *Electoral Democracy*, eds. Michael MacKuen and George Rabinowitz. Ann Arbor, MI: University of Michigan Press.

Zamora, Karen. 2018. "Former UMD Women's Hockey Coach Wins Discrimination Case, $3.7 Million Award." *Star Tribune*. www.startribune.com/former-umd-women-s-hockey-coach-wins-discrimination-case/477007603/ (July 31, 2019).

Zarrett, Nicole, Philip Veliz, and Don Sabo. 2020. *Keeping Girls in the Game: Factors That Influence Sport Participation*. New York: Women's Sports Foundation.

Ziegler, Mary. 2015. *After Roe: The Lost History of the Abortion Debate*. Cambridge, MA: Harvard University Press.

Zimbalist, Andrew. 1999. *Unpaid Professionals: Commercialism and Conflict in Big-Time College Sports*. Princeton, NJ: Princeton University Press.

Index

abortion rights, gendered policies on, 10,
  185–87
academic personnel, on NCAA
  committees, 109–10
Affordable Care Act (ACA), public support
  for, 71
amateurism doctrine, myth in college
  sports of, 37–41
Association of Intercollegiate Athletics for
  Women (AIAW), 14–15, 52–53, 186
athletic administration
  challenges for women leaders in, 115–17
  competency bias against women in, 115
  data analysis of women administrators
    survey, 120–24
  decrease in women's proportion of,
    20–22, 24–25
  demographic data on, 110–11
  gender disparities in athletic
    departments, 110–11, 120–24
  gender equality recruiting requirements
    for, 24–25
  male dominance in, 165–67, 177
  on NCAA committees, 109–10
  NCAA policy and governance in relation
    to, 109–10
  organizational culture and, 175–78
  promotion of gender-balanced structure
    in, 135–37
  reform proposals for equity in, 20–22,
    30–31, 120–24, 194–95
  sampling-based data on, 54–56
  Senior Woman Administrator (NCAA
    designation), 29–30, 108

student-athlete trust in, 95n.39
support for policy change, data analysis
  of, 112–20, 130–31, 177
Title IX compliance and, 114
top-down policy change and, 28–32, 50,
  105–106
women leaders' support for gender
  equity in, 112–20
women's minority status in, 30–31
women student-athletes and women in,
  117–20
attendance at games, fan behavior
  measurement with, 154–57
attitudinal measurements
  analytic strategy for, 65–66
  inter-personal contacts and,
    171–72
  male student-athlete attitudes, changing
    of, 74–78
  market-driven fan support, weakness of,
    157–62
  policy change and, 62–64
  policy feedback and stakeholder support,
    178–80

Baylor football sexual assault cases,
  59–61
Big Ten Conference, 37
binary logics, gender equality in sports
  and, 43–45, 168–75
Black student-athletes
  representation in college sports,
    70–71n.4
  revenue produced by, 37n.37

Hypothesis 3–2 (male-female student-athlete contact and trust in schools linked to gender equity policy support)
development of, 76–77
imagined contact study, male respondents, 91–98, 101–102
predictions based on student-athlete survey, 80–84
results of student-athlete survey, 85–89
sex-based identity and cross-sex contact and, 86–89
Hypothesis 4–1 (female coaches/athletic administrators' equity policy support greater than male counterparts)
data analysis of coaches and athletic administrators survey, 120–24
overview, 112–20
Hypothesis 4–2 (Impact on gender equity, coaches and athletic administrators, student-athletes impact compared to)
data analysis of coaches and athletic administrators survey, 120–24
organizational culture as factor in, 131–34
overview, 117–20
Hypothesis 4–3 (women head coaches support for gender equity vs lower-lever coach-administrator support)
data analysis of coaches and athletic administrators survey, 120–24
overview, 119
Hypothesis 5–1 (women's greater support for gender equity *vs.* men, all else constant)
disparities in support, 148–51, 157–62
overview, 119
Hypothesis 5–2 (families with daughters as student-athletes, gender equity support among)
disparities in support, 157–62
overview, 143–44
survey data on, 148–51, 162–63
Hypothesis 5–3 (male participation in high school sports linked to less support for gender equity), 144–46
disparities in support, 157–62
overview, 144–46
survey data on, 148–51
Hypothesis 5–4 (fan investment in college sports linked lack of support for gender equity)
disparities in support, 157–62

overview, 147–48
survey data on, 147–48

identity conflict
gendered roles and, 169n.7
for women coaches and administrative leaders, 115–17
imagined contact approach
debate over, 89n.31
in-group or out-group contact and trust, male respondents and primers of, 90–94
participant demographics, 90–92
results of student-athlete survey, 95–98
in student-athlete survey on gender equity, 89–98
incremental change, in organizational cultures, 115–17
India classroom intervention study, gender equality support and, 102n.50
in-group dynamics, male respondents in imagined contact study, 90–94
institutional barriers to gender equality. *See also* educational institutions; organizational culture
in college sports, 8, 113
contribution to and acceptance of women's marginalization and, 157–63
inter-personal contact and, 172–75
mechanisms for changes to, 103–104
reform proposals for, 185, 190–99
status quo bias and, 30–31, 34
Intercollegiate Athletic Association, 138–39
intercollegiate athletics
NCAA oversight of, 52–53
organizational culture in, 115
Title IX implementation and role of, 105–106
interest group coalitions, 27–28
inter-personal contact
coalition building for policy change and, 74–78
conditions for, 75–76n.13–14
families of student-athletes and increase in, 143–44
imagined contact approach and, 89–98
non-judgmental narratives and persuasion and, 76n.16
partisan segregation and, 170
political factors in choices for, 84n.28
segregation reduction and, 170–75

market forces impact on, 178–80
on NCAA committees, 109–10
opposition to compensation for, 37–41
policy advocacy by, 67–70
sampling-based data on, 54–56
self-selection into college sports by,
84n27
sponsorship and endorsement deals for,
138
survey data
demand effects in, 89n.31
on gender equity initiatives, 49–52
large-N, quantitative survey approach,
50–52
public and fan-base research using, 56,
148–51

team-branded clothing, fan behavior
measurement and, 154–57
television contracts
policy change and revenue from, 37,
138, 164–67
viewership of college sports events and,
154–57
women's sports coverage and, 180–81
"37 Words" (ESPN documentary),
182–83
"Three-Part Test"
data challenges with, 48–49
parity logic in, 186–87
proportionality criteria and, 19
Title IX enforcement and, 15–16, 38,
114n.15
Title IX (Education Amendment of 1972)
absence of revenue calculus in, 40–41
administrative compliance with, 28–32
alternatives to, 188–90
backlash and resistance to compliance
with, 10, 59–61
civil rights policies and, 9–12
cultural context for compliance debates,
114
data measurements for compliance,
48–49
educational impact of, 9–13, 187–88
enforcement enhancement for, 25,
35–36, 182–83
familiarity with, 59n.13
federal enforcement of, 106–108
future politics of, 171–72, 180–85
gender gap in support for, 142–43
high school sports and, 144

historical framework for, 5–9
impact assessment of, 5–9
legacy of, 166–67, 180–85
market pressures and, 146n.8
media 50th anniversary coverage of,
180–85
NCAA ambiguity in support for,
106–108
noncompliance with, 113
Office for Civil Rights virtual hearing
on, 138–40
passage of, 1
perceptions *vs.* actual compliance with,
114n.16
policy feedback theory and, 71–72
public support for, 32–34, 140–46
scholarship on impact of, 11–12
sexual assault policy guidelines, 59–61
single-sex higher education and, 99
spillover effects, limits of, 21–22
status quo enforcement and policy
design in, 7–8
women's leadership role in
implementation of, 113
Title VII (Civil Rights Act of 1964),
197n.4
top-down policy change
absence of, in college athletics, 134–37
athletic administration and, 28–32, 50,
62–64
descriptive representation and induced
preferences, 112–20
organizational culture as barrier to,
30–31, 105–106
organizationally induced preferences,
112–20
transgender girls and women
co-ed sports and, 192–93
college sports research and, 44
fan resistance to sports participation by,
147–48
legislative challenges to rights of, 32n.34
politicization of participation by, 60–61,
183n.17, 184–85
Republican party focus on, 141
Trump, Donald, 10, 24
trust conditions
imagined contact study, male
respondents and, 90–94
inter-personal contact for policy change
and, 77–78, 171–72
policy change and role of, 74–78, 171–72

Printed in the USA
CPSIA information can be obtained
at www.ICGtesting.com
LVHW051212041223
765471LV00004B/332